heavyhands®
WALKING

heavyhands®
W A L K I N G

WALK YOUR WAY TO A LIFETIME OF FITNESS WITH THIS REVOLUTIONARY, COMMONSENSE EXERCISE SYSTEM

BY LEONARD SCHWARTZ, M.D.

Rodale Press, Emmaus, Pennsylvania

Everyone—particularly those over the age of 35 or who have known heart or blood pressure problems—should have a complete physical examination by his or her physician before beginning a strenuous exercise program such as Heavyhands Walk.

Senior Editor: Ray Wolf
Editor: Catherine M. Cassidy
Copy Editor: Linda Harris
Book Design: Acey Lee
Cover Design: Acey Lee
Cover Photo: Carl Doney
Photography: by Carl Doney except for the following: pp. xiv, 10, 20, 126, 136, 154, 194 by Tom Auble; pp. 108, 118 (bottom) courtesy of Mac Good; pp. 94, 120, 125 by Michael Hopkins/Photographs by Gerlinde; pp. 14, 133 by Ed Landrock; p. 141 courtesy of John McKean; p. 123 by David Madison; p. 143 courtesy of Ginny Miller; pp. 23, 25, 34, 46, 60, 80, 180, 188, 202 by Leonard Schwartz; p. 163 (left) by Margaret Skrovanek; p. 165 (left) courtesy of Team Russell; p. 160 (left) by Christie C. Tito; p. 15 by Sally Shenk Ullman.

Source for illustrations: Leonard Schwartz except pp. 69, 104, 125, 129, 184 courtesy of Tom Auble.

Library of Congress Cataloging-in-Publication Data

Schwartz, Leonard, 1925–
 Heavyhands walking.

 Includes index.
  1. Exercise. 2. Arm. 3. Weight lifting.
4. Walking. 5. Physical fitness. I. Title. [DNLM: 1. Exertion— popular works.   2. Health Promotion—methods—popular works. 3. Physical Fitness—popular works. QT 255 S399h]
GV508.S39   1987   613.7′1   86-33885
ISBN 0-87857-692-4   paperback

2 4 6 8 10 9 7 5 3 1   paperback

To the exercisers of this world—actual and potential, obsessive and casual, gleeful and curmudgeonish, consistent and fickle, devout and heretic, leader and follower, veteran and novice, impassioned and phlegmatic, graceful and klutzy. Long may you serve as visible reminders that all we really own is a form of energy called Life!

CONTENTS

Acknowledgments

Acknowledgments are difficult because any such list ends up shorter than it ought to be. It would take several pages to thank those who have made substantial contributions over the past five years. Literally thousands of fitness instructors are more than casually involved with combined exercise, and teach it with expertise and sensitivity. I'll mention a few names that represent various categories of the kind of support I've enjoyed. Thanks to:

Judy Shasek and Tom Auble, superfit compatriots with enthusiasm and skill and know-how and wall-to-wall need to explore these uncharted waters.

Bonnie Voss of Chicago, Rich Boggs of Atlanta, and Sylvia Lambert of the University of Ottawa, teachers *extraordinaire*.

Ginny Miller of Atlanta and John McKean of Pittsburgh, super representatives of the strength and bodybuilding legions.

Bob Farentinos of Boulder, Colorado, the famed cross-country skier who has helped bridge the gap between sport and fitness; and rowing champion Mac Good, of Croton-on-Hudson, New York, who continues to bring new insights into this challenging area.

Dr. Richard Kalla, who brought wisdom and friendship.

Dr. Fred Marks of Pittsburgh, for his unremitting personal and professional involvement.

Endless thanks to Jean and Saul Chosky, who make most of my days a bit sweeter.

Masters Jeremy David Bailey and Ryan Matthew Lindner, 70 pounds (total!) of dutifully pumping grandchildren, who showed me that kids can and should be included.

Herb Cygan of San Francisco and Commander Nick Janus, for real friendship and real help over these years.

Drs. Phil Bishop and Joe Smith, researchers at the University of Alabama.

Rick Silberman and Debbie Cassinelli, young physiologists who labored hard, long, and intelligently at the Human Energy Laboratory at the University of Pittsburgh.

My Rodale Press editor, Catherine Cassidy, who brought talent, diligence, and cheerful care to a knotty project; and Acey Lee of Rodale Press's art department, for his good instincts and excellent taste.

And finally, my family: my wife, Millie, who has continued for over 40 years now to share each of my projects with the wise tolerance of a modern Mona Lisa without neglecting her own active career; and my daughters and sons-in-law, upon whose support I can depend.

Introduction

A great deal has happened since the publication of the original *Heavyhands* text five years ago. A number of researchers have joined in the many-faceted study of the combined aerobic exercise I call *Panaerobics*. I coined the term Panaerobics to stand for three main ideas. First, it is exercise that mobilizes as many muscles as possible simultaneously. Second, it brings as many *kinds* of fitness—things like strength, speed, and a combination of the two, called power—to those muscles. Finally, Panaerobic training involves versatile movement. Given identical working muscle groups, varied movement options make exercise more interesting and therefore more pleasant for most of us. And this is important, considering the discouragingly high quit rate among exercisers. Reducing the ordinary discomfort and risk of injury during good exercise should go a long way toward keeping people motivated to maintain fitness throughout their lifetimes.

Of course, novelty is a major part of what ignites interest in something new here in America—particularly on the fitness front. But I don't believe combined aerobics is a fad. I think of it as aerobics "in a new key." The research done at the University of Pittsburgh's Human Energy Lab and elsewhere seems to generate two kinds of excitement about combined aerobics. One has to do with the seductiveness of numbers: Numbers supply the "stamp of proof," the shield of evidence that the academic community requires. (They're also anxiety reducers for authors!) The other kind of excitement is nameless, soft-edged, and qualitative, and you needn't be a physiologist or coach to sense it. It's the kind of excitement that comes from doing something that you know is good.

This book evolved out of new information gathered over the last four years. The core issues are these:

- Heavyhands Walk can help the vast majority of you attain at least the same level of cardiovascular fitness as can any current popular exercise method.

- Heavyhands Walk can make you stronger without sacrificing cardiovascular training.
- Heavyhands Walk, performed properly, can have a telling effect on the control of body composition—more specifically, on how much fat and muscle allow us to perform and look the way we do.
- Heavyhands Walk can be as diverse a movement adventure as anything you can do in quest of good fitness.
- Heavyhands Walk is the most convenient and least expensive means—in terms of both time and money—of gaining all of the above!

After observing it closely for a decade, I think the fitness revolution enjoys more luster than substance. We're a bit fatter than we were a generation ago, and our kids apparently are more at risk for cardiovascular disorders. We've been deluged by an abundance of beckoning gadgets and machines manufactured to make hard work seem comfortable. But the *body-machine*, whose skills alone determine our movement options, seems a bit underprogrammed nowadays. The intensity factor—or how *hard* we go at it—isn't receiving a fair shake, either. Too many of us are not fit enough for hard work, not healthy enough to risk it, or needlessly afraid of it.

I believe the next phase of the fitness movement will find us tuning our hearts with more muscles and programming our brains with an open assortment of movements. Once that happens, our measurable national fitness could easily soar 15 to 20 percent. Three kinds of improved intelligence could bring us closer to success: better exercise, with all that implies; more interesting exercise, to keep us at it; and surer ways of identifying those for whom exercise is dangerous. The material in this book addresses the first two issues.

I've tried to keep the introductory chapters as brief as possible without neglecting information I feel is vital for beginners. After that, the chapter headings should direct the reader's picking and choosing through the text. I hope that you, the reader, will be adventurous here: My aim is to help to make an exerciser of you in as many good ways as your freedom and willingness will allow.

Thumbing through these pages, you will immediately notice that considerable space is devoted to boxes, or "sidebars." They are not extraneous material: On the contrary, they are an essential part of the book! I have tried to speak to the reader with two voices. One speaks logically, matter-of-factly presenting the book's basic arguments. The other voice is less structured, less stiff, highly opinionated—sometimes too personal, I'm afraid! These two voices give you the option at any cracking of the book to receive information two different ways. The sidebars may or may not be relevant to the book's argument of the moment. This second voice was intended to moisten the lethal dryness with which most exercise books are afflicted and from which mine can claim no immunity.

Some may find my approach unusual; this is, after all, an exercise manual. But the effects of a long career as a behaviorally oriented physician cannot be quickly erased! I hope you will be able to jog cheerfully between my shifts from concrete detail to attempts at cosmic overview. I'm trying to transmit what I know about exercise: I remain convinced that knowledge and interest are the motives that will keep us willing to chance this complicated art that aspires to make energy part of health.

About the Author

Leonard Schwartz, M.D., has been a physician, psychiatrist, and psychoanalyst for the past 35 years. He was chief of the Division of Psychiatry in the Department of Medicine at Montefiore Hospital in Pittsburgh from 1963 to 1985; is a member of the faculty at the School of Medicine at the University of Pittsburgh; and is a staff member at the Western Psychiatric Institute. He is an adjunct full professor of physical education and health at the University of Pittsburgh. For more than a decade he was consultant in psychiatry to the Jewish Home for the Aged in Pittsburgh and has been consultant to the Veterans Administration Psychiatric Hospital of Pittsburgh. He is a member of the American Medical Association, the American Psychiatric Association, the American Geriatric Society, and the American College of Sports Medicine.

Besides his involvement in the physiology and psychology of fitness, Dr. Schwartz finds time for the classical guitar and is particularly interested in choreography for the combined forms of exercise he pioneered. He is also actively engaged in research. The Leonard and Millie Schwartz Foundation funds research in the field of exercise physiology and in other areas of medicine and wellness. His first book, *Heavyhands: The Ultimate Exercise,* was published in 1982. Dr. Schwartz developed the Heavyhands weight and has invented other devices for combined exercise.

About the Models in This Book

The two younger people who join me in the exercise photos are not professional models; both are esteemed colleagues. Judy Shasek, 38, is a wife and mother of two beautiful children (who are, incidentally, excellent "Heavyhanders" in their own right). A former schoolteacher, Judy has taught Heavyhands seminars around the United States to people of all ages. She is a superb athlete, excelling in swimming, tennis, windsurfing, and cycling, among other sports. I have watched Judy pump 'n' walking 10-pound weights high both in and outside the laboratory. Judy continues to teach the Heavyhands technique to aerobics instructors and professional athletes. She works with a Florida pediatrician, and is planning postgraduate work in exercise physiology.

Tom Auble, 36, is a career engineer turned exercise physiologist. Now working toward his doctorate at the University of Pittsburgh, Tom has been more intimately involved in the laboratory investigation of Heavyhands exercise than anyone else in the country. He has completed the first precise and comprehensive study of the energy cost of pump 'n' walk movements (to be published), and has measured directly the energy cost of many other varieties of Heavyhands exercise. A former distance runner, Tom has developed, as has Judy, incredible total body strength-endurance. He has lectured widely on Heavyhands and teaches classes in the method.

What Is Heavyhands?

The Heavyhands principle is really quite simple. It merely involves putting as much muscle as you can into all sorts of movements: walking, jogging, calisthenics, shadowboxing, dancing, special movements for stubborn body areas like the belly and lower back, even exercises that mimic various sports-related moves. All of the exercises are *combined.* This means that the arms and legs move *simultaneously*, and that the trunk muscles are usually put into action, too.

Handweights are used in Heavyhands—hence the name. That's because the arms are excellent exercise drivers, even in their typically untrained state. A number of studies showed that subjects were capable of armwork that was 70 percent of their leg-alone capacity. This is especially surprising when you consider that the arms have only one-fourth to one-third of the legs' muscle mass!

The Arms as Muscle Mobilizers

The hands are loaded with handweights for two main reasons. One is to slow them down to make them good working partners for the legs. If we trained our arms without weights, they would soon be able to move faster than our legs do while running! What happens in Heavyhands training is just what you might expect: Early in the game, the arms have a hard time keeping up; later the situation reverses. Hand-weights are the great equalizers.

The other reason for using handweights, oddly enough, is to "teach" the arms strength and speed. Weighting them down with variously sized weights works the entire upper torso, with its large mass of muscle that gets little continuous action during typical work and play. While arms are small compared to legs, the upper body contains fully 65 percent of our total muscle mass! And most of it is as conveniently available to the fitness seeker as are the muscles of the legs—which, in fact, may be handicapped by their continual chore of simply carrying a large, upright body.

What Is an Exerciser?

As I see it, there aren't many of them around. There are lots of people who exercise, but an *exerciser* is of a different species! A runner exercises but may not fulfill my definition of an exerciser. An exerciser who runs may or may not fulfill your definitions of a runner. Exercise is the more inclusive term. One definition of an exerciser is one who can remain at a target heart rate doing one of a dozen or more movements comfortably. Or an exerciser may be one who can switch the emphasis on muscle groups or fitness factors easily while continuing to get the "work" done. Asked what they do for exercise, specialists have staccato answers: They run, walk, swim, bike, etc. When I'm asked, I'm so confused by the question I just sputter. Exercisers have few fixed loyalties. We are jacks of many exertional trades, masters of none. At least for now.

How Fit Do You Want to Be?

My experience tells me that most people wouldn't know how to answer that question. It's a lot more difficult than, "Would you like to be as fit as possible on reasonable expenditure of time?" That one is easier because a quick "yes" does it. Few of us know *how* fit we want to be because we don't know how various fitness levels could change our lifestyles. I identify two distinct groups of people who discover fitness through exercise. Things don't change much for the first group. The fitness they produce becomes "potential energy," something they may call upon when the need arises. The other group continually alters the events in their lives to make use of their growing energy reserves. It's just like algebra or Russian: If you incorporate them into your day-to-day life, you will feel more changed by them. No one abandons algebra or Russian if they've become tools for living. Once you learn any particular exercise skill, as with algebra or Russian, it's easy to reclaim it after a brief layoff.

Take the latissimus dorsi muscles. The "lats" are the largest single muscles of the body; they're the ones that broaden the upper back. If you're not a swimmer, kayaker, rower, or cross-country skier, chances are your lats probably cannot perform hard, continuous work, the kind that trains your heart muscle. But a muscle needn't be huge to be strong and work-capable. Once trained, lots of little muscles add up to a large total mass of trained muscle, and that's what's needed to perform the hardest exercise you can do comfortably and safely during extended workouts.

Heavyhands training works to create the most efficient relationship possible between the heart and the body's muscles. When the heart beats, *all* of it beats. It functions as a unit, all of it contracting during each "cycle." But—perhaps to our disadvantage—we enjoy the option of working just a few muscles with given exercises and virtually ignoring others. Take running, for instance. While an excellent heart conditioner, running fails to be a good exercise for all of the skeletal muscles (those muscles that are attached to our bones). Since running uses too few muscles, a relatively large task is thrust upon a small percentage of the body's muscle. That limits the muscle mass that goes into a workout, which could lead to more vulnerability to injury.

Including as much muscle as possible in aerobic workouts pays handsome dividends in terms of heart function. Regardless of the condition of the heart muscle itself, the more work-capable the skeletal muscles, the easier becomes the heart's work at any level of difficulty. Delivery of oxygen becomes more efficient once more muscles are trained to use it well. This simple logic looms even larger when the heart pump is limited for any reason, as in coronary artery disease.

So Heavyhands aims to exploit the enormous additional potential of the entire upper torso and trunk, within the framework of *combined exercise*. But while the upper body experiences great physical gains, increases in legwork capacity as a result of Heavyhands training can be as great or greater than those derived from leg-alone exercise. Heavyhands exercises are designed purposely to activate what *isn't* included in conventional exercise. Trained Heavyhanders become able to jump, kick, and knee dip in ways that would be difficult for most elite runners. At the same time, Heavyhands training can make a better runner of you (more about that in Chapter 11).

When it comes to mobilizing muscle mass, the Heavyhands concept is unrivaled by any other exercise method. And while orchestrating lots of muscle, it is heedful at the same time of the need for grace, comfort, and practicality. With four limbs and the trunk involved, the number of good movements is practically endless. If you choose, Heavyhands exercise can be endlessly varied.

Greater Benefit—With Less Injury Risk

Surprisingly, most healthy hearts are easily trained. With conventional exercise programs, the rub ordinarily lies in various weaknesses and subsequent injuries of the body—the muscles, bones, joints, tendons, and ligaments involved in movement. Heavyhands exercises are designed both to optimize cardiovascular effects and to lessen the risk of injury.

This diminished risk of injury is most likely due to the fact that the work is distributed to all the body's muscles *evenly* enough to prevent overuse problems. As a result, the work of exercise feels easier at given levels of intensity in those who become trained. Here's an example: A person who can run a 10-minute mile at a heart rate of 130 beats/minute may, once well trained in combined exercise, accomplish *exactly* the same work level at a heart rate of 100 or even lower! That means that by mobilizing lots of trained muscle, your heart can do in only 100 beats the amount of work it requires 130 beats to accomplish with leg-alone exercise.

Heavyhands Fitness: What's Special about It?

Heavyhands's claim to being an "ultimate" exercise is double-pronged. Everything else held constant, like your genes and your willingness to invest time and gristle, I believe once you're a trained Heavyhander, you will be doing *more* exercise than you would be likely to do any other way. That might be measured as calories lost per average hour of exercise. You'll also be doing more *kinds* of exercise: Things like strength and speed and power and flexibility will become part of each workout, and thus lend more kinds of fitness to more muscles. Less measurable, but equally important, is the *diversity* you will bring to these noble efforts. I suspect that all of us are subtly looking for reasons to give up anything as tough as good exercise! So any system worth its salt will exclude as many of those reasons as possible. Until recently, the best heart and muscle trainers were also apt to be the most boring of exercises. We're looking to change all that. In sum, Heavyhands will give you a higher level of *total* fitness, with plenty of variety. Now in greater detail:

1. Increased maximum capability. When we did a study at the Human Energy Laboratory at the University of Pittsburgh

Fitting in Fitness

My guess is that fitness won't really come of age as long as it remains isolated from our lives. I learned that from my own experience. Any workout that is directed toward some sort of measurable gain is automatically more fun and interesting to me than the one that I do because I'm following a deeply rooted motive. Recently, I've noticed that I get ideas about tomorrow's workout while I'm executing today's. That makes for a sense of continuity, and that's a good thing. Two things are necessary for good fitness: getting it, and using it. It's just like learning Chinese—you have to use it or lose it. A decade from now, best-selling fitness books will deal mostly with the applications of fitness for an already fit population— I hope!

recently, we got some surprises. We tested subjects two ways: by a conventional treadmill test, and by a similar test, in which the subject pumped tiny handweights while walking "uphill." We found that on average their performance was the same. At the end of several weeks of Heavyhands training, the same two tests revealed that (1) the leg-alone capability of the Heavyhanders had increased significantly, and (2) their combined (arm + leg) workload had increased greatly. Another group, who simply ran for an equal total training time, showed an expectable increase in their leg-alone capability, but little change in their combined test. What was especially striking was lower heart rates of the Heavyhands group during combined exercise as compared with the running controls. The gains in leg capability experienced by the Heavyhanders were surprising, since that aspect was not emphasized during their training.

2. Increased intensity of comfortable exercise. Trained Heavyhanders spontaneously select four-limbed exercise intensities for their workouts that are significantly *higher* than the known averages for most serious exercisers. This increased intensity is important, because it brings together the psychological factor (comfort) and the physiological elements. A small increase in the average moment-by-moment work intensity, multiplied by 150 or so hours each year, will produce important cumulative effects.

3. Maximal strength-endurance. We've found that Heavyhanders who train a reasonable amount of time with larger handweights consistently outwork other athletes at tasks requiring rapid, generous limb movement of "heavy" handweights along with leg movement. "Heavy" Heavyhanding, unlike conventional weight training, is an excellent cardiovascular conditioner.

4. More varied aerobic workouts. Heavyhanders enjoy a wide assortment of combined movements for their workouts. Those of us who walk or run for our exercise usually become overspecialized; these specific exercises become our *only* way of generating the continuous workloads that keep us fit. The Heavyhander may have dozens of ways of doing it, using imaginative combinations of movements and muscles, and bypassing injured parts when necessary. The notion of versatility without sacrificing intensity should prove to be an advantage that will reduce the awesome quit rate among exercisers.

5. More fat-fueled exercise. It is likely that well-trained Heavyhanders will come to use more *fat* to fuel their exercise at higher workloads than conventional aerobic practitioners.

6. High oxygen pulse. Trained Heavyhanders use more oxygen at progressively lower heart rates. That translates as more oxygen consumption per heartbeat. It's merely a convenient way of describing a better teaming up of heart and skeletal muscle to do work. You can also think of this in terms of calories of heat expended per beat of the heart. This is important for those who want to be healthy and look good by way of their fitness program. A powerful oxygen transport system means melting fat faster while using a relatively slow heart pump.

7. More total exercise. That just means the most effective multiple of *intensity* times *duration*. Physiologists will continue to argue the merits of "how hard" versus "how long" we should exercise, but the fact is we need some of both! Regardless of how you look at the intensity-duration riddle, Heavyhands can provide the best range of solutions for you. Since more vigorous work can be done comfortably, and since this work is distributed in a fashion that's less likely to cause injuries, the trained Heavyhander can log larger weekly totals of exercise than can conventional aerobic exercisers. That fact ensures both ultimate cardiovascular benefits and body-weight control.

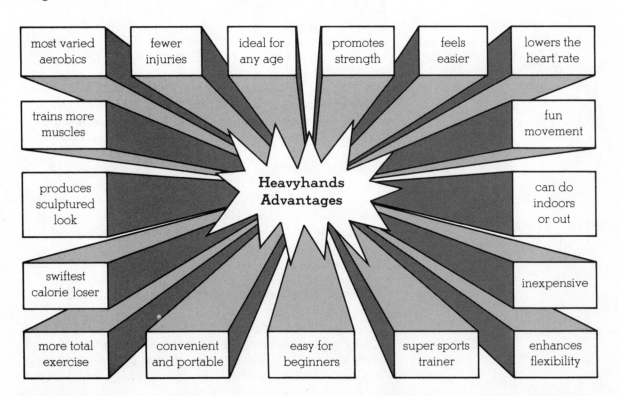

Structural Changes from Heavyhands Training

Three major changes take place in muscles as a result of endurance-type training. I'm not talking now about the possible addition of some new muscle fibers, and the evident enlargement (called hypertrophy) of those already present. I'm speaking of increases in the number and size of *mitochondria*, the tiny structures within the muscle cells that regulate the production of energy; in the number of *capillaries* that lacé the muscle cells and supply them with oxygen; and in the amount of energy-producing *enzymes* (chemicals called catalysts) in muscle tissue, which decrease rapidly when regular training ceases.

These changes are not hypothetical. They have been observed with the electron microscope in both animal and human tissue samples. Indeed, they occur in all sorts of exercise we call aerobic (endurance). We believe these changes are potentially greatest during Heavyhands training, simply because more muscle gets into the act!

Important Cardiovascular Benefits You Can Anticipate

The past several years have given us an opportunity to study the changes that make the bodies of Heavyhanders fitter. Take the matter of a slower heart rate. We have collected lots of data from anecdotal material and in the laboratory showing that Panaerobics has the most profound slowing effect upon the heart when compared with any other aerobic exercise. Elite athletes whose resting heart rates had long since leveled off have found them slowing even further following Heavyhands training.

Some cardiologists and other exercise experts don't believe a slow heart rate is an advantage. But a bit of basic physiology suggests that, other things being equal, a slow heart is a more effective heart-muscle supplier and safer than a fast heart. Why? Because the heart muscle fibers receive their oxygen-rich blood *between beats*; essentially, a slower heart rate means more opportunity for the heart itself to receive life-giving oxygen. That becomes even more crucial when the heart's coronary artery "suppliers" become closed to some extent.

A heartbeat trained to a slow resting cadence is safer as well as more efficient because it can typically work more slowly during heavier exertion. A trained person can cover a 12-minute mile at a slower heart rate than he could at the outset of training. And here's where health and fitness interact: High heart rates may contribute to the increased risk of exercise. Since many people aren't aware of the actual state of their coronaries, it might be a good idea to exercise at the slowest training heart rate possible. If you choose a fast, sedentary heart over a slower trained one, you're also opting for a dangerously fast heart if you should forget yourself long enough to chase a bus!

One well-known cardiologist-author prescribed a 15- or 20-minute/mile walking pace for a mile or two, feeling that was sufficiently intense. His own exercise routine included tennis. Brisk singles tennis can be nearly twice as demanding as the doctor's walking prescription. Does it make sense to train at an intensity *half* that at which you play?

I've had dozens of people tell me they simply weren't interested in cardiovascular fitness; fitness for them was purely a matter of good looks—being slim and tightly wrapped, mostly. Given a half-hour, I'm usually able to convince them that a slow heart rate derived from training is their best guarantee of shaping the best body they could ever own! A slow heart won't show in your mirror, but its visible by-products will: an improved work capacity, the ability to lose

Slow Heart Rate: A Good Thing?

The matter of the slower heart rates that come from exercise is quite interesting. I know physicians who don't make much of it, and don't seem convinced that it's an advantage. But common sense dictates that, other things being equal, a slow heart derived from regular exercise (there are other causes) is to be preferred to a fast one. For some of us, fast heart rates could be a bit risky, and often those who are at risk don't even know it. So having a heart that pumps lots of blood with each contraction does whatever you require of it at a slower rate.

The heart muscle actually receives its blood supply (doctors call it "perfusion") *between* beats. The slower the heart rate, the more total "in-between" time for the heart to receive its needed oxygen. And most would agree that there is a strong relationship between how fast your heart's beating and how hard you feel you're working. So training your pulse downward means more comfortable exercise.

I sincerely believe that, over the long haul, Heavyhands exercise will produce the slowest heart rates. Dozens of dedicated runners have written to tell me of marked lowerings of their heart rates—heart rates that had remained stable for a

decade or more of running— once they began Heavyhands. Our own brief training study in the lab, which involved only about 2 hours of weekly exercise, showed striking heart rate lowerings in the Heavyhands group. Several years ago, I did a more casual study on a group of nurses, who are excellent pulse counters! The more sedentary members of the group dropped as many as 25 beats/minute (that's resting heart rate) after five weeks of training, at 3 hours a week. Allowing for plenty of error, that's still a lot of slowing for 15 total hours of training.

calories at a slimming rate, and the production of work-capable quantities of well-sculpted muscle. Additionally, for most of us, training lots of muscle and the heart toward a more efficient working relationship produces parallel changes for the better in both the working *and* resting blood pressure.

A Quick Summary of Heavyhands Advantages

A lot of information to digest, isn't it? Just to make sure it all makes sense, here's a brief rundown of the main advantages of the Heavyhands exercise method.

Cardiovascular Benefits

There are two main cardiovascular benefits. One is a lowering of the heart rate; the other is a lowering of blood pressure. These effects are realized *after* training is well under way. Heavyhands training is used rather routinely in cardiac rehabilitation, because these cardiovascular effects can, in the long run, be an advantage for patients in whom the heart muscle's blood supply has been reduced by coronary artery disease. But you can see why a gradual, cautious approach—sometimes involving constant surveillance—would be necessary. While these beneficial training effects are frequent, they may require additional medical treatment.

Metabolic Changes

After a few weeks of a properly conducted program, certain changes take place in the body's metabolism. More fat is used to fuel the exercise, more calories are usually lost per minute of exercise, and more calories are lost per heartbeat. In addition, trained Heavyhanders can usually perform more total exercise comfortably. So Heavyhands is the premier method for controlling body composition.

A crucial and unique metabolic effect of Heavyhands exercise comes from mobilizing combinations of large muscle groups: the utilization of a greater muscle mass than is possible with other exercise. Microscopic structural and biochemical changes occur in hundreds of muscles, the combined effect of which produces the ultimate circulatory, metabolic, and mechanical advantages associated with exercise.

Psychological Advantages

The best exercise is only as useful as the exerciser's willingness to stick with it for a lifetime. Heavyhands exercise is so varied that, once skilled, you needn't work out the same way twice in a given month! By its nature, the method spawns inventiveness, and diminishes the boredom that proves lethal to so many other programs. The strength-endurance factor, more highly developed in this method than any other, works to improve simultaneously the look of your physique and those body functions that have proven value in the wellness-health area.

Heavyhands should be a learning experience. Its physiological effects and the focus on skill make it potentially the most pleasurable of the aerobic exercises. Its logical use in a group situation, its lowered risk of injury, and its visible effect of producing muscle while reducing fat, add to that pleasure. For trained Heavyhanders, *any* workload feels easier than if performed by conventional aerobic methods. And that's a pleasurable plus!

The Ultimate in Practicality

Heavyhands is practical. Its equipment is inexpensive, and its space requirements are minimal: A cube of space 8 feet on each side is large enough to accommodate the most intense exertion imaginable! Heavyhands is suitable for sports training, adaptable to TV watching, and is *the* comprehensive exercise since it includes all the important fitness factors in each workout. Heavyhands is a highly controllable format, easily altered to fit the exerciser's changing needs, and works equally well indoors and out—for either gender and for any age group.

That's a capsule statement of Heavyhands advantages. It's a large mouthful admittedly, and should evoke your healthy skepticism. Please play devil's advocate from here on in! In a sense, I've written the book in anticipation of the questions and doubts these claims should raise.

For Those with High Blood Pressure

There are many people who have a powerful aversion to taking medicine—even the potentially life-saving kinds that doctors prescribe for high blood pressure. Some people prefer exercise to taking medicines, and come to believe that their blood pressure will automatically be controlled so long as they remain faithful exercisers. Blood pressure is such an important health issue that you must be careful about allowing any single factor to control it. Good exercise may indeed control slight or moderate elevations of blood pressure; or it may lower the dosage of appropriate medications. In any case, allow a health professional to help you plan a strategy that could add years to your life. Incidentally, no one should take medicines unnecessarily. But even if your exercise doesn't solve your blood pressure problem completely, you still need its "medicine" for the host of other benedictions it confers.

Why Heavyhands Walk?

Walking is here to stay! While everyone walks, it is estimated that around 55 million Americans do it for exercise. A constitutional was certainly good enough for some of the world's great intellects. Bertrand Russell and Sigmund Freud were known for their long walks. Harry Truman loved to walk and walked quickly, it is said. Racewalking is a respected sport and becoming more popular these days.

Walking is a useful alternative activity for injured athletes for whom the airborne state of running may mean risk of reinjury. It's also good for senior citizens and those whose heart function limits exertion. Walking in a strange city whole days at a time can be educational and stimulating. But young, healthy people merely *strolling for exercise* is plain nonsense.

You probably can't get a quicker fix on the general condition of your cardiovascular system than by counting your resting and working pulse rates. The lower the count per minute of the resting heart rate, the better—provided you don't suffer from some impairment of the heartbeat that keeps it slow. Now, if you counted the resting heart rates of 100 consecutive people who "stroll" for health, my guess would be that the percentage of those with a resting heart rate below 60 would be low, and I'd want to look at their electrocardiograms to decide what indeed was slowing their hearts. Strolling alone—without pumping weights—won't do the trick. And it wouldn't matter much whether they strolled 1 mile each day or 10, except that the long-distance walkers *might* come out slimmer! That's because no matter how slowly you stroll, a mile of walking nets you pretty nearly 100 calories of heat loss. But the facts are nonetheless unassailable: If you're *healthy* and *stroll* for cardiovascular conditioning—somewhere in the range of 2.5 to 3 mph—your ticker probably isn't getting a fair shake!

Actually, ordinary walking could be reasonably good exercise if many decided to train themselves to walk *quickly*. At paces above 4.5 mph, some people could get respectable heart training. Of course, there are those who can walk 7-minute

Some Curious Research on Walking with Weights

The reluctance of some to acknowledge the notion of active arms while walking emerged at a recent meeting of the American College of Sports Medicine. Researchers insisted upon measuring the energy expended when subjects walked on a treadmill merely *holding* small hand-weights at their sides. They found what they should have: insignificant work increases. Even huge weights don't evoke much aerobic work when hanging inertly. On the other hand, walking forward four steps and then backward four, while pumping 3-pound weights 3 feet up and down at 110 beats/minute converts a 2.5-mph walk to the equivalent of a 6-mph jog! We've practically *begged* people to try these simple movement recipes in their labs on their standard equipment. What's even more curious is that some of these researchers, usually scrupulous to a fault, utterly ignore crucial measurements like stride-stroke pace and pump height as though they don't matter!

Walk Plus!

For those who might find "Heavyhands Walk" a large mouthful, I thought "Walk Plus" might be a good equivalent. It merely means that conventional walking is just the beginning. The pluses are useful, interesting additions that increase the work in innumerable ways. For the upper torso, they include everything from pumping higher, heavier, and faster to leaning and flexing about your middle. For the legs, added work is in the form of knee dips and strides that bear only casual resemblance to the walk patterns we normally use to get around. I find the "plus" idea fetching because it conjures an open-ended option toward growth.

miles and even faster! Once at those fast paces, the work of walking gets harder at a faster rate. That makes it good exercise! I don't know how many of the alleged 55 million American walkers move at 7.5 mph (the equivalent of 8-minute miles or 200 meters/minute), but it has to be a minuscule percentage. A recent count estimated that there are only 10,000 to 15,000 racewalkers in the United States.

Perhaps there are fitness benefits other than cardiovascular considerations that come from regular long, slow walks. How about things like muscular endurance, power, strength, balance, coordination, grace, weight loss? Modest ratings everywhere, I'm afraid. If you calculate the upper torso benefit from walking, the answer is near zero—unless you're talking about racewalking, which does include a moderate level of armwork.

Well, then, how about backpacking, hill climbing, walking in foot-deep snow, or slogging through loose, wet sand at the beach? A couple of years ago, some Israeli investigators reported the beneficial results of walking regularly while carrying several pounds of bottled water on their backs. The *Journal of the American Medical Association* published their article, eager to let their readers know that adding work to walking would generate more training effects. How could it be otherwise? Fact is, *any* load you carry while you walk will

A Fitness Comparison:
Heavyhands Walk and Other Exercise

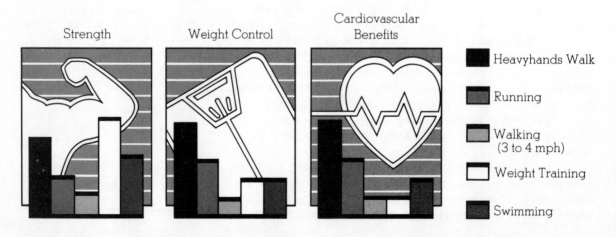

Strength   Weight Control   Cardiovascular Benefits

Heavyhands Walk

Running

Walking (3 to 4 mph)

Weight Training

Swimming

increase your heart rate for the length of your usual constitutional and train you to some extent. And, of course, that applies to walking faster, up hills, loaded down, or belaboring yourself with a duck walk!

There's no arguing the fact that walking can be good exercise. Whether a carefully designed study would show that it's good exercise as *currently practiced* is another question. I have scientific data that suggest there are more beneficial ways for people to walk for exercise—from octogenarians to hip-wiggling marathon walkers.

"Walking" with Your Upper Body

Having experimented with hundreds of combined exercises over the past decade, I am continually perplexed by our general willingness to throw the job of getting and staying fit upon the legs alone. Two kinds of mythology are probably responsible. One is a negative kind that implies that no other muscles can cut the physiologic mustard; the other, more positive, says, "Legs are such great aerobic drivers—why ditch 'em?" After several years of looking hard at the problem from lots of angles, I'm not too impressed by either argument.

First of all, the upper torso is a veritable aerobic gold mine. For their size, the arms are incredible exercise drivers. If you begin a leg-dominated aerobic program today—like jogging, fast walking, rope skipping, or biking—you'll do well if you can increase your work capability over your lifetime by as much as a full 20 percent. Armwork, generally neglected because of our lifestyles, can increase by as much as 100 percent. But what is more important is that trained legs *plus* trained upper torso, back, and abdomen make for greater overall progress and can be fueled simultaneously by a trained healthy heart. There's no *need* to choose!

Another side of the argument is that in conventional leg-dominated exercise, the legs aren't always heroic. Legs have been declared by experts in the exercise field to be ideal for heart training because of their large size, and this theory held sway for some time. But this argument neatly sidesteps the fact that the massive legs are underused in typical leg exercise like running because lots of leg muscles never get a piece of the action, and because the range of motion involved is modest. The muscles that *are* used are prone to injury because running, indeed, *overuses* the few doing the lion's share of the work.

Interestingly, the runner's overworked legs may not be very strong. In one study, elite runners, following a brief

---

Heavyhands Walk: Movement "Au Naturel"

It occurred to me long ago that Heavyhands Walk movements were not only the best way to begin combined, four-limbed movements, but they were logical, albeit outrageous, extensions of our natural limb movements while walking. The automatic associative movements feel right when the right arm swings while the left leg strides, and vice versa. The "work" of the exercise builds from there: faster action, more action in the form of range of motion, and heavying the hands with weights. So no matter how weird a Heavyhands Walk movement appears in its final form, it all "grew" from what we did as toddlers!

period of detraining, were able to jump higher than they could at the height of their running capability! The runner's training is so specific—moving the body horizontally swiftly and efficiently—that it excludes the kind of power needed for vertical acceleration of the body, as in jumping. It's a theme you'll hear me rant about repeatedly: how the motives of sport and fitness may be at odds with one another.

There's no question that our legs, trained moderately by a lifetime of getting around on them, are a logical choice for working the heart to a better state of fitness. The trouble we encounter, especially when we're seeking fitness levels of a *total* sort, is that conventional leg-driven exercise regimens don't get the job done for the majority of us. Those who do train to superior fitness through running constantly face the risk of lower body injury, **while** their relatively inert upper torsos usually remain "**healthy**" but unfit! Gurus in the field, like Dr. Ken Cooper, are beginning to believe that we don't need to run as much as we formerly thought. He has been suggesting lately that excellent fitness levels can be achieved on 15 miles of running a week. Dr. Cooper was also quoted

In running, the entire body is airborne. During Heavyhands Walk, the arms do the flying while the body stays on terra firma!

The Walk-Jog Gap

Anyone who is able to run is able to walk. But the reverse proposition doesn't hold. While walking, one foot always stays in contact with the ground; in running, however, the entire body is *airborne* for part of the stride. This airborne state requires a greater energy level than low-impact activity such as walking. Even a slow jog requires more endurance than most nonrunners enjoy when just starting out. And so you will see beginners jog along until breathless, slow to a walk until they catch their breath, jog again,

and so on. As training proceeds more time is devoted to jogging, less to the walking "relief phase." Finally, they can jog continuously through the entire workout.

What's happening during these intermittent jog-walk "intervals"? As you might expect, the jogging phase is really a "sprint" of overwork that gets the heart rate quite high—at the same moment breathlessness occurs. Then the walk phase allows the heartbeat to recover to a slower rate. The "gap" between the energy requirement of jogging and that of walking

makes it necessary to run a little at a time until the system trains itself.

Heavyhands Walk takes that gap out of training. Here's what I mean: Using four limbs and handweights while walking we can, from day one, gradually increase your training "load" without ever tampering with your working heart rate. That is, we can decide on a comfortable heart rate that is appropriate for your age and condition and keep it constant while gradually making your workouts more intense!

recently as saying, "Running 5 miles a day doesn't do a thing for your upper body strength." A couple things seem to be happening at once: some subtle easing of the need for the noncompetitive fitness seeker to log big weekly running mileage; and more emphasis being placed on the upper torso and other muscles, most often in the form of either weight training or in low repetition work with dumbbells.

Putting Arms and Legs to Work—Together

The arms, as I've said, are excellent exercise equipment. Because of the way our upper body is built, the arms are free to move in ways the legs can't. These include freewheeling actions about the shoulder joint—an assortment of 12 movements in all. Since arms don't support the body weight, they aren't reduced to the relatively lumbering movements of the legs. Supporting the body is a practical but unimaginative chore. Only athletes and dancers seem to venture beyond conventional legwork.

Arms can enjoy complicated movement options. Hands can reach enormous velocities because of their smaller mass

Rowing works specific muscle groups in the upper body; the many variations of Heavyhands Walk let you call lots of muscles into the exercise act.

How Heavyhands Walk Sizes Up to Running and Weightlifting

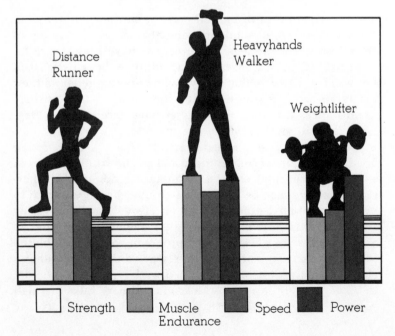

Distance Runner

Heavyhands Walker

Weightlifter

☐ Strength ▨ Muscle Endurance ▨ Speed ■ Power

**The Question
of Sudden Death
during Exercise**

I think they'll be wrangling long and loud over this one. The sudden deaths that occur during jogging bring that matter into sharp focus, naturally. Most of us don't hear about sudden deaths during walking, so we presume that jogging's intensity is the culprit. I remember reading a quote from runner/doctor/philosopher George Sheehan right after Jim Fixx's untimely death while running. It went something like, ''Walk if you don't want to run. No one dies while walking.'' I don't know whether that's true or not.

Of the hundreds of thousands of sudden deaths from heart attack each year, some must occur during walking. They are no more newsworthy than deaths in other situations—like during sleep, in the bathroom, during sexual activity, playing tennis, or at dinner. I've heard of many of each of those; I've even been present at a few. I remember, as a young doctor, pronouncing a man dead whose fatal heart attack had followed someone's making an almost imperceptible scratch on his new white Chevy station wagon.

One of the *New England Journal of Medicine* studies on the jogging/sudden death bit indicated that the group of victims studied did not exercise at high intensity. By the way, I've never heard of a sudden cardiac death in someone capable of high oxygen uptake capability, say, the top 5 percentile among runners. One study suggested that running did increase the risk of sudden death by sevenfold. I can't interpret that number with confidence unless I know how risky it is to get your new white Chevy station wagon scratched. There have been some statements in the popular literature that suggest going slow longer can be the equivalent of higher intensity exercise. Codswaddle! You simply can't eradicate the danger of exercising by dismissing the intensity factor. We simply need to learn how to better identify those for whom standard training intensities are extraordinarily risky.

and the great range of motion possible in the shoulder joint. Arms can engage in subtle movements that are simply out of the question for the legs. Physiologists have been aware for some time of the immense work capability of the arms. It's well known, for instance, that many swimmers can generate their maximum work capabilities using their arms *alone.* And there are instances when trained athletes have exceeded their leg-work capability using *only* their arms.

Our research suggests powerfully that unless there are good reasons for *not* combining arm, leg, and trunk muscles in exercise, there are substantial advantages in doing so! Furthermore, walking may be the best all-around format in which to practice combined exercise. Though Heavyhands is a varied system, if you had to choose a single movement theme and its variations for your Heavyhands program, walk would be the logical choice. To put it another way, our research shows clearly that a variety of four-limbed walking movements can, in time, generate steady workloads in ordinary folks that will equal or surpass the intensities they could expect to achieve with running!

Heavyhands Walk— Exercise That's Interesting!

The fact is that most healthy, intelligent, motivated people can become fit within a single year, at the outside, with aerobic exercise. Once fit, they can probably stay that way on two hours of exercise per week or less—for a lifetime. But if it's that simple, why aren't we all paragons of ultimate fitness? Probably because another characteristic of the human ego is its awesome susceptibility to boredom. I'm always perplexed by the fact that the major endurance training exercises—those allegedly best for our health—are the ones most likely to bore us. Once conditioned, many people quickly lose interest in exercise. Some abandon fitness programs for sports simply because the latter include the unpredictable: surprises and challenges that are more stimulating than the tedium of a 5-mile run.

Some facts of human psychology could rescue us. One is that people who are interested aren't bored! Practice allows us to improve our skills. Improvement keeps us interested. Interest keeps us directed toward further enhancing those skills. Exercise can be a glorious self-perpetuation, spinning off health, fitness, and fun along the way—but often it's not. (It's ironic that dance exercise, the one aerobic preoccupation that most emphasizes skill, sadly produces too many sidelining injuries and oftentimes not as much measurable fitness as the experts would lead you to believe.)

From a physiologic point of view it's easy to design a comprehensive exercise program that would keep us maximally fit; it's the *psychology* of exercise that poses the major hurdles. This book starts with the premise that anyone who persists at exercise will indeed become physically fit. But it goes a step farther: This program is designed to bring skill, interest, and imagination to the process of creating fit bodies.

When I decided to do a Heavyhands Walk program, I worried that some people might be put off by the word "walk." While there's not much doubt that this is walking, that's just the beginning of the story. In a physiologic sense or in kinesiologic terms (*kinesiology* is the science that deals with muscle actions), Heavyhands Walk might be more likened to cross-country skiing, swimming, or rowing. But it differs from *those* activities as well, because it's less regimented by standard movements that are constantly repeated. On the contrary: Heavyhands Walk allows you to experiment with a myriad of different movements. The more kinds of movements at higher intensities you can perform enjoyably, the less likely you are to become bored—and the fitter you will become!

The Embarrassment Factor

Don't discount the importance of embarrassment as an exercise inhibitor. Running went through its own embarrassment phase. I remember clearly hitting the roads and track at odd hours to avoid exposure! And there's no doubt that large numbers of participants represent the best antidote to shame anxiety. Other things help: confidence as to the benefit of what you're doing; technical skill; tangible results from training; and pride in "belonging" or subscribing to some method or strategy.

Pumping handweights while striding through a normal American urban community hasn't yet become standard procedure. It can't be compared with other combined exercises like rowing, swimming, or cross-country skiing: Each of those activities require special conditions and/or hardware that effectively isolate the exerciser from conventional trappings. But the nice thing about social embarrassment phenomena is that, in America at least, they disappear as fast as they emerge. And so it will be with pump 'n' walk. When people discover that the odd movements associated with pump 'n' walk produce exhibitable muscular rips and cuts, the embarrassment will vanish. You can count on it.

The Rational Phases of Heavyhands Walk Training

The first addition to general fitness comes by conditioning the badly deconditioned arms. That always works, because no sport can train the arms the way a variety of Heavyhands strokes can. The upper torso fitness adds to combined work capacity. Upper torso means more than arms: It means the huge muscle mass consisting of lats, delts, traps, pecs, and smaller accessory groups. During the upper torso "induction" phase, the legs have as much work as they can manage supporting the upper torso's output. As the upper torso fitness begins to level off, the Heavyhander begins to add strength-endurance loading to the legs. Adding strength to ordinary walking calls for knee dips, cross-strides, long strides, hamstring flexes, side-kicks, karatelike kicks, struts, duck walks—all radical departures from ordinary walk. As heavier hand-weights become more comfortable, these stride variations will generate even more strength-endurance, and at comfortable tempos. Interspersed speed drills make the program complete.

The Universal Exercise Solution?

I've scratched my head trying to decide if there is some individual who might not benefit from a steady program of Heavyhands Walk. Except for those who are too ill to exercise, I'm pleased to report that I can't think of anyone! The inclusion of the most muscle mass possible in continuous exercise is the fundamental tenet of this program, and nothing can mobilize more "beef" immediately in the average exerciser than the working together of all four limbs. That happens most easily by walking while adding handweights to a freewheeling upper torso. All the advantages of basic Heavyhands exercise apply to its walk version. And even if you prefer dance or calisthenics or shadowboxing routines, walk is a good place to gain your Heavyhands "sea legs." Heavyhands Walk involves natural movement, and provides a skill-base from which many interesting modifications can spring. With variations of four-limbed walk, all of the important fitness factors can be realized: strength, speed, endurance, strength-endurance, flexibility, agility, balance, and coordination. The movements, as you will see, can be as simple or as complicated as you wish. Every major muscle group can be mobilized in four-limbed walk.

As I've suggested, you may be struck by the notion that this *isn't really* walking: It doesn't *feel* like it or *look* like it, and others might glance quizzically at you now and again as you pass them, arms and legs going full throttle. Don't fret. Hundreds of thousands of Americans will soon be walking this way for health and that number should skyrocket during our lifetimes. While there's always resistance to the establishment of a new idea, the research findings here are too compelling to ignore for long.

I don't want to sound blasé about beginner's self-consciousness. For the past three years I've had literally thousands of encounters with supposed Heavyhanders whose pumping actions were low to nonexistent! With little 1-pounders it certainly wasn't a matter of weakness. And when I took their pulses I knew they weren't overworking. It had to be partly self-consciousness. A nice man visited me one day while I was on tour in Houston. "Doc," he said, "there are 5,000 runners in Memorial Park every day, mebbe more on weekends. And there are a thousand carrying Heavyhands. I don't think I've seen five of them doin' it right!"

Hardly a remark I could ignore. One day, at the Human Energy Lab at Pitt, we measured my workload just "carrying" 10-pound weights while walking on a level treadmill. The work increase over plain strolling on the treadmill sans hand-weights wasn't even worth mentioning. The other side of the coin: Pumping those 10's to a modest height or pumping 1's high and fast while walking, Heavyhanders have done better than the work-equivalent superb runners can do at a 5-minute/mile pace! But whether you're armed with heavy or light weights, you have to act boldly!

Another advantage of Heavyhands Walk is that it can be performed aggressively. Those who have tried pumping weights while running may not have been stalled by embarrassment alone. When vintage runners complained in a chorus that pumping weights "knocked them off stride," I had to stifle a small chuckle. Pumping high and fast with small weights while remaining faithful to your running pace will inevitably back you into a physiologic corner. The workload increases so much that something has to give. To bring the upper torso into the act and remain at a reasonable heart rate, the tempo of the whole procedure *has* to slow. If the runner stubbornly keeps to his habitual pace, the pumping effort must slacken—thus the Heavyhanding runners who protest they've been knocked off their stride. As it turns out their stride is the least of their problems!

Since most recreational walkers don't worry much about stride, they can experiment more freely with arm movements. If they discover they must walk a bit more slowly to pump their arms more, that's not a problem.

Now it's time to get you started on a system of exercise that hopefully will be user-friendly enough to keep you hooked for life.

Energy Revisited

I can empathize with anyone who shudders at the mere mention of laboratory data. Some years ago, an article in the *Washington Post* took a whack at my first book, saying you needed a graduate degree in theoretical physics to figure out what I was talking about. I pouted to myself that the guy was unfair—that an undergraduate degree would have been enough. But if I say that the energy you get from Panaerobic training—just pump 'n' walk—makes you able to do more than you were able to do before you were trained, what kind of a degree do you need to comprehend that idea?

Even so, since most of us have become comfortable with our movement habits, we are not enthralled with the idea of doing *more*, or doing the same thing more easily. So I think the way to kindle a legitimate fitness revolution is to pay the largest premiums on work. *Pay* our citizens to be slim and muscular, and they'll work toward more active lifestyles in a flash. How hard do you think it is to mobilize Sly Stallone, Arnold Schwarzenegger, Jane Fonda, Bruce Springsteen, or even a bush leaguer like Lennie Schwartz to work out?

Getting Started

On the next few pages we'll talk about your health and the equipment you'll need to get started with your own Heavyhands Walk program. Like learning to dance, play a musical instrument, or even work your personal computer, Heavyhands Walk is much more enjoyable if you go slowly at the beginning.

Medical Sanction for Heavyhands Walk

There are many different opinions on this subject. Of course, if you suffer from a chronic illness or have recently recovered from a brief illness, you should ask your doctor's opinion about this program as it relates to *your* health. Some

---

"Silent" Heart Disease

We generally expect coronary artery disease to announce itself through characteristic discomfort: a choking or constricting sensation under the breastbone, a radiation of pain into one or both arms and into the jaw or neck, and other kinds of pain. Those symptoms usually occur when the heart's work capacity is being challenged in some way—by physical activity, emotional strain, or even a large meal. These "anginal" symptoms usually occur because the openings in the coronary vessels, the ones that supply the heart muscle, are virtually closed off by "atherosclerosis," a collection of fatty material that develops along the inner lining of the vessels. That characteristic warning is what gets the patient to the doctor where, hopefully, the diagnosis is established, and treatment, either surgical or medical or both, is administered.

Sometimes, however, these warnings don't occur. A person may accomplish a surprising amount of physical work without the typical anginal signals. And sometimes even an exercise ECG doesn't locate the problem (called a "false negative" test). No one is quite sure why silent coronary artery disease occurs. But this absence of angina makes us particularly nervous about people in their middle and later years who start exercise programs without benefit of a preliminary checkup. Sometimes after a sudden death in an apparently fit, youngish jogger, doctors discover that the symptoms were not, in fact, silent—and death might have been prevented. A high total cholesterol level and a low HDL level (HDL is a form of beneficial cholesterol), a suggestive family history of early coronary heart disease, high blood pressure, heavy smoking, and diabetes should alert us to the possibility of heart disease, even if there are no symptoms.

doctors believe everyone over age 35 needs an exercise electrocardiogram. I'd also be inclined to ask for a stress test in a 20-year-old who is overweight and has led a sedentary life.

I think I'd like to see the exercise electrocardiogram (also known as an ECG) used for reference data, something you can look back at when charting your progress (or lack of it, as the case may be). We have noticed that a preliminary test measuring a person's capacity to use oxygen often serves as a graphic stimulus for their continued interest in exercise. They learn a great deal in a few moments about the nuts and bolts of "exerscience," and we usually give them their printouts for later reference.

When you consider the people who exercise at 700 cardiac rehabilitation centers in the United States, you wouldn't think that exercise is prohibited for many people. What does become a problem is the too-prevalent belief among compulsive health-seekers that obtaining medical advice is unnecessary; often superb performance makes a consultation with the doctor seem unimportant. Super health and fitness are a lifetime commitment. But no fitness level absolutely excludes the possibility of latent disease, and almost no disease altogether excludes the possibility of exercising. Periodic checkups make hard-won fitness more meaningful, and remove subtle doubts about your state of health.

An exercise ECG can provide valuable information: Often it reveals the first indications of coronary artery disease in patients who haven't yet experienced symptoms. Having detected those signs early, the doctor can prescribe safer exercise that falls comfortably within that person's observed work capacity. You can also use blood pressure readings and ECG results to evaluate improvements gained through your exercise program.

Another cautionary note: There are those who should be re-evaluated periodically (perhaps each year, or more often) despite their apparent good health, superlative work capacity, and total absence of symptoms during exercise. I refer to those people whose total blood cholesterol levels tend to be high despite their investing time and energy in good exercise and good nutritional habits. If there is a strong family history of heart attack and/or stroke before the age of 60 in either parent or their siblings, this evaluation is even more important. Exercise is a potent preventive measure, but it cannot always move mountains without some medical support and careful monitoring under actual stressful conditions.

In my experience, those who are "at risk" often deny a lurking medical problem by virtue of their apparent excellent

A stress test equips you with the information you need to gauge the very specific and positive changes your body undergoes through exercise.

health—in which case a visit to the doctor becomes invaluable. I have also discovered that evaluations such as exercise ECGs usually leave the individual enormously relieved, despite their annoyed comments suggesting that the procedure was an unnecessary expense and an inconvenience. Perhaps many of us are more worried than we admit about the "real" state of our health, and are understandably but foolishly afraid of the truth—which is seldom as bad as we suspect it will be!

Last-Minute Miscellany

Once assured you're in reasonably good health, you're ready to gear up for your Heavyhands Walk program. While this program is probably as simple as any you'll ever undertake, there are a few preparatory steps that will help make your Heavyhands experience even more enjoyable.

Appropriate Clothing

In warm weather or indoors, shorts or sweats with light shirts or tank tops are all you need. Since we differ in our response to heat and humidity and in our enjoyment or distaste for sweating, I'm not going to tell you exactly what to wear. Generally speaking, most people feel that cooler is

Holter Monitoring: Promise for Those at Risk

This new technique for monitoring heart activity over a 24-hour period may hold new promise for identifying those at high risk of sudden death during exercise. The subject carries a comfortably worn monitor, which records a 24-hour ECG that can be played back in concentrated form in a few minutes by computer. The monitor can print out particular samples from the record, as during certain moments of exertion, anxiety, or stress. The record collates the frequency of rhythm deviations, or moments when the heart muscle isn't receiving enough blood. An enormous amount of information can be pooled to identify what's happening to the patient's circulatory equipment during a normal day's life—some of which may not surface during the standard, brief exercise ECG. And it looks like the price will be right.

The Challenge of Pump 'n' Walk

Pump 'n' walk is a natural movement, and thus an easy movement. Obtaining a sense of grace is important—moving with four limbs as automatically as you steer your body on a crowded sidewalk, for instance. But once you've accomplished that, it becomes literally impossible to make a mistake; you can't stride and stroke easily with the limbs on the same side. It doesn't *feel* right. If I asked you to walk, swinging your arms easily, with the arms and legs on each side moving simultaneously, you'd have a very tough time of it!

The hitch in pump 'n' walk comes when the arms are asked to do exaggerated things, like stroking high and/or fast, or doing so with heavy handweights. We're used to effortless, spontaneous arm-swings of small amplitude, the pace ordinarily dictated by the legs' power and the brain's ambition. Once you're able to switch handweight sizes and hang in at your target heart rate through subtle adjustments of stride-stroke pace, you're a Heavyhander!

better. Your core body temperature will soon rise and you'll probably start peeling layers after about 10 minutes of vigorous movement.

The Right Place to Work Out

Our Heavyhands group meets at a gym in an ancient schoolhouse in our neighborhood. We work out inside during the cold months of each year, then outside during warmer weather. At the gym, we're preceded one night each week by a group of young male volleyball players, who've worked up a sweat by the time we get there. But they keep the windows shut! Before we start the music, all the windows are opened wide!

The point is that team sports—even a very spirited and well-played game of volleyball—may not make the same demands as the continuous, apparently modest activity of four-limbed exercise. The combination of cool ambience and evident sweat is a strong indicator that the intensity factor isn't being neglected.

Once you're trained in Heavyhands, you will be able to exercise long and hard in hot weather at a much lower heart rate. By mobilizing more muscle, you'll be working hard without *feeling* like you're working hard. In cold weather, your greater heat production will make you comfortable. Also, since Heavyhanders work at relatively high levels, slowing down a bit because of the heat will still leave you working at a respectable clip.

Shoes

I have little to say about the shoes that are appropriate for Heavyhands Walking. I have used an assortment of running shoes, and all have proven satisfactory. I have also used a variety of implements to weight my feet, and will address that subject when we deal with Strength Walk in Chapter 12. I don't think you need to change the exercise shoes that have proven themselves during ordinary walking or jogging once you add handweights. I would mention, however, that I would choose running shoes over aerobic shoes, as the latter do not seem to provide the kind of support needed for continuous *walking* with weights. There are dozens of excellent brands of *walking shoes* available, in a large price range.

The Question of Weights

Handweights are the next thing to be considered. The Heavyhands strapped handweights were developed when it became clear that, once trained, 5,000 to 10,000 or more continuous repetitions were as doable by arms as by legs. The strap simply made things easier for the small muscles of the hand and forearm, and made hard gripping unnecessary. The option to change the weighted ends was essential for a combined program that trains for speed as well as strength and range of motion. Once I was armed with strapped weights, both the comfort and the duration of steady workloads were extended measurably. Now my *hands* never gave out. My experiments also showed that using the strapped handweights at a given workload produced lower average increases in working blood pressures.

If you decide to use the Heavyhands weights, be sure that you select the handle size that fits snugly without constricting—only the largest hands need the "large" size handles. Also make sure you're using them correctly. After two years, we continue to see people wearing the weights improperly. The strap should ride over the *back* part of the hand.

If you use standard strapless weights (small dumbbells), try to practice your walking movements, being conscious of your tendency to overgrip, which is normal in the beginning. In a few days you will learn just how much gripping is necessary. During pumping movements you can relax your grip somewhat during part of each stroke so that the gripping action is intermittent.

Eventually, you will want to use a variety of weight sizes to work on several fitness factors like strength and speed. One other reason: The exercises that you are about to add to "ordinary" walking vary in difficulty. Some invite heavier handweights than others do. But using heavy weights is not necessarily an indication of more work. In our class I occasionally spy someone—typically a strong, young man—pumping big weights high and handsome. When I check his pulse, it becomes evident that all that apparent heavy labor was really a piece of cake. His pulse is often below what's appropriate, and the fact is, he's *resting* while most of his classmates are green-eyed over the hefty hardware he's sporting.

It is vital early in the game to gain a clear mental distinction between *work* and *strength*. If I suggest to this young man that he switch to weights half the size, pump high, and stick to the musical beat, he finds himself puffing usefully by the song's end. With smaller weights there's less "pure" strength involved, but much more work, more increase in aerobic capacity, and more fat incinerated per minute.

But I would not discourage my young friend from working with his heavy weights altogether. Working with heavy weights will build a bit more muscle mass and the kind of strength that ultimately will add to your aerobic capacity.

The strap is designed to relax your grip and lower your blood pressure during exercise. Make sure it fits snugly and squarely over the back of your hand.

A Word on Wrist Weights

I happen not to like wrist weights. I've tried them all, and I can wear them satisfactorily until I try to use them for Heavyhands exercises at meaningful intensities. For those exercises, they're uniformly too light, too bulky for their small mass, too loose, or too scratchy. Were I to do 120 to 140 punches or hi-pumps each minute with wrist weights, at the hand velocities I generate, I'd need a skin graft by the end of a week.

Some say wrist weights are preferable because they leave the hand free during upper body exercise. Free for what? When I want hand exercise, which I almost never do, I play my guitar, or a bit of piano. I've even tried 5-pound wrist weights and larger. It simply doesn't work. And if you need wrist exercise, the better way to get that is to put the weight where it belongs: not over the joint itself but smack in the palm of your hand. It feels good there, there's a sense of control. Feet are made to wear things like shoes because they're passive. *Hands* are a different story. They're what we *manage* with, our tools for handling things—and very handy ones at that.

Tiny wrist weights foreclose on the mighty upper torso's work capacity. In fact, possible *underuse* and some discomfort are my chief criticisms. I'm probably spoiled from using the strapped version, which to me fits like a glove.

"Strength-endurance" is the best way of describing it. The bulk of your Heavyhands time, however, should be spent using weights that optimize your steady work capacity. That weight changes as training proceeds, but a handy rule would be that any weight too heavy to generate a solid target heart rate and the increased breathing volume that goes along with that for at least five minutes is too heavy to be part of your Panaerobic workout. Next year it may be comfortably included in your routines.

Keeping the Beat

A metronome of some sort is useful—much more useful, incidentally, than in conventional walking or jogging. That's because the frequency of arm movements is more crucial to the Heavyhands workload than is stride pace in the absence of armwork. Timers can take the form of one of the popular "pacer" watches, the musical beat from your stereo, or your Walkman when outdoors. The beat keeps you honest and the workload constant when you're doing a specific movement with weights. It also helps keep track of your training progress; you'll begin to notice greater ease and lower heart rates with given workloads.

Warming Up and Cooling Down

There is still a good bit of confusion over the problem of warming up for exercise. For a long time many considered the words "stretch" and "warmup" to be synonymous. But the newest thinking on this is that a warmup should actually be a form of lower-than-target aerobics, performed to actually "warm" the body, to get its temperature up. Stretching is thus best performed following this increase in the body's core temperature because the stretchable tissues respond best then.

"Cooling down" is reducing the workload gradually from target heart rates; its importance is said to derive from the danger that blood will "pool" in the lower extremities if we stop vigorous work too rapidly. This pooling reduces the circulating blood volume so that the blood returning to the heart may be substantially reduced. When cardiac output falls, you might experience symptoms ranging from lightheadedness to chest pain. Some experts advocate lying down. Some don't bother with cooldown at all. I tend to play the odds. Since neither warming up nor cooling down can hurt, and since it makes some physiologic sense—and since there have been a few post-exercise deaths reported—I vote "yes."

Tracking Your Responses to Heavyhands Walk

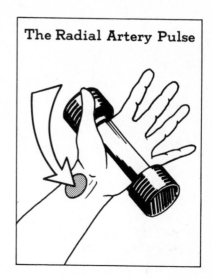

The Radial Artery Pulse

You're probably aware of the importance of heart rate in aerobic exercise. Well, it's equally important in Heavyhands Walk. But if you don't want to be bothered with pulse checking, there is a useful alternative. It's called the RPE, meaning the "rating of perceived exertion." A researcher named Borg (who, incidentally, invented the scale of the same name) decided people could usefully rate the difficulty of their exercise on a moment-by-moment basis—from very, very light to very, very heavy. After counting your pulse for a few days, taking reasonably frequent samples, you may decide to go the perceptual rating route, and you may find that you've become able to estimate your heart rate quite accurately.

Nonetheless, pulse checking can be a valuable guide, especially early in your training. Though most exercise manuals give you plenty of choices, I believe in using the radial pulse. The radial pulse is located on the thumb side of the palm surface of the wrist. Use the tips of your middle and forefinger to find your pulse, and count for 6 seconds, calling the first counted beat "zero," not "one." Then you simply add a zero to your 6-second count and you have a minute count. Some count 15 seconds and multiply by four, and I've seen a half and a whole minute recommended.

Truckin' with Your Radio Headset

I prefer the radio headset because I find the connecting wires on conventional tape recorders an impediment to my freewheeling arm action. Working with various musical beats is a wonderful way to become a superb Heavyhander. You're out on the road with only one set of weights. That means the resistance element can't be varied. The challenge now is to juggle ranges of motion to accommodate a tempo that's changing about every three minutes with the music.

Look at the things you can do to keep your heart rate happily constant:

- Alter pump height
- Switch to punches, alter the force of the pullbacks
- Add snap to ordinary punches
- Go to semi-ducks
- Do a side lean with each pump/punch
- Any combination of the above!

It's hard to convey the thrill that combination of utter control and wide-ranging variety ignites! You become a moving gymnasium. You've got your whole fitness world in your hands! You can even change the quality of the stride-stroke pattern according to what enters your ears: rock, bebop, heavy metal, jazz, bluegrass, opera, symphonic, rhythm and blues, ethnic, baroque. You can pump and stride to German lieder if you wish! And if the neighbors think this gyrating old man with a headset is playing with less than a full deck, why, what's new?

As you become more aerobically fit, your weakish pulse will gain some impact as it moves against your fingertips. If you take a six-second count, it's important to start the count immediatedly upon stopping your exercise. That's because your heart rate starts slowing once you stop. Early in your program it's not that important, because your heart rate doesn't "return" as fast as it will once you're trained. There are recommended target heart rates that are related to your age. You've doubtless seen this chart dozens of times. These values are approximations, of course, but good for rule-of-thumb application. Again, if for one reason or another your range of heart rates doesn't seem right while you exercise, don't worry. All rules except moderation are to be dropped for your initial trials with Heavyhands Walk.

I think it's good to get a fix on where you are from a cardiovascular standpoint; that means checking your resting heart rate regularly, and your resting blood pressure when possible. Contrary to what you might believe, the resting heart rate is elusive; that's because it's rather volatile. It jumps a few beats on the slight provocation posed by a meal, an anxious moment, a tinge of temper, or even a bit of good news. Just

Determining Your Target Heart Rate

You have probably seen a chart like this before; it will simply be a quick reference for you. To determine the average target pulse range for your age, draw a vertical line from your age on the bottom up to the shaded area. Where the line crosses the shaded area tells you the pulse rate range for that age by reading across a pulse table. For example: Age 45 gives you a target heart rate range of 122 to 148.

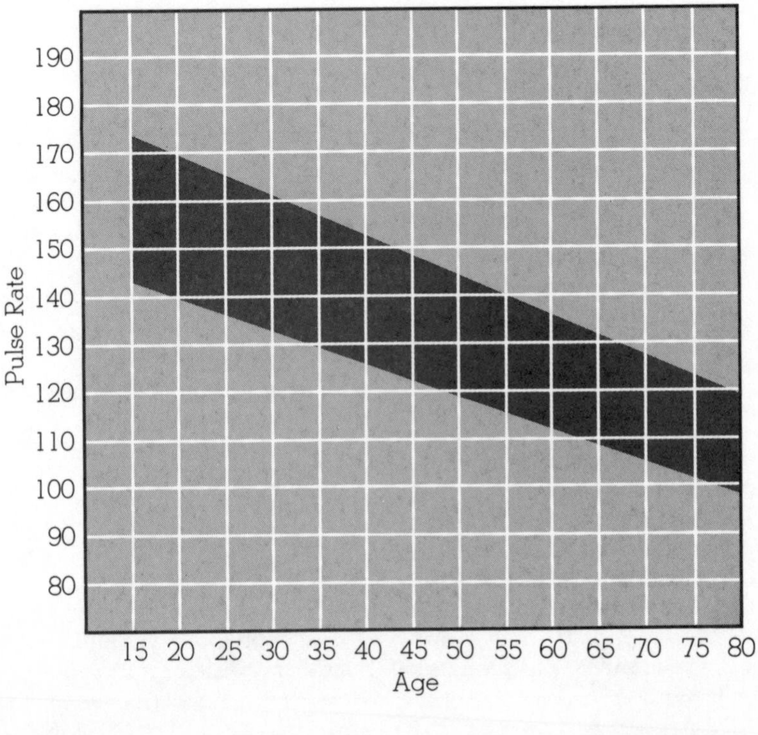

standing up may cause your heart rate to increase by a full 20 percent or so. It's higher for a few hours after prolonged exercise, and surprisingly, it's not always at its slowest when you awaken in the morning.

The best way to get a good representative resting heart rate is to sample it several times during the day, not close to meals, exercise, or a battle with your boss. Unless you're a health-care professional, chances are you'll need help in determining your blood pressure. Your resting blood pressure should parallel resting heart rate lowerings as you gather "training effects." And since Heavyhands exercise has such a dramatic effect on the circulations of regular "users," you can enjoy these heart rate and blood pressure drops often as early as three weeks into your training.

And while you're at it, there's nothing wrong with noting other body "specs," like your weight, skinfold fat, oxygen consumption values your doctor can give you after a stress test, maximal heart rates recorded during "max" testing, and blood fat levels, including HDL cholesterols and total cholesterol. That sort of data gathering makes sense, and can help to get you more interested in your own body and personal health.

My Static Stretch

I do one static stretch. It was designed to be the best stretching bargain I could conceive. It stretches simultaneously the hamstrings, the inner thighs, the lower back, the groin muscles, and much of the upper torso to boot. The photos tell all. I do it for a few seconds anywhere from 0 to 10 times a day depending upon my disposition and my body talk.

An easy stretch

Heavyhands Pump 'n' Walk: The Basic Movement

Five minutes after you read this you'll probably know how to do it! The reason is that we merely are extending what comes naturally to us bipeds. The ordinary "automatic associated movements" of walking involve swinging the arm *opposite* the striding leg. That's basically all there is to pump 'n' walk. Taking a pair of your 1-pounders, begin to walk as shown in the photos. Your right arm will "pump" in a forward and upward arc while your left leg is swinging forward in its stride; then the alternate—your left arm will pump while your right leg swings forward. If you get mixed up, stop and start again. Soon it will become as second nature as ordinary walking.

Workloads in Heavyhands Walk are determined by at least three factors—or at least we can content ourselves with just three for now. One is tempo. How many pump-strides can we perform in a minute? Most pop music has a tempo that's about 120 beats/minute, but most people strolling walk fewer steps than that each minute. Some people can stride as frequently as 200 steps/minute or more, but that's very diffi-

Basic pump 'n' walk

The wrong way

cult and not sustainable by many. Walking at very fast stride frequencies becomes "inefficient." That means that at 160 strides/minute, it's easier for most folks to jog than to walk; as you might expect, you can lose more calories walking at that pace than you can jogging.

The second factor determining how hard we work at Heavyhands Walk is range of motion. At a given tempo, stridelength becomes a significant variable: The longer your stride, the harder you're working. That makes good sense, because at a given tempo, when you're striding fast, you're covering more territory—more miles per hour.

The pump height of the weight is the best indicator of workload. Chances are good that most of your striding will vary only slightly—perhaps an inch or two—unless you consciously alter it. But variations in pump height change the work of Heavyhands dramatically. For convenience we measure pump height in feet: Level 1 is 1 foot, Level 2 is 2 feet, Level 3 is 3 feet, and so on. Measuring with the hands hanging straight down at your sides, if you're about average height, Level 1 hits you about belly button high, Level 2 near the front of the shoulder joint, Level 3 about the top of your head, and Level 4 about as high as most of us can pump without losing the limb! Those relationships obviously change as your height approaches the extremes of 4 or 7 feet. If your height nears 7 feet, for instance, pump heights of Level 5—or 5 feet—are possible.

This awareness of pump height is an important concern in "standardizing" Heavyhands workloads. But there's another consideration. As you will learn from experimenting with pump 'n' walk, each of the pump levels works the upper torso somewhat differently. Levels 1 and 2 work the muscles of the arm itself. At Levels 3 and 4 you're mobilizing plenty of muscle mass from the shoulder, chest, upper back, etc. Generally speaking, your Level 3.5 pump 'n' walk ventures will use nearly twice as much energy as will Level 2, although there is apt to be some individual variation.

Downwork

This is a term I apply to a unique characteristic of Heavyhands exercise. This is the special quality of the pumping movement in which the workload—and therefore certain training effects—can be increased by forcefully *pulling* the weight downward, and not simply allowing gravity to do it for you. Downwork can become an important part of your four-limbed training. We have measured the work involved in

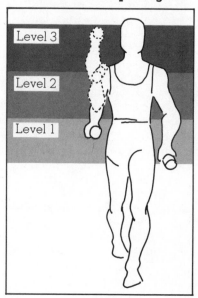

The Basic Pump Heights

Level 3

Level 2

Level 1

Heart Rate vs. Intensity, One More Time

It looks to me like for lots of people, heart rate and work intensity mean the same thing. Can we talk? Pulse rate is a good measure of work intensity, maybe the best, surely the least expensive, for you—right now, that is. That means "relative" intensity, relative to what your heart rate at near exhaustion would be. Like 60 or 80 percent of your maximum effort. That's the most important measure of intensity because while exercising you should remain, physiologically speaking, in your own little private, noncompetitive world.

But part of our quest for fitness is in relation to the demands of the world around us. The things we do require energy and some of those things require absolute amounts of it. Time and space make for absolutes. You can't stroll toward first and expect to arrive there safe! You can't win at good singles tennis or play soccer if you walk leisurely for fitness. You can't lope, even slowly, up a steep grade without the wherewithal, or hit the green on that four par with your second shot unless you can make that club-head whistle! If you stop to think about it, life is full of situations that are "go or no go": You either have the stuff or you don't. Every bit you add to your capability introduces innumerable little abilities that were absolutely out of range before. That's why the categorical "walk at such-and-such pace at a pulse of such-and-such and you'll be as fit as you need to be" is pure rubbish. How can anyone know?

different sorts of downstroking and have been surprised at the increase that comes with an enthusiastic downward "snap" of the hand, even when the tempo remains unchanged.

Downwork increases dramatically with fast tempos; depending upon the size of your weights, it may become unavoidable. You'll discover that at tempos above 130 or so you *must* snap the hands downward lustily in order to be ready for the next upstroke. A metronome or music with a spirited beat will help make a fine downstroker of you. Downstroking produces, of course, regional advantages. It develops the lats, triceps, and pectorals nicely.

Downstroking can be practiced deliberately at various pump heights. It becomes necessary even at slower tempos when you're pumping high (Levels 3 and 4), simply because the weight has to travel farther. Hard downstroking at Level 2 happens for me at around 160 beats/minute; at Level 3.5 I'm downpumping hard at 120! You will probably experience a bit of soreness at the back of the arm and perhaps in your lats the day after your first shot at purposeful downwork. Downwork is an added touch to Heavyhands, like "hanging 10" if you're a surfer or learning to switch your backhand grip in tennis.

What You Can Expect from Heavyhands Walk— and from Yourself

If I didn't believe this method of getting and staying fit had solid merit—and something no other exercise method has to offer—I would not have devoted a sizable part of my life to ferreting out its benefits as well as its real problems. There's no magic here; the claims are simply ones we've learned to anticipate as part of the process.

A recent training study undertaken at the Human Energy Lab disclosed things that went beyond the measurement of training effects, things we could have expected instinctively beforehand. Heavyhands Walk, like any other kind of activity that calls for continuous application, lends itself both to the best sort of diligence and the most flagrant copping out you can imagine. Most subjects who "hung in" nobly until the movements really became easier went on to bigger workloads and logged phenomenal gains in a few total hours of training. Two didn't. Their minimal gains reflected their lagging enthusiasm, probably lower training heart rates, shorter pump heights, and falling behind the prescribed exercise tempos. Like just about everything else in life, you get from exercise precisely what you put into it.

Naturally, if you add *any* work to conventional walk you will make gains that walking alone couldn't have produced. These movements, hardly bizarre, are also hardly usual. Part of the plan here has to do with the way muscles work together (kinesiology), and part involves keeping the exercise as interesting as possible for lots of people.

The physiologic aim seems simple: to move in ways that will cause alterations in the heart and the entire musculature that no single exercise menu or machine or sport can duplicate. Given that, trained Heavyhands Walkers should develop the leanest, hardest-working body they can have on an equal investment of training time. In a nutshell:

- Heavyhanders' strength-endurance, the capacity to continue at rather "heavy" chores for a prolonged time, should be second to none.
- Their running times should improve or remain the same on a quarter or less of their weekly mileage.
- Strength athletes and bodybuilders should sacrifice little strength or muscle mass while improving muscle definition, again, on a fraction of their previous training time with heavy weights.
- Athletes should expand their skill and the work capability they bring to their sport.
- Injuries should be fewer, across the board.
- New agility and balance should accrue.
- Blood pressure and pulse rate should drop, even in those maximally trained previously by other techniques.
- The trained Heavyhander should gain the best overall control of the distribution of muscle and fat in his or her body.

In subjects whose work capacities were high to begin with, we have seen substantial gains (in excess of 20 percent) on less than two total hours of weekly training in just eight weeks! The training was limited to walk. The subjects were never airborne—not for one moment!

I'm sure you're more interested in what Heavyhands Walk holds in store for you. So we're ready to try our pretest to locate you properly on the spectrum of aerobic capability. Then you can measure your own training effects as things begin to happen!

Walking Strong

If you'd have suggested to me 10 years ago that walking could be converted into an exercise that makes one more mechanically strong and aerobically powerful than any other combination of exercises could, I would have guffawed. But it's true. Some recent studies from our lab showed that an untrained, healthy subject pumping 8-pounders to Level 2, at a modest 120 paces/minute—or 3.5 mph—with a bit of a knee dip added, could generate a greater workload than is required to run 11 mph! The terrific potential of the legs is seldom unleashed by mere walking or running; but the combination of heavyish handweights and knee dips makes it happen. We already know that sprinters, supposedly the fastest humans, do not record the highest continuous work capabilities. But it would never have occurred to me before our research began that slow, heavy work would do the trick.

Finding Your Fitness Level: A Five-Minute Test

Now you can make use of pump 'n' walk to do a combined exercise that will tell you a lot about your current physical condition. Knowing that will enable you to make a close estimate at a beginning Heavyhands exercise prescription for yourself.

It's really quite simple. In the laboratory we measured the amount of aerobic work required to do a moderate intensity of pump 'n' walk. Knowing that value, you can determine how readily your body accomplishes that much work by doing five minutes of it, then immediately counting your pulse. The lower your pulse rate upon completing the test (providing you've played by the rules, of course), the more efficient your performance of this task and the fitter you are. Another advantage of a "pretest" is that it gives you a base-line level against which you can measure your training gains. Remember, though, that if the test produces any sort of unusual discomfort—breathlessness, dizziness, or any chest pain, for instance—good sense dictates that you stop at once.

What You'll Need and How to Test Yourself

To get the most accurate test results, you'll need a watch for pulse counting and something that cues you as to how fast to pump 'n' walk. And you'll need some 1-pound weights. The test simply requires that you pump 'n' walk to Level 2 (you'll recall from Chapter 3 that means up 2 feet and down again) with these 1-pounders for five full minutes. The *number* of pumps and strides per minute is important to combined exercise. So, ideally you should have a pacer watch that will beep for you at the rate of 120 beats/minute. Your natural stridelength will also help to determine how hard you are working, but not enough to worry about if you simply stride as usual and do it the same way each time.

If you don't have a pacer watch, there are some pretty good though somewhat less accurate alternatives. Most people

METs!

I've become obsessed with the notion that I can, or should be able to, teach anyone what a MET is. I worry a little that people may regard themselves as unintelligent after many brushes with the word without the foggiest notion of what it means. (Actually, it might be simpler just to let it stand for a professional baseball team and banish it from exercise terminology forever.)

In any case, rest is 1 MET. Don't ask me why. Someone decided that the amount of work the body does at rest should be called 1 MET. It's known that big bodies produce more heat than small bodies. But when each pound of us is working at the business of *rest*, each of those pounds or kilos or tons produces the same amount of heat if you average it all out. You need to average it out because it would hardly be fair for big people to be thought of as harder workers merely because they're bigger. That would be like matching heavyweights with flyweights.

So it's always how much work per unit of body weight, and since metrics are "in" in scientific circles, we think of oxygen used per each kilogram (2.2 pounds) of body weight. If you're moving along at 2 METs, you're working twice as hard as when you're at rest; at 10 METs, you're doing roughly the work of running 6 mph, or 10 times the work of rest. That's all there is to it. It's nice to understand it, but I'll let you in on a secret: The issue is mostly academic, because if you're at your target heart rate and comfortable, you're spinning off all the METs you can—and being a mathematical whiz won't lose you an extra calorie!

feel comfortable with 120 strides/minute when they are walking with a stridelength that would cover a mile in about 15 to 20 minutes. If a quarter-mile track is located conveniently, practice walking until you do one whole lap somewhere between 3 minutes, 45 seconds and 5 minutes. That translates into 15- to 20-minute miles, 4 mph and 3 mph respectively. If there's anyone around who is using a beeper watch, try pacing at a 120 pace to get the feel of that tempo. Better still, if you own a musical metronome, or can borrow one, practice stepping around the house or the backyard at a 120 tempo for a few minutes. Even if your first test isn't done precisely, you can do it again within a day or two with more accurate equipment.

To "standardize" the test, you should pump your 1-pounders 2 feet high at this 120 pace. Use a tape measure or yardstick and measure from your middle knuckle when your arm is completely extended downward. See where 2 feet comes to (probably the point of the shoulder or thereabouts), practice a few pumps in front of the mirror to check your pump height, and you're set to go. While the pacer watch makes for better accuracy, even an approximation done without one will give you a fair idea of your present condition. Another way of getting to pace is to merely count the paces you "self-select" for a minute to gain a rough notion of whether you need to speed or slow a bit to get closer to 120 beats/minute.

Another alternative to buying a beeper watch is to use a portable stereo headset. Some Heavyhanders have made audiocassette recordings of various tempos, which work nicely for their outdoor Heavyhands routines. Eventually you can make use of all sorts of musical accompaniment with various stride-stroke combinations. And almost any tempo can be translated into an exercise intensity that suits you. You merely adjust the range of arm motion or the weight you're pumping to make the music work for you: You pump higher at slow tempos, lower at fast ones.

For testing purposes, those who own a Walkman or facsimile can scout around for a song with a tempo of 120, then simply pump 'n' walk the test at five minutes of that. Just remember to use the same song when you decide to retest! You can tell by all this that I'm eager to see you get some sort of beginning values in order to measure your subsequent gains. Rest assured, there will be gains!

More Exercise Lingo: "Mls of O$_2$"

If we were testing you at Pitt's Human Energy Lab, we'd hook you up to our gas analyzing equipment. A couple of large hoses would connect those machines to a mask you'd wear during the exercise. Before starting we'd weigh you and plug that number into our computer, along with other numbers like the air temperature and barometric pressure since they affect the volumes of the gases you'll be breathing—oxygen "in" and carbon dioxide "out." After each half-minute of walking or pump 'n' walking or whatever, the computer would print out a bunch of numbers that tell us what and how you're doing. Among them would be how many milliliters—"mls"—of oxygen you had used up out of the room air. Another col-umn would divide those numbers by your weight in kilo-grams, expressing it as mls per kilo per minute.

After you'd "steadied out," meaning your body had caught up to the moment-by-moment work you were doing (that takes a few minutes), the ml figure would reflect how hard you're working. If you were pump 'n' walking with 3-pounders, lifting them 3 feet high at about 130 stride-strokes/minute, the mls per kilo column would read about 35. If we wanted to read that in METs to know how many times the body's work at rest you were doing, we'd merely look at the MET column as it was printed out. To give us that, the computer is simply programmed to divide the mls per kilo by 3.5 because there are, in fact, 3.5 mls per kilo in a MET! The column would read "10." 35 mls = 35 ÷ 3.5, or 10.

To finish the story: If you weighed 70 kilos, the O$_2$ column would read 70 × 35, or 2,450 mls of oxygen. If you want to think of your exertion in terms of calories, it's easy to convert the 2,450 to calories per minute. I do it by dividing the first two digits mentally by 2 (or you can multiply by 5). Half of 24 is 12—about the number of calories you'd be losing each minute at that work rate. When experts discuss work they usually speak of mls and *always* mean mls per kilo per minute. The average 55-year-old male, for example, has a VO$_2$ max of about 25 ml/kilo/minute. That means his maximum work capacity is 25 "mls," or a little over 7 METs (25 ÷ 3.5 = 7.14).

There's Nothing Like Knowing

Knowing, even if it's often only academic, is fun. These number games will become second nature after a while. I sometimes think newcomers to the world of exercise physiology are put off by the fluency with which the experts speak the language of numbers, and kind of retreat from it. The first two, admittedly bulky, boxes in this chapter are a concentration of the high-tech elements of this book. Take it or leave it. It can't add much to your excellence as a Heavyhander. And it won't make you stronger or more graceful. But there's a wonderful, proprietary feeling that comes from being able to "talk that talk"!

Suggestion: Don't try to buy it all the first time around. Read these "sidebars" every few weeks or so. Let the information grow on you. You'll be reading and hearing more and more about METs, O_2 consumption, calorie loss per minute, mls per kilo per minute, VO_2 maxes, and such from now on. Goethe said, "What one knows, one sees." Numbers such as these are already flooding magazine articles dealing with exercise and fitness. Rarely does a day pass when there isn't an article in *USA Today* on some facet of fitness. Quite sophisticated, too.

We've rigged the test to make its difficulty about six times the work of rest. While your body may be inert, the various metabolic activities of the body buzz on uninterrupted. We call that state of apparent bodily rest 1 MET, or one unit of metabolic energy. Our test is a 6-MET test. This level wasn't chosen arbitrarily: 6 METs happens to be the average intensity level of an aerobic-dance class, for example, or the work involved in walking at 4 to 4.5 mph for most people. Not a leisurely level, to be sure, but also not sufficient to "max out" most healthy folks.

To review: Pump 'n' walk to Level 2—or 2 feet up—averages out at 6 METs when your stride pace is following a tempo of 120 beats/minute. It is not important that your test be precisely 6 METs. Consistency, or making sure that subsequent retests are done the same way, is more important.

Presuming you are proficient at pulse counting, take your six-second pulse *immediately* upon completing the test, add a zero, and record that number. If you didn't note your age-related target heart rate range, return to the chart on page 28 and find it now. A good percentage of sedentary folks will find that upon completing the 6-MET test, their heart rates are either within their target range or very near it.

Try to be reasonably accurate with the pump height, but also remember to follow through—bring the handweight *all the way down* to the bottom of the arc; your elbow should be extended when your arm is down. If you chop the armstroke, or don't follow through its downward travel, you'll change your test value. More importantly, you want to establish good pump habits early in the game in order to maximize benefits and diminish the chances of discomfort while exercising.

Determining Your Pump 'n' Walk Prescription

Now let's consider an example: You are 40 years old, and calculated a 130 heart rate from your pulse check after the test. Consulting the chart on page 28, you note that your average exercise heart rate range is 126 to 153. That means the 6-MET test got you there, so to speak. Somewhat toward the low end of your range, actually. And you may not have felt any discomfort—you really were cruising easily for the entire five minutes.

The test itself could then serve nicely as your beginning pump 'n' walk prescription. Our aim, first off, is to get you to do a half-hour of that continuously—say, 1-pounders at Level 2 pump height to music with 120 beats/minute, at a stridelength comfortable for you. If that poses a problem—not because you're panting but because you're arm-weary—take the 30-minute prescription in divided doses for a few days; like 10 minutes three times a day or 15 minutes two times daily. It won't be long before 30 minutes at your 6-MET prescription at target heart rate becomes easy to manage.

There are two other kinds of test results we have to deal with. If you came in *above* your target range, you simply need to back off and use another work combination. Thus, if the average range for your age group is 126 to 153 and you hit 160 during the test, or you hit that target range and found it too difficult, lower the load. Walk slower and/or pump lower; try the revised combination for five minutes, then take your pulse. On the other hand, if you're in better condition than you realized, or know yourself to be fit, your post-exercise heart rate may be quite low after five minutes at 6 METs. For instance, if you're used to running at an 8-minute/mile pace, 6 METs is apt to produce a low heart rate for you—perhaps between 90 and 120! In that case we have to rev up your Heavyhands prescription, adding a faster tempo, higher pump height or more weight in some combination.

Note: If you're a well-conditioned runner or do some other leg-dominated exercise like cycling, don't be surprised if your test-generated pulse is higher than you expected. That's simply because untrained muscles—in this instance those of the arms—will stir a proportionately higher heart rate. That's just a physiologic fact of life. If you train at Heavyhands Walk for a while, that situation will reverse itself: Working lots of trained muscles will produce *lower* heart rates than a similar amount of leg-alone work previously had. That's an idea worth repeating because it's worth remembering.

Moving Up

Moving up means increasing the workload. If you're a runner you simply run faster. Heavyhands, with its multiple ways of activating lots of muscle, makes moving up a more interesting and controllable process. To increase the workload, you merely "up" one or all of the components: pace, pumps, or weights. If the weights feel very light and the armwork seems negligible after five minutes, you might move up to 2-pounders. If that doesn't elevate your heart rate, either go to 3's or push to a full Level 3 pump height—36 inches—or even higher (Level 4 if you're tall, ambitious, and able!). Even if you've recently gotten a medal for rowing or swimming or cross-country skiing, I think I can safely say that 99.9 percent

Oxygen Pulse

The oxygen pulse is really a sleeper. Imagine: It's a number that tells you how much oxygen your body is using per heartbeat. All this business of exercise physiology is related to what's called *oxygen transport:* getting the oxygen out of the air, through the lungs, into the heart pump, through the blood vessels, and out to the capillaries that supply the contracting muscle fibers. The oxygen pulse neatly couples heart pump action with oxygen utilization or energy production.

It's easily calculated: If you know how much oxygen you're using per minute (our O_2 analyzer in the lab does that) and your heart rate (by anything from a pulse count to an ECG tracing), you're in business. Divide oxygen per minute by heart rate for that minute. The number you get is the oxygen pulse. Since big folks tend to have higher resting oxygen pulses because they use more oxygen at rest, some have taken to dividing the oxygen pulse by body weight (just like with mls, remember?).

Pulse Rate	Condition
Less than 70	Excellent
70–90	Good
90–130	Fair
130–150	Low Average
Over 150	Poor

of you will have more than you can handle using weights no heavier than 5 pounds, stepping no faster than 150 beats/minute, and pumping no higher than 42 inches (Level 3.5).

In this early stage your target heart rate should help guide your exercise intensity. Heavyhands exercises provide a means of reaching it in almost endless ways. Using pump 'n' walk as a basic, you can achieve your target range by merely juggling your stride-pump pace, the range of your arm movements, and the weight. That's why pulse checking is so important in the early stages of your training. It's the most reliable way of learning what combination of "how fast, how far, how much" produces a comfortable workload that will generate training effects. After a while you will know your responses to exercise well enough to make pulse checking a rare thing. You probably should return to it when moving up or starting out with a new movement.

The more varied your workouts and the more combinations of muscle groups involved, the better control you'll have over various fitness factors and body regions. These factors are not isolated: speed augments strength and vice versa; both help endurance; and all make for more general interest in the exercise. That in turn leads to skillful execution. This applies equally to all of the walk moves you'll be learning as you move through the book.

High Pumps While Walking

The biggest reason for the failure of some Heavyhanders to achieve optimal fitness lies in their persistent failure to pump their hands, and thus the weights, high. Even if your pretest at 6 METs gets you comfortably to target, you are probably ready to experiment with high pumps. Why am I eager to get you pumping high? Because of the benefits that accrue from including *more muscle mass*. The higher you pump, keeping the workload constant, the more of those generally unused muscles of the upper torso you'll be including in your exercise. So the sooner you get started, the better.

To keep things at 6 METs you'll have to go slower. Experiment striding at 100 beats/minute while pumping your weights 3 feet up and down (this is Level 3) instead of just 2 feet. If five minutes of that leaves you comfortably at target, you've got yourself a wonderful alternate for your Level 2 walk at 120. Experiment! It's all good exercise anyhow, and you will soon feel the fine mastery of your exercise "load," in the form of subtle variations of pump height and tempo.

Your first alternate exercise is crucial. It's what distinguishes the dutiful, often stereotypical exerciser from those who intend to exploit the "system" for all it's worth. It means you're launched in the direction of establishing a repertoire of moves that makes you as individualized at exercise as you'd wish to be at everything else. It's the beginning of freedom and imaginative ability—and thus variety and optimal benefit—in your training strategy.

Theme and Variation: Building on the Basics

The next three chapters will serve as a quick reference guide, allowing you to easily locate a number of Heavyhands Walk movements. Chapter 5 will concentrate on arm movements, Chapter 6 on stride variations, and Chapter 7 on Heavyhands Walk movements especially for the back.

The photos are important; I tried to make the text a useful accompaniment. An illustration of the body's muscles is provided here so you can locate and learn the muscle combinations used in each variation. With most exercises we will point out: (1) which muscles get the most action; (2) how to "extend" the exercise, or increase either the range of motion or the number of muscle groups involved; (3) a range of suitable

The Body's Muscles

The illustration below shows, of course, only the most superficial layer of muscles. Huge masses of important but invisible muscles lie underneath these. But since this is hardly a text on human anatomy, I thought I'd spare you all the Latin while reassuring you that once you're into an assortment of stride/stroke combinations, you can't avoid using lots of muscles that you may not know by name! The long spinous muscles that lie deep beneath the middle portion of the lats are good examples of important muscle groups Heavyhands Walk will mobilize even though they don't show up on this drawing.

The Body's Muscles

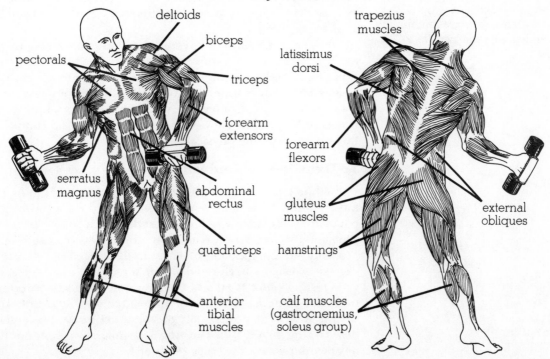

deltoids
biceps
pectorals
triceps
forearm extensors
serratus magnus
abdominal rectus
quadriceps
anterior tibial muscles

trapezius muscles
latissimus dorsi
forearm flexors
gluteus muscles
hamstrings
external obliques
calf muscles (gastrocnemius, soleus group)

Why No Schedule or Program?

Some designers of exercise methods are fond of telling you what to do on a day-to-day, week-to-week basis. I'm not. Rigid programs comprise averages that apply only occasionally and only to certain individuals. Besides, there's no good reason for asking anyone to adhere to a bunch of abstract numbers. To me, it's reminiscent of the new parent anxiously consulting child development schedules. Schedules unavoidably introduce a painful competitive element. Depending upon your personality, you're apt to compete with the average values, sometimes to your detriment. I'm giving you the basics—enough, I think, to get you moving in the right direction. Then the ball's in your court: It's up to you to make your Heavyhands exercise routine complement your own lifestyle.

tempos; (4) specific muscle groups or certain fitness factors that are emphasized (speed, strength, strength-endurance, etc.) by a particular exercise. I've tried to go from the simple movement combinations to the more complicated.

If you did nothing but master the basic pump 'n' walk from Chapter 3, you could, in a few months, bring yourself to superlative Panaerobic fitness! Missing from your workout, though, would be an assortment of muscles that the basic move doesn't reach. Training of the cardiovascular system would suffer little from those omissions, especially if you spent a fair amount of workout time pumping high. But some important regions like various trunk muscles, the belly and lower back, and some sizable muscles of the inner and outer thigh would receive moderate treatment at best. Conventional walk doesn't optimally train the hamstrings, hip flexors and extensors, and many muscles that surround and mobilize the shoulder joint.

To review: Before launching into more exercises, you should feel comfortable with basic pump 'n' walk and its variations. If you are able, you should have acquainted yourself with Level 3 pump 'n' walk, or learned that even at a slow tempo, that produces a too-fast pulse rate, or makes you too breathless for comfort, or bothers your left shoulder or something else. For the time being at least, you may have excluded that pump level and wisely backed off to Level 2 or even 1. Perhaps you've discovered that 30 minutes of continuous exercise, seemingly impossible at first, was quite manageable after a short time.

I hope you've also discovered that you're not likely to be usefully competitive with anyone else at Heavyhands. Your experience, body structure, genetics, level of enthusiasm, fitness ambition, discipline, state of health, athletic prowess, etc., make you unique. Competing with some other unique soul makes little sense in view of these differences. And competition can increase the physical risk of injury.

To Overdo—or Underdo?

While I must issue the usual warnings about overdoing it, these should be a matter of greatest concern for the older population, the utterly sedentary, and those who have health problems of one sort or another. Most healthy exercisers probably err on the side of chronically *underdoing*. Aerobic exercise is usually performed within a range of pulse rates. If your resting pulse is 60 and your prescribed steady working heart rate computes to 150, you have a range of 90 heartbeats within which to do the job of conditioning yourself and maintaining those gains. Training boils down to squeezing the most work possible into those 90 beats!

A Word about Warnings

Articles on fitness are full of warnings. Some articles contain little more than a series of presumably well-intentioned no-no's written in a mother-hen tone. If you want to write something that's generally worthless while remaining protected from criticism, be sure to insert plenty of warnings! "Remember, hand-weights of more than 2 pounds are too heavy for aerobics" or "5-pound hand-weights may injure the biceps muscles," or "3-pound hand-weights will knock you off your running stride."

By its nature, a warning can't be wrong. Anything that sounds as caring and as au-thoritative as that could be right. I often call the authors of such articles to find out how much *they* know about the things they're warning against. The warning remarks inevitably are quotes from experts they usually have inter-viewed by phone. Same kind of thing happens in medicine, when the manufacturer of a pharmaceutical has to list everything that *might* happen when you take a dose of the drug. Panic producers, I call them. You find that an appar-ently innocuous and popular nose drop produces convulsions, or a dangerously low white cell count. But how often does that happen?

Trouble is, we often believe what the experts say even if it isn't based on hard data. Experts are probably responsible for more needlessly painful rumors than anyone has time to investigate. Do warnings work? My guess is that many warnings inhibit most those who are already inhibited.

But you can fake it. You can plateau at a certain workload, stick to a certain heart rate, and stay put indefinitely. Too many exercisers do precisely that: If you sample their work three years down the line, you may find them doing *less* than they had been doing a year earlier but at a similar heart rate. This process of "self selection" is a fascinating one. Some researchers are studying the factors that determine what workload an exerciser settles into and to what extent this choice is a psychological one rather than one based upon measurable physiologic factors.

Indeed, there comes a time when your exercise work capacity will reach its ceiling. I worry more about this leading to a premature plateauing of function. It would be like quitting learning at a young age! You must always challenge the system realistically. That amounts to sneaking a bit "extra" into a workout when you feel up to it and adventurous, then gradually including a larger dose of that intensity level into your everyday exercise prescription. Intelligence, good judgment, and what I think of as "flexible diligence" are at least as essential as are heart and muscle in making exercise a lifetime friend.

How Many Movements Are Enough?

You needn't use all of the movements that follow. You should sample them just to gain a preliminary "feel" for them.

Avoiding Injuries

Injuries during exercise are a very different species from those associated with sports. If you play a fast sport that requires even intermittent spurts of power—and play to win—the chance of injury looms constantly. True enough, within a given sport some get injured more than others. Some running backs are on the injured list more often than not, and others ring up thousands of career yards while remaining injury free. The individual factor is important and so complex that I surely can't discuss it intelligently.

In exercise, especially the rhythmic aerobic kinds, the problem changes dramatically. While accidents can happen, the exerciser's control is greater than the athlete's. A jogger can land on a pebble, a cross-country skier can slip on an invisible piece of ice, a cyclist can fall while cornering on a patch of sand. If we eliminate those kinds of accidents, we're left with the injuries that aren't caused by some unfortunate miscue between exerciser and environment. What's left are things we do to ourselves. I divide those into injuries that occur from doing the same thing too much (overuse), and injuries that occur after we've made some change in our exercise plan. Heavyhands Walk, I believe, can cause injuries both ways, depending upon the character of the exerciser!

The people least likely to get hurt will be those who

The likelihood of your using them will change with your changing skill and level of conditioning. They all have some special albeit at times subtle usefulness. Remember, though: Better to master a few moves and their variations than to tackle them all the first day. Recently I decided to take a crack at rowing. I was surprised at the awkwardness I experienced first time on the shell. After watching a few of the experts on the lake, I knew it would be a while before I could master their graceful stroking movements. Each part of the stroke had to be practiced "separately" before they could be brought together to resemble that powerful harmony that allows one to row with authority!

The parallel between rowing and learning combined Heavyhands movements may be a pretty good one. Why should I concern myself with grace and why indeed is grace important during Heavyhands Walk movements? Several ideas come to mind. Being graceful makes movement fun in ways that I can't explain well but feel strongly about. There is a sense of being very much "in one piece." The whole movement becomes much more than the sum of its parts. Once you've got it right, one cycle seems to propel you smoothly

work at an intensity low enough not to tax their body. Problem there is they may end up with less than ideal cardiorespiratory training effects. For those willing and able to work at heart rates that are 80 percent or more of their maximal heart rates, common sense dictates that their body will be taxed more. Heavyhands Walk is probably the way to generate this high-intensity, continuous work with the lowest risk of injury. But this is based on mere averages. The risk of injury will always be there.

Certainly some caution should accompany anything new: different moves, bigger weights, faster tempos. But *too* much caution can cause prob-

lems, too. The best thing to do is to learn precisely what "just enough caution" means for you. That involves intelligent experimentation, and I've found that people who can do this end up with the fewest injuries. Impulsive behavior carries a high risk for obvious reasons: The impulse-ridden exerciser isn't thinking well. An impulse to action is like an explosive mental sprint, which is apt to pull a very fleshy hamstring! The ideal pattern for an exercise life with few hurts would be one that includes frequent cautious experiments, and plenty of practice with extreme situations. The body seems to injure least when it's been there before!

into the next. The sense of mastery is greater, of course, as the complexity of the movements increase, just as in dance.

I think some of the combined movements presented in the following chapters are at least as difficult as rowing or a given swimming stroke or cross-country skiing. There's one obvious difference: In these sports you are apt to be reminded, often in harsh terms, that you're doing it wrong! Each has a standard that we work to achieve. Because the signs of poor execution will be less evident in performing these Heavyhands Walk movements, bad habits can sneak into your routines. All of which adds to the challenge, as I see it.

Each movement was designed to serve as a Panaerobic workout in itself, or to be a part of a succession of movement sequences called Medleys. Your heart training should not be affected by how you choreograph your workouts. That's why you don't have to hurry to include many moves. (On the other hand, using one or two *exclusively* can and perhaps should lead to boredom.) More movements also become a definite biomechanical advantage. A large repertoire used imaginatively may lessen the hazard of injury, and make earlier return to exercise possible following injury.

You may find you like a new move so much that you want to work exclusively with it for weeks. Suit yourself, so long as it's not so easy that your work level collapses when you "indulge" yourself with it. And don't stick unyieldingly to your first impressions. Keep your options open, and don't forget to try sometime later those movements that didn't quite enthrall you the first time around.

One thing more. Experiment. It's *your* body, and your uniqueness can never be perfectly matched to any combination of movements that someone else devises. These exercises, built upon a base of walking, were an attempt to assemble movement combinations that are extensions of things most of us do naturally. You'll soon realize that everything here is merely an exaggerated version of something familiar to us all. The exaggerated choreography implemented with hand-weights simply welcomes lots of muscle to join in the act of *controlled overwork*, which is what exercise is all about. By listing strokes and strides separately I would like to stimulate those readers who haven't done so before to experiment, and those who have to do more of it!

On the Blessings of Having an Available Laboratory!

We literally can "run off" a new move or a variant of an old one about as quickly as you can say Jack Robinson. So our curiosity never lasts long. If we want to know how the workload (oxygen uptake) with a given movement varies with weight size, range of motion, or frequency, or any combination of those, we just hook ourselves to the equipment and let the computer deliver answers. Tom Auble has things rigged so that pump heights can be assessed accurately during the action; we can also reassess things afterward by taking video footage. We can run or walk with and without upper torso "add" to get a notion of the contribution of upper and lower body, or we can just carry humongous weights to see how that adds to the work of walking. If we wonder how variations in body-build affect the economics of a given movement, we can borrow people with those structural particulars for the few minutes it takes to find out. The convenience makes us more willing to pose more questions because the answers are within a stone's throw. Another advantage of a laboratory is that you learn quickly the kinds of questions it can't answer!

More Heavyhands Walk: Strokes

Here are several ways to vary the arm movements that can accompany ordinary walk or be matched with other strides. Each will do something a bit different for your upper torso. Remember: Each movement combination can serve as an entire workout in itself or become part of a Heavyhands Walk Medley. In this chapter, we'll be concentrating on armwork, so all the photos will depict various strokes performed with *conventional walking strides*. Chapter 6 will detail various strides accompanied by simple pumps.

Hi-Pumps

This exercise forces you to pull the weight as high as you comfortably can. I won't assign an absolute level to it, because our bodies and sleevelengths vary so much. I merely want the muscle-joint-ligament-tendon combination to act in this maximum extension upward and back down again. You probably won't care to do much of it at first because it can be quite difficult even when accomplished at relatively slow tempos with light weights. Arcing upward to their highest reach, your deltoids (shoulder muscles) may actually brush your ears! Don't fudge on the downstroke; merely give yourself enough time for complete raising and lowering of the weights by selecting a tempo that provides enough time while getting you to target heart rate.

Muscles worked: A whole host of uppers: latissimus dorsi, deltoids, trapezius muscles, triceps, pectorals.

Variations: Nothing much to add in terms of range of motion; once trained, you can add side leans, but you'll have to lower the tempo to cover the additional work involved.

Tempo: Hard to assign tempos for this one—70 or slower may get some to target.

Pumping vs. Swinging Weights

I don't see anything wrong with swinging weights. Rudimentary physics tells us that it shouldn't make much difference how the weight gets to where it's going: The work, measured over a long stretch, will be about the same, although I prefer more action. I like the sound of "pump," "punch," or "stroke" because an element of motor "purpose" is implied. "Swinging" sounds a bit less ambitious to me. Also, once you've mastered the arm moves, you'll want to snap the weights out, up, and down—and that's anything but swinging. Just use your target heart rate to guide you toward the proper intensity level.

Hi-pumps

Knuckle-Up Pumps and Throws

Just that. You merely rotate the hand some 90 degrees counterclockwise so that your thumbs are pointed *inward*, toward your body. The arm is pumped knuckles up, outward and to the side slightly, so that its downstroke can pass behind the body; at the end of the downstroke, then, your hand should be right over the top part of your butt. Caution! In all moves in which the weight's shaft is oriented horizontally, take care not to strike yourself. After a time that care will become embedded in your movement. When you've got the feel of this it will feel more as though you're actually throwing or *snapping* the weight out and up. Allow the elbows to relax during these movements. Keeping the arm rigidly extended may in time cause soreness not unlike tennis elbow.

Muscles worked: Excellent for delts, lats, pecs, and traps.

Variations: Alternate between pumps and throws; alter

Knuckle-up pumps

angles; increase range of motion; juggle tempos and weight sizes.

Tempo: 80-plus.

Punches

There are definite fitness advantages to arm movements that have a punchlike quality. The dynamics of punching make a single punch more like two separate strokes: the punch "proper" and its active, hard return. Punches can be thrown comfortably during ordinary striding. Punches will naturally combine speed and strength to make for power, and thus more work. Punches can be performed so as to include lots of upper body muscle. You can also fine-tune upper torso workloads when using punches, by subtly altering how hard you punch when you feel either below target or too much above it. Most punches are best thrown as an opposite maneuver while walking: The right arm punches while the left leg strides and

Pump 'n' Walk Workload Increases

Bar chart titled "Pump 'n' Walk Workload Increases." Vertical axis labeled "METs" ranging from 5 to 16. Horizontal axis labeled "Pounds in Each Hand." Bars from left to right: No Weight; Arms at Side; Arms Swinging Level 2; 1 lb.; 2 lbs.; 3 lbs.; 4 lbs.; 5 lbs.; 6 lbs.

vice versa. Later, you can try the same combinations as same-side versions. Don't neglect punches when doing the eight-count routine described later in Chapter 13.

I must admit to being a punch-stroker more than a pump-stroker. While I don't want to influence your choice, the high-velocity option and great versatility of punches have me hooked. I have punch 'n' walked many a continuous hour into a cool breeze. For me it's an improved vertical expression of what I do horizontally while swimming, and it's a great training aid for rowing. It also adds a triceps element that rowing lacks.

Muscles worked: Muscles of the arms and shoulder girdle; important contribution by pectorals and the serratus magnus muscles attached to the rib cage and shoulder blades. At fast tempos, punching can be an excellent trainer of the respiratory muscles. Practice exhaling sharply with each stroke, with every other, and even with every fourth punch.

Variations: Cross-punches—thrown *across* the midline toward the opposite side; add hard leans to the side toward which the punch is thrown; high and low punches, both uncrossed and crossed versions; punches thrown with the hand held in various rotations; punches out to the side; short and long punch strokes, determined both by size of handweights and stride-stroke tempo. Since many sports injuries occur during sudden twisting movements of the body, punch-stride variations can be used to train the torsion mechanics of the body. While punch-striding, simply twist your entire trunk assembly enthusiastically about an imaginary axis that travels vertically from the top of your head into the ground.

More variations: Cross-punches plus knuckle-up pullbacks. Try this: After throwing a hard knuckle-up cross-punch, pull the punch sharply back so that the hand ends up behind you, *palm up!* It will soon earn a permanent spot in your walk repertoire. It does unique things for all the muscle about the chest, upper back, and shoulder joints, and is a wonderful triceps developer besides.

Tempo: 80-plus.

Punching variations

Lateral Flings

This exercise can be used as a change of pace during long sessions of Level 3 walk, for example. It's especially good when these muscle groups are a bit weary. Note from the photos how the hands are held in the thumb-up position and pulled hard laterally without locking the elbows at the end of the fling. While lateral flings can be hard work, they will give you a little

Lateral flings

Varying Pump Height for Maximum Control

Especially at brisk paces—120 paces/minute and up—2 to 3 inches added or subtracted from the pump height or other strokes can make a big difference. Once you learn to ''read'' your intensity level well, you can do the same thing to your workload that a steep incline does to your conventional walk or run, and you won't need the hill! Usually your sense of respiratory effort is the best tip-off as to when to use these variations, either up or downward.

breather while working other muscles. To balance the exercise it's a good idea to occasionally switch the foot that strides with the lateral fling. Otherwise, your body becomes too accustomed to a one-sided pattern. Begin each fling with your elbows close to your sides, not extended outward.

Muscles worked: Pectorals and deltoids mostly, but trapezius muscles and some of the smaller muscles of the upper back also get work; triceps.

Variations: Try these on for size: (1) Pull the hands vigorously backward so they actually end up behind the body when extended fully laterally. That stretches the pectorals and works the deltoids and upper back muscles. (2) Vary the angle of the fling itself, i.e., high in front to low at the sides; low in front to high at the sides. (3) Change the tempo, which means going to ''heavy'' or ''light'' weights to remain at target. (4) Match the flings with other strides (see Chapter 6). (5) Include a bit of a bend forward during the lateral fling portion, returning to the erect position as the arms approach the midline.

Tempo: Anywhere between 80 and 160, depending on hand-weight size and how fast you can walk.

Lateral Fling Crossovers for Tennis Players

I can't resist including this because it's so regionally right for the muscles that hit forehand and backhand shots in tennis. Instead of the hands coming together in the midline as usual, they cross hard in front. It's best to orient the weights horizontally (knuckles up). Alternate your crosses so that first one arm and then the other is the "top" arm. It's a good idea to vary both that and the order of the stride every so often, to keep things symmetrical. I include side leans to get the abdominal obliques into it, by leaning laterally toward the side toward which the top hand is traveling.

Do not overdo! This is an unusual movement and works the delts in an extreme way. So use little weights and do the move for a few seconds at a time at first, so as not to injure.

Exercise Intensity

After most of us have done our last workout, there will be those who will continue to debate the big issues that confront the exercise theoreticians and practitioners. Duration versus intensity is a major theme that's been argued over the years. Marathoning got popular during a surge of interest in duration—going long; a running death or two caused experts to suggest cutting back on intensity. Then again, physiologists who downplayed the intensity factor a decade ago are now preaching its necessity. As you get older, the question of intensity becomes even stickier. If you don't get intense, your condition may resemble that of a nonexerciser. If you do get intense, you're probably at greater risk of developing problems that sometimes surface near maximal heart rates, especially if you have coronary artery disease. Until the day when peeking at your coronaries is as easy as slapping a stethoscope on your chest, quality exercise will always be something of a gamble. The size of the gamble poses the crucial question. So the exercise game boils down to learning better ways of matching specific fitness strategies to the assorted talents, needs, penchants, deficiencies, and risks that each individual possesses. This considered, I believe that trained Heavyhanders exercise in the best of physiological worlds: They work at higher intensities than they could with any other exercise method; they can exercise at given workloads at heart rates at least as slow as they could generate other ways; they can go long enough at given intensities to generate training effects; and they feel they're working more easily than they would if they performed leg-alone exercise.

Carrying and Pumping Handweights: Two Different Animals

Tom Auble came up with this graphic note from rummaging through the literature and comparing the numbers obtained by other studies with ours. Some researchers measured the oxygen uptake when subjects just carried 15-pound handweights. The oxygen consumption increase over just plain walking at an equal pace was calculated to be about 13 mls of oxygen per pound of handweight per minute. Pumping measly little 2-pounders high (42 inches), the increased O_2 consumption per pound of handweight jumped to 422 mls! Pumping 2's high will train more muscles, including the heart pump, and shed four times the calories per minute as would lumbering along with 15's held at dead hang. Think of what's happening to your body when you're up to pumping those same 15's at a brisk walk!

Lateral fling variation

A Nation of Walking Jocks?

I read in this morning's newspaper that when it comes to fitness, walking will do it all for us during the coming years. Maybe. It's clear that the experts at both ends of the exercise spectrum are concerned. They're mostly worried about the sedentary types. Get them mobilized and you reduce one big risk element in the population. At the other end they worry about the victims of "silent" heart disease for whom the risk of overdoing is great. So walking becomes a kind of universal antidote, curing the risks of both under- and overdoing in one simple prescription.

Unfortunately, that quick fix leaves too many questions unanswered. We are also a nation that dips heavily into sports. Most of the games we play, not good aerobic training in themselves, may be aerobically demanding at "peak" moments. Will training with 3- or 4-mph walks prepare us for those moments? Should no one seek higher levels of fitness? Don't higher fitness levels, in fact, confer psychologic and physiologic benefits and pleasures that add to health and the quality of life? Galvanizing the sedentary "low end" will surely have merit. But neglecting the "high end" could present problems in a nation in which the fitness movement has fluctuated about as uncertainly as the economy! In our concern about sudden death during exercise, may we not be trad-ing a few tragic episodes for more less-visible tragedies?

How fast should the National Average Resting Pulse be? Would heart attack, obesity, and hypertension numbers be no better with a 60 average than a 75? How many 60s can we expect if we make walking our mainstay exercise? What happened to those interesting anecdotes that suggested that the chance of a heart attack with a resting pulse more than 90 was five times greater than with one of 65 or slower? What concerns me most is that selling something that's "easier," other things being equal, has a better overall chance of acceptance in our population. But does acceptance mean success?

Also, I should warn that there is danger of bumping the hands during the swift crossing maneuver. The Heavyhands strapped weights are especially useful here because of the protective foam strap. Even so, pay attention to your hands to avoid collision. I noticed myself occasionally bumping weights when I tended to overdo the move to the point of fatigue.

Swoops

This is another favorite variation that includes lateral arm movement but much more. I call it the "swoop" simply because the word occurred to me when I first experimented with it. It's really a tintype of the arm move in the old-fashioned breast-stroke: The hands push forward in the midline, then make circles outward (parallel with the ground) and return to the midline at chest level. The swoop part comes in the downward dip of the knees during the initial "push." The knees straighten during the lateral and return phases of the stroke. It works the delts, pecs, quads, lats, and many lesser groups.

This move will be difficult at first, but with the right combination of weights, tempo, and heart rate, you'll learn to do miles of it. This move is a nifty model of the Panaerobic way: It demonstrates that enormous quantities of muscle can fit into movements that make some sort of traditional sense, and

Swoops

Beating the Heat
Once you're Panaerobically fit, it's probably a good idea to pump 'n' walk during mid-summer heat and humidity. Why? To take physiologic advantage of all that trained muscle. At a given workload, you'll cruise at a lower heart rate and a lower level of perceived exertion, and will probably do more total work with less residual fatigue than if you did some conventional leg-alone physical exercise.

are doable by those of us who aren't inherently graceful! Add some forward leans with the swoop, straightening up as the knees straighten.

Alternate Lateral Raises

Merely move your weighted hands alternately upward from dead hang to shoulder height or higher. This movement goes well with cross-strides and quick kicks (see pages 67 and 68). The advantage of going the "alternate" route with lateral raises is that you can really get the trunk into the action.

Muscles worked: Lateral delts; trapezius muscles; obliques.

Variations: Raise the weights higher; seesaw the shoulders and do side leans; use heavier weights during slow striding.

Tempo: 90-plus or so, but as you'll see again and again, tempo is linked to other movement variables, like range of motion and handweight.

Alternate lateral raises

Kids and Heavyhands Walk

Seems to me that as children we quickly learn to walk, then run, and that's really it as far as forward movement is concerned. The evolution of rhythmic, four-limbed activity is excluded early on. It may be resumed later as combined movements associated with sport—swimming, cross-country skiing, or rowing, for instance—but that's usually delayed quite a while. When I watched my preschool-age grandchildren smile as they pumped 'n' walked, I knew it couldn't be any more wrong than a dog's tail wag. Why did they enjoy it so? Probably because Heavyhands Walk is a natural "next step" in the ambulatory process for them. The ape in my family tree tells me it's right. The effect on my own activity pattern—and the smiles on my grandchildren's faces—proves it.

Forehand-Backhand Alternates

This movement sometimes appeals to tennis players and to throwers. While it's not identical with the forehand and backhand strokes of that game, it will work many of the muscles used to hit a tennis ball. Don't try to duplicate proper forehand and backhand tennis "form" at first because the extended elbow required in the sport might present a problem when performed with handweights heavier than a tennis racket.

In this movement, each arm strokes twice in succession: First the forehand, which is actually executed more like a throw, and then the backhand, which can't be like a throw because no one throws backhand except a Frisbee thrower! What makes the stroke combination especially rewarding are things like the stride you pair it with and the degree of side leans you throw in. Be sure to go with little weights until you get the feel of this.

This simple stroke combination demonstrates something I've found to hold true consistently: The more complex the move, the more numerous the variations one can fish from it. And so it is here. It works well indoors, too; like around the perimeter of a gym to a thumping musical beat. Note: In this

Forehand-backhand alternates

walk combination, the stride-for-stroke rule is broken. It's best to start with a forehand-backhand sequence accompanying *each stride*. Actually, the stride begins with the forehand shot and reaches its endpoint as the backhand is executed! I'm sure that sounds distressingly complicated, but don't worry about it. By the time you're comfortable with the arm sequence, your legs will know instinctively what to do.

Muscles worked: Virtually all of the muscles of the upper torso!

Variations: There are endless variations of tempo, range of motion, and subtle variation in the direction of strokes; it's easily matched with several strides, including karate kicks, for those looking for something both demanding and dancelike.

Tempo: 90 to 150 (that's counting *each* stroke), depending upon weight size and completeness of each stroke.

■■■■■■■■

So much for standard strokes. Whereas they don't begin to exhaust the stroke possibilities, they should hold you for a while! In the next chapter, we'll present various stride patterns that can be paired with these or used with the basic pump motion from pump 'n' walk. Putting strokes and strides together in interesting combinations is part of the fun of Heavyhands Walk.

And you needn't stop with this sampling. Improvise! You can do no wrong so long as you stick to the cardinal rules. Unless we indicate otherwise, go stride for stroke. Get used to that from the outset. Some try to fudge it, going two strides for each armstroke. Keep the idea of *mobilizing the most muscle mass* foremost in your mind. Change to your heart's content work-load components like tempo, range of motion, size of hand-weights, and length of your still "ordinary" strides. Don't forget that target heart range. Remember to consciously relax your grip on the weight until it becomes automatic. Bring the often neglected trunk into your work with the leans and bends I've already mentioned. There are more!

Stride
Variations

You'll recall my sermonizing earlier about the benefits the legwork specialist can get from Heavyhands Walk training. This chapter is part of what makes that true. In many ways, strides are more difficult to make inventive than strokes. Unless we're dancers or athletes, most of us don't experiment much with our legs. Actually, the arms and legs pose very different sorts of problems during combined exercise choreography. Our arms loaf generally, and our legs tend to loaf, too, except when we're traveling by foot. Heavyhands training brings spectacular physiologic work gains to the upper body, and new grace and qualities of motion to the legs, along with greater fitness. The combination comes across as a vigorous upper body in sync with legs that possess agility, strength, and endurance you just can't get from conventional leg-driven aerobics.

In designing these strides, I tried to (1) get every muscle, even the obscure ones, into the act; (2) create strides that can readily be paired with all or most of the previously described strokes; (3) make a range of difficulty that allows the work emphasis during Heavyhands Walk to be shifted from the upper to lower body and vice versa; (4) make sure that the resulting stride-stroke combinations mobilize the trunk muscles. Again, there are enough strides here that you needn't become enamored of all of them. But you should try to include a sampling that will work each of the major muscle groups—hamstrings, quads, abductors, adductors, and hip flexors.

> ### Strides and Strokes— Always Together?
>
> We thought that was a reasonable question and one that would lend itself to a quick answer in the lab. It happens that pumping 3 feet up half as often as one strides produces only *one-third* the work of equal numbers of strides and strokes at the same stride pace. We reasoned that there's a lot of work tied up in the downstrokes. I've known a couple of Heavyhanders who've pump 'n' walked a couple of years, sticking religiously to a less energetic pump pattern. Sure enough, their training effects were less than they might have been if given the full treatment.

Stretch-Strength Strides

These are long strides that stretch the hamstrings of the "back" leg and muscles of the groin. These also strengthen the quadriceps of the front of the thigh, as the front knee alternately flexes and extends. Of course, you'll manage this gait only slowly at first, and it never will become one of your speediest steps! Even modest armstrokes (there are many you can match with this stride) will bring you to a nice pant.

Stretch-strength strides

Muscles worked: Quadriceps, hamstrings, glutei, hip flexors a bit.

Variations: Gradually increase the length of your strides; add leans opposite to the pumping arms; you can also lean slightly backward.

Tempo: For these movements, tempo is necessarily slow, about 80 to 120.

Hamstring Flexes

It takes time to feel comfortable with this exercise. It sometimes feels harder to flex hamstrings in "kickbacks" during walk than during airborne jogs. Anyway, you bring the foot of the flexing leg up toward the opposite buttock, where it touches the downside handweight of the opposite arm! If that mouthful isn't absolutely clear, I'm hardly surprised. The

Strokes Compatible with Stretch-Strength Striding

Lots of combinations will work here. Start with pumps and punches. Then you can add variations on hand position (knuckles out or up). Cross-punches also work well. Most of all, I enjoy adding side leans with just about any movement combination. They're great for training the belly; try it and note that pleasant discomfort in your obliques the next morning. Gradually the angle of those leans will increase, and with it will come greater strength and suppleness in the "love handle" area.

Hamstring flexes

Striding toward Leg Strength-Endurance

The strides in this chapter were concocted with your training future in mind. After you've built a healthy amount of work capability into your upper body with pump 'n' walk and other strokes, you can redirect your emphasis upon training your legs. You will be doing lots of legwork even with conventional walk strides, but the best is yet to come. The strides you learn will allow for more legwork even at slow tempos, because of the substantial increase in strength-endurance they gen- erate. Each stride can be up- graded by increasing its range of motion (such as the depth of knee dips), its length, the number of strides per minute, and the foot velocity. And, of course, the gradual addition of handweight further increases the legwork.

Embarrassment, Again

Of course, these strides bring the embarrassment issue back into focus. The question is: Do you want to sneak around unperceived by your friends and neighbors when you dare attempt these things outdoors? Or do you wish to confront them proudly and cheerfully? Perhaps you're a born pedagogue, merely eager to teach! Sometimes the best attitude I can muster to stifle my essential shyness in all things is to play researcher; my odd movements act as an "experimental stimulus." Occasionally, a group of us pump 'n' walkers at the track will encounter a jogger doing his thing who looks like *he's* the embarrassed one! My prediction of things to come: Someday joggers will appear on Sunday afternoons like one of those redone Model T's, all spit and polish, to remind us of the good things of the past.

photos should be self-explanatory. Next-day soreness in the back of the thigh and the butt, even if the move is accomplished at a snail's pace, will tell you where you've been working. As you improve, the action can be facilitated to the point of grace and enjoyment!

Muscles worked: Hamstrings, glutei; a real specific for these.

Variations: Increase the effectiveness of the kickbacks; add enough armwork to keep to training pulse.

Tempo: Try a pace of 70 or so for starters. When you can negotiate this stride at 100 beats/minute, consider yourself a pro!

Same-Side Kicks

In this stride, you merely kick what would normally be your forward foot gently toward the side (at about a 45-degree angle, actually), return a bit, then place it on the ground. For most of us, accustomed to ordinary forward stepping, this move will seem foreign at first. But with practice it will become easy and graceful—while still working you hard.

Muscles worked: Good for the quads (collectively the most massive muscle group you own); to some extent the abductors of the thigh, the ones that pull the leg outward.

Variations: Increase your stridelength; make your kick to the side more dynamic; just plain go faster.

Tempo: This can vary, depending on what your arms are doing and on the total workload, from 100 to 150 or more.

Same-side kicks

High Knee Lifts

This adds hard work to pump 'n' walk. It's not a gait that will move you far quickly. The leg lifts work muscles that are not mobilized much in regular ambulatory exercise like walking or running. You'll find yourself at a relatively high heart rate at a given walking pace because the "vertical" component (leg lifts) makes for a very inefficient way to travel. (It's thus an excellent exercise, but a terrible way to win a footrace!) Try this in relation to various strokes, doing *both* on the same side (called ipsilateral) and then on the opposite (contralateral). You will probably find the same-side version easier to execute at first.

Muscles worked: Hip flexor exerciser deluxe; also works the quads.

Variations: Lift your knees higher—when they're up to waist high or higher you're getting there; point your toes to bring the calf into the move; in the opposite pattern, bring the

**Energy by
Any Other Name...**

Physical work is *energy spent*. Energy has been defined as the capacity to do work. So when you hear people rhapsodize over their newfound "energy" since starting an exercise class, that should mean something besides some sort of psychic lift it gives them, and all that. It should mean they *can*, and better still, *do* work harder. They can generate more watts, foot-pounds per minute, calories per minute, METs, mls of oxygen (either total or per kilo). It means they can shop, walk, wash the car, carry in the groceries, make love, sight-see, or play three sets of tough singles tennis in hot, humid air more efficiently and/or more easily than they could before.

High knee lifts

lifted knee slightly toward the opposite side of the body; add some forward bending at the waist to increase the difficulty.

Tempo: A good pace is 100.

High Kicks a la Karate

A difficult move for most beginners. It will help add flexibility, speed, and strength to the lower extremities—but it is also hard work. It's best performed as a same-side stroke-kick pattern. I prefer to use a punch, either straight forward or up high, to parallel the martial-art feeling that goes with the fast high kick. This way, the weighted hand and the kicking foot reach their destinations at about the same instant. The body turns slightly with each kick, the face and body directed opposite to the side of the kicking leg. If you want to try something different, do karatelike kicks with the lateral fling variation for tennis players demonstrated in Chapter 5 on pages 54 and 55.

Muscles worked: Great for quads and hip flexors; leans develop abdominal obliques.

High kicks a la karate

Variations: Kick higher and higher; alter your arm accompaniment to allow for a variety of effects.

Tempo: A pace of 80 is fine.

Cross-Strides

These do for legs what cross-punches do for uppers. The striding foot crosses the midline, landing flat with the toes pointed toward the side of the hip that's doing the striding. The whole leg swings in a large arc from the hip in initiating each stride (a movement called "circumduction"). Try it with a number of strokes. I happen to enjoy opposite cross-punches with it, so you end up twisted by the fact that your leg is striding in one direction, your arm punching the opposite way! The local police may check your breath for alcohol if you're found doing this in public. But you never know—next year it could be an "in" way of walking for fitness!

Muscles worked: The adductors of the thighs; the hip muscles that circumduct the leg; glutei; obliques; great shoulder girdle work if you do the cross-punches I suggested.

Working Out to Music

Working out to music may pay off in some ways beyond the obvious. I call it a "motor identification" with the music. Listening to music when it's purely passive and sensory is one thing. But when your muscles are mobilized by it, you "lay down" a special kind of memory. Working to a tape full of favorite selections, you will soon start to move to each successive song before a single musical cue. Your muscles will "hear" it first! I have a notion that after some hundreds of hours of exercise to music, you don't listen passively anymore, even when you're attending a concert! "Listening" with your muscles will become a reflex. By the way, if you've never worked out to the strains of Vivaldi, try it. I find his music transporting. Vehicled by Vivaldi, my dumbest movements make me feel balletic.

Cross-strides

Variations: Make the crosses more extreme and therefore more demanding; add more side-leaning to the whole complex.

Tempo: 100 is an excellent pace before you're trained for cross-striding.

Quick Kicks

These are somewhat different from the first kicks described. They are quick, snapping movements; what you're actually doing here is adding a power component to conventional striding. The feet move very rapidly without the necessity of covering ground faster. I often use it while chatting with a fellow Heavyhander who is somewhat less work-trained; it keeps my heart rate up even at a slow walk pace.

Pump 'n' Walk 'n' Dip!

Once you add knee dips to ordinary strides and strokes, you will have launched yourself into another dimension of exercise. Depending upon the depth of your dips (as in the two downs, two ups stride) and the pace, you may add 5 or more METs to the work of or-dinary walking. Varying your strokes makes it, again, another ball game. Be imaginative about it. Use light, high, and snappy strokes with deep dips one day, and heavier, slower armwork with less ambitious dips the next. Add side leans whenever you can. As the graphic here illustrates, you will be able to do enormous work at slow tempos this way—once you're up to it, of course. Starting with ordinary strolling as the basis, you can literally walk your way to a form of superfitness that non-Heavyhanders will never find.

Heavyhands Triple Treat: Pump 'n' Walk 'n' Dip

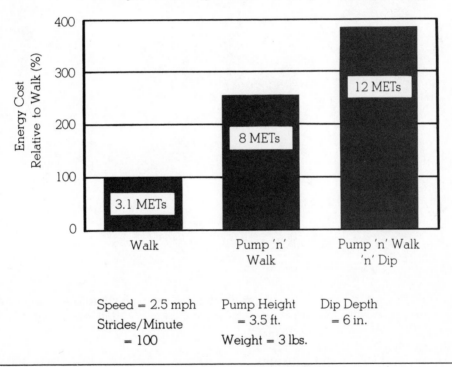

Speed = 2.5 mph   Pump Height   Dip Depth
Strides/Minute   = 3.5 ft.   = 6 in.
       = 100   Weight = 3 lbs.

Similarly, the quick kick can be very good for those in group Heavyhands workouts who don't want to sacrifice good training for good company.

You will feel it the next day in your quads. Quick kicks add a power component that trains the front of the thigh like conventional walking can't. I believe this stride would make a better runner of you, and a better hill-climber, too. You can check out its heart-training potential by noting how it increases your pulse rate much more than would conventional striding at a similar pace.

Quick kicks

Muscles worked: Quads!

Variations: Go faster!

Tempo: Start at 120; if you don't find that a challenge, try stroking and quick kicking at 150 for about four minutes nonstop!

Struts

A strut is in reality a knee lift followed quickly by a little kick. It's an excellent, enjoyable trainer for the runner. Struts go well with cross-punches, hi-pumps, and alternate lateral raises. You put the trunk muscles into action by side leaning while strutting. If everything else remains constant (hand-weight, pump height, tempo), strutting will increase the work-load and hence the calorie cost of your Heavyhands Walk combinations.

Muscles worked: Hip flexors, quads, calves.

Struts

Variations: Lift your knees higher and harder; point your toes.

Tempo: Try to move at 110 or better.

Double Same-Side Kicks

This exercise is not easily pictured! As the name implies, this stride tactic is best paired with same-side armstrokes. You simply kick twice per stroke. The first kick is an aggressive kick-stride from the hip and knee in that order. The second kick comes strictly from the knee, now suspended in the air in front of you. The combination works well with high, heavy pumps or punches. I often use cross-punches with side leans toward the foot on the ground. This walk exercise creates another interesting paradox: The average foot velocity, even at 65 or 70 double kicks/minute, is very high—even though the whole body is moving pretty slowly. So it's a good one for strolling with grandma while keeping at a fast heart rate.

Muscles worked: Quads, hip flexors.

Variations: Increase the tempo and the briskness of your kick movements; switch matching strokes.

Tempo: 90 to 130 (double kicks with each beat).

Skip Steps

I'm sure you skipped when you were a child. Skipping has re-emerged recently, and I got to experimenting by adding the upper torso to skipping. It's a sure winner as an exercise, perhaps because it brings a joyful, childlike quality to our "adult" exercise! If you've ever skipped, you will be able to pick it up again in a few moments, I'm sure.

Skipping is really nothing more than stepping, then hopping. You simply add a tiny hop to the end of each step during ordinary walk. The hopping foot can do little variations: It can cross in front of the other foot or it can land a few inches to the outside to make interesting variations. When you're ready, you can increase the workload by making the strides longer or faster. And the height of your pump can make the crucial difference between the ordinary skipper and the

Skip steps

jock! If you skip on a cinder track they'll hear you scraping along a hundred yards away. I think skipping could be an important link between walk and dance. Try pumping 'n' skipping to the music provided by your stereo headset if you don't believe me.

Muscles worked: Bunches of leg muscles.

Variations: Increase the tempo, the range of foot motion, the vertical height of the hop; add side leans—you name it.

Tempo: 100 to 140 or even faster, once you're good at it.

Fast Walk

Fast stepping should become part of most Heavyhands Walk workouts. By "fast walk" I mean something faster than 130 beats/minute. Paces in excess of 200 beats/minute are possible, but the work becomes very hard, since walking becomes less economical than running after about 4.5 mph. When pushing yourself to fast walking paces, pump heights naturally must lessen in order to keep the total work within your capability. Most untrained subjects will find that pump-

Fast walk with low pumps

Good Strokes for Semi-Ducks

Here's a good chance for you to learn some solid "clinical" exercise physiology. The hard work of duck walking means you may have to reduce the stroke workload somewhat. Side leans go nicely with anything that flexes the hips like duck walking. You may have to content yourself with a slower tempo in the initial stages (like 100 strokes/minute or fewer). And it wouldn't be prudent to pump big weights at the outset, unless you're at a largo tempo (funeral march stuff). You can design a great interval by going a minute or two duck walking with modest stroke workload, then pushing the load "upstairs" while you recover from the duck walk with conventional striding.

ing 2-pounders to Level 3 is difficult if not impossible at a pace of 140; but I know of Heavyhanders who can pump 4 pounds high at paces in excess of 160! Fast stepping can make up an entire aerobic workout, or can be done intermittently as part of Medleys or intervals (see Chapter 8 for more on that). Early in training you should pump low. You'll find Level 2 pumps and light punches are all you need to get you to your target heart rate while fast stepping. (For more detail on fast walk, see Chapter 10.)

Muscles worked: Good for the legs.

Variations: Pick up the pace; exaggerate the movement of your upper torso as you continue to train.

Tempo: 130 to 200! Depends on many factors.

Hamstring Press-Backs

This is another good leg trainer, although it's not readily photographed because performers look as though they're walking conventionally. During conventional walk one leg literally strides past its planted mate. The planted foot rests. I devised this one while pondering the much-discussed imbalance between the powerful thigh-front and the weaker hamstrings behind. Why not actively pull the body forward with force exerted by the planted foot? After some experimentation I discovered it was doable. Here's how the complete leg cycle would go: The leg strides, plants, then pulls the body after it. The alternate leg begins its stride while the first leg is in its "pulling" phase. This makes both legs simultaneous partners in the act of transporting the body. I'm not sure yet, but my guess is that this practice would make for more efficient walk, and lessen the quad-hamstring imbalance.

Of course, it's all done while engaging in various strokes. You'll have to concentrate at first because the natural tendency is to revert to the pattern of striding past the passive foot. And if you've been doing it diligently, you'll feel it the next day in the hamstrings and buttocks. The "pulling" can be exaggerated by striding slightly to the side rather than straight ahead, and alternatively planting the ball portion of the foot. Steve Reeves mentions something quite similar in his book, *Power Walking*.

Muscles worked: Hamstrings mostly, but an assortment of other muscles that cross the hip joint also.

Variations: Go faster, and execute longer strides; vary the footstrike from the ball to the heel then to a flat foot.

Tempo: 100 to 140; about 5 beats/minute slower than ordinary pacing with Heavyhands.

Semi-Ducks

These are for folks who want leg strengthening as well as endurance. The knees remain flexed during the striding, the thighs angling at about 45 degrees. The exerciser is essentially sacrificing the great mechanical advantage that comes from keeping the knees locked; that forces harder quad work. This kind of training is great for skiers of any persuasion. Insert semi-ducks into Medleys when you feel the impulse to work the legs harder at relatively low stride-stroke frequencies. Incidentally, these strides can be accompanied by a variety of strokes and go well with side leans and trunk twists.

Muscles worked: Quads and calves, mostly.

Variations: Go faster, dip lower.

Tempo: 90 to 140.

Semi-ducks

Two Downs, Two Ups

This stride is performed as though you were simply walking down two steps, then up two. The first two strides find the knee bending a bit more; then they straighten on the "up" two strides. This can be done with a variety of strokes. It works well with lateral flings, though it is a little tricky to get the strides and strokes matched perfectly at first. The arms fling outward on the first "down" stride, return on the second, fling again on the first "up" stride, and return on the last. This also works with all sorts of punch and pump strokes, and with body flexes such as double ski poling.

Muscles worked: Plenty of quads and calves and hip flexors and extensors; even a bit of abdominals if you're especially body-flex inclined.

Variations: Exaggerate the downs and ups and the body flexions.

Tempo: Slower than a regular walking gait, obviously; try 90 to 140.

Now you have a starting repertoire of strides and strokes that can be hooked up in almost endless ways if you count the varied striding and stroking angles, range of motion combinations, rotation of the knuckle orientation during strokes, etc. I've done all of these and more outdoors, sometimes in rather staid urban residential settings, and no one, to my knowledge, has phoned the authorities. Nonetheless, you may not wish at first to trot out the most unorthodox of these combinations on a Sunday afternoon in your neighborhood. I have high hopes that that sort of understandable embarrassment will disappear soon. Running went through a similar phase.

The more "far out" Heavyhands Walk combinations could bring more of us into the sphere of movement adventure that is traditionally reserved for the specialists—athletes, dancers, and the like. No one speaks much of the *art* of exercise, and that could be missing a good bet. If you step back from the field of aerobic exercise to gain perspective, here's what you find: The best body-training tactics tend to be least imaginative; the most imaginative tactics generally produce the least scintillating training effects. Heavyhands Walk is an attempt to gain the best of both worlds.

Two downs, two ups

Mix It Up!

Variety in exercise is good protection against leaving muscles out, for one thing. And you don't have to have a variety of sizes of handweights to work at your target heart rate in many interesting ways. By switching tempos and pump heights with a single weight, altering strides and strokes, and interspersing side leans and knee dips, you can convert any ordinary stroll into a kaleidoscopic ensemble that is interesting and enjoyable, and that gets the job of keeping fit done.

Stride-Stroke Combos

This chart was designed for your quick reference. Putting it together took a couple of days, hopping from my breakfast table to the living room to try out each movement! I selected a dozen strides and a dozen strokes. If they all worked well together, you'd have 132 Heavyhands Walk combinations. However, you'll notice that a few were left blank either because they didn't work at all for me, or because I thought their inherent awkwardness made them expendable. Deletions notwithstanding, no one will remain unfit because of a scarcity of Heavyhands Walk movements. And every combination sporting a diamond contributes to a sizable indoor repertoire of in-place movements which beat the bad weather rap.

Summary of Stride-Stroke Combos

- ☐ **On Move**
- ⛉ **Both Opposite and Same-Side Combos Okay**
- **s** **Side Leans**
- ◇ **In-Place Okay**
- ○ **Difficult Combo**

	Low Pumps	Hi-Pumps	Knuckle-Up Pumps and Throws	Straight Punches (Knuckle-Out)
Stretch-Strength Strides	⛉ [s]	⛉ [s]	⛉ [s]	⛉ [s]
Hamstring Flexes	⛉ [s] ◇	⛉ [s] ◇	⛉ [s] ◇	⛉ [s] ◇
Same-Side Kicks	⛉ [s] ◇	⛉ [s] ◇	⛉ [s] ◇	⛉ [s] ◇
High Knee Lifts	⛉ [s] ◇	⛉ [s] ◇	⛉ [s] ◇	⛉ [s] ◇
Karate Kicks	⛉ [s] ◇	⛉ (s) ◇	⛉ [s] ◇	⛉ [s] ◇
Cross-Strides	⛉ [s]	⛉ [s]	⛉ [s]	⛉ [s]
Quick Kicks	⛉ [s] ◇	⛉ [s] ◇	⛉ [s] ◇	⛉ [s] ◇
Struts	⛉ [s] ◇	⛉ [s] ◇	⛉ [s] ◇	⛉ [s] ◇
Double Same-Side Kicks	⛉ [s] ◇	⛉ [s] ◇	⛉ [s] ◇	⛉ [s] ◇
Skip Steps	⛉ [s] ◇	⛉ [s] ◇	⛉ [s] ◇	⛉ [s] ◇
Semi-Ducks	⛉ [s]	⛉ [s]	⛉ [s]	⛉ [s]
Two Downs, Two Ups	⛉ [s] ◇	⛉ [s] ◇	⛉ [s] ◇	⛉ [s] ◇

	Cross-Punches	Lateral Flings	Lateral Fling Crossovers	Swoops	Alternate Lateral Raises	Forehand-Backhand Alternates	Swing 'n' Sway

Heavyhands Walk for Your Back

I decided to keep the next three movements and their variations separate from the rest because they are different mechanically and will do special things for your fitness in enough ways to merit special attention. If you have reasons to be concerned about your back, I suggest you read the entire chapter through before trying any of these exercises.

DSP: Good News for Bad Backs

Trudging pumpingly around our neighborhood, I got to thinking the other day that my wife and I and other fellow Heavyhanders find an astonishing number of pennies. There are two major reasons for our uncommon good luck, I theorized. One is inflation—or more specifically, what it's done to the value of pennies. The other, I mused, was the high incidence of back problems. Given the small value of copper coins and the danger inherent in bending over, people simply don't pick up pennies! We find 'em mostly while doing back-training exercises that keep our eyes riveted on the ground much of the time!

Which leads me to the first of this trio of back-training exercises, modeled in spirit after the sport and exercise of cross-country skiing. It's called "double ski poling." It seemed to me that the essential characteristics of this movement would go a long way to further our resolve to train lots of muscles simultaneously. But it's also true that doing this exercise poses a conflict: We're immediately dealing with the pros and cons, the benefits versus the risks of vigorous exercise as they apply to the vulnerable lower back. It's a challenge because we're required to be bold and careful at the same time.

Cross-country skiers are known to develop enormous levels of aerobic capability. Furthermore, cross-country skiing activates a high percentage of body muscle. Beyond those essential parallels, double ski poling—we'll call it "DSP" from now on—is a marvelous exercise for the back. If the pollster's numbers are accurate, there are more than 100 million Americans involved in the mainstay aerobic exercises like running, walking, swimming, and cycling. But these exercises do little to strengthen our backs. Two years ago, one poll listed the back as the number one problem area among runners. Swimmers, presumably because of the tendency toward "hyperextension," suffer commonly from "swimmer's back." As for walking, some who walk may manage to continue despite their back problems, but few would think to walk because of walking's usefulness in curing or preventing back ailments.

All this might not be worth mentioning were it not for these simple facts: We need to exercise, but we also suffer terribly from an assortment of back disorders. Curing the 75 to 95 million of us who have bad backs already is very "iffy" business. But the best cures for the next generation, the young with apparently healthy backs, will come from *prevention through maintenance.* Not overly cautious prevention—like a series of defensive, self-conscious preoccupations with how not to offend the back—but, rather, an aggressive assault on the weakness problem that seems to have been built into our modern lifestyles. I submit that the best preventive is not heavy weight training, but *strength-endurance* training, designed to allow you to train aerobically while strengthening your back at the same time.

I designed Heavyhands DSP to do just that: to get my back (along with lots of other muscles, of course) and heart well trained, and to keep them trained on the smallest investment of time possible. I recall an article in a geriatric journal suggesting that back problems in this country had reached the stage where it might (and I'm paraphrasing) be wise to lessen the focus on aerobics and instead devote some of that time to the maintenance of the back. With DSP, that kind of choice isn't necessary because it handles both of those issues *simultaneously.* An hour of DSP, inserted in divided doses into each week's exercise program, would do a number of good things for your back without interrupting your ongoing cardiovascular training.

There are essentially two kinds of people who should learn to like DSP for as long as they pursue fitness: One *has* back problems already, and the other doesn't *yet!* But while I recommend DSP for back sufferers, I do it nervously and never without a list of precautions and provisions. Here's why: For the great majority of us, the back is a very weak piece of equipment. Since it's weak, it's vulnerable. Because we decide now and then to do something with it that we haven't done for a while, it's apt to be unprepared for it. Aware of that, I can't simply allow my unbridled enthusiasm about DSP as a back

The High Energy Cost of DSP—and Its Consequences

You can see why DSP is great. A lot more is being lifted with each arm cycle than the little handweights: The whole body is actually being moved along. While that's happening, the knee and hip joints are flexing and the spine is flexing, too. Then it all "unwinds" in the extension phase and straightens out again.

With all its benefits, though, I consider it a *dangerous* move for those who are sedentary or have heart-based work limitations. Here's why: Not only does DSP use energy at a rapid rate, but the energy comes in large measure from untrained muscles. A highly fit runner might find DSP shockingly difficult for this reason. His legs aren't trained for this sort of movement extravagance. Beyond that, he's likely to be completely unprepared for the upper torso "add." I learned that by rude experience one warm day in Florida when a young neighbor decided to work out with me. He followed my lead while I double ski poled, and promptly fainted! He was fine, but I noticed a pulse nearing the 200 mark—even though he was using only 3-pound handweights moved in a modest range of motion.

I urge those teaching Heavyhands Walk at cardiac rehab centers to avoid DSP until a patient is quite advanced. The work can sneak up on you quickly: Any increase in tempo or range of motion, like moving from 30 to 35 cycles/minute or passing the weights past the legs at a lower level, say, nearer your ankles than your knees, will increase the amount of work significantly. I know of no disaster resulting from double ski poling, and I'm not an alarmist. And I believe the exercise is an absolute boon to any exercise program. But its physiologic effects must be respected and approached gradually.

conditioner to take over. I think I'd be more willing to prescribe it boldly if I had your complete medical history, perhaps an X-ray or two, and providing I could join you in your first attempts. There is much to be gained from making DSP a regular part of your training. But there is much wisdom in going easy at the start if you suffer from a normal lifestyle-induced back vulnerability—*and* in checking with your doctor before you start.

Heart Trainer par Excellence

During a recent study at Pitt's Human Energy Lab, a group of trained Heavyhanders were given three exercises: pump 'n' walk to Level 3, faster pump 'n' walk to Level 2, and DSP. In almost every instance, the fastest training heart rates were generated during the DSP segments. That's because the work is inherently difficult. It may also be related to the use of a lot of muscle mass, a good bit of which normally remains untrained—namely, the delts, biceps and triceps, pectorals, trapezius muscles, latissimus dorsi, abdominals, glutes, quads, and calves. (Quite a mouthful!) The heart rate during combined exercise is determined, other things being equal, by the average level of training of each of the muscles involved. So in your initial experiments with DSP, don't be surprised if you hit your target zone very quickly, or if you exceed it before you realize it.

The photos should be a help to you, though moving pictures would be even better. Like all Heavyhands moves, this has a kind of natural tempo at given weights and ranges of motion. Use your smallest weights. Even your unweighted arms should be regarded as weights.

The Basic Four-Step

We start with a four-step version of DSP. With your weights high in front of you, knuckles out, take four small steps. While you're doing that, your hands execute a 270-degree arc (three-quarters of a circle), traveling down and backward, then returning. So the end of your first stride finds your weights passing downward; at the end of the second stride your hands have completed their movement high in back; after the third stride they're coming forward, and will have completed their cycle at the end of the fourth step. Of course, this soon will become a smooth flow of movement. The other big variable is the matter of knee bending and spine

flexions during DSP. In the latter, discretion is the better part of valor. Sometime in the future you may be bringing your chin close to your knees as you coil and uncoil your spine! For now, it's wise to exercise due caution.

If you're not in good condition generally, you will find DSP hard work. It *is* hard work. And the ever present embarrassment factor may cause you to remain on your patio or in your basement while you gain expertise. In Pittsburgh, I see more "closet" DSPers hit the road and track as time goes by.

As you improve and train, you will find yourself settling into a nice 30 to 35 cycle/minute cadence (the four-step sequence equals 1 cycle). To do 30 cycles, your watch can be set at 30, beeping you at the same point in each successive cycle; at 60, once for the forward arm movement, once for the return move; or at 120, 2 beats for each half-cycle. If you are strong of back and quite flexible, deeper bends during DSP will find 25 cycles quite demanding initially. Take my word for it.

Don't spoil things for yourself by overdoing the first time. A couple of minutes are plenty. Include some DSP in warmup

Warning for Back Sufferers

If you're the victim of a bad back, you enter the world of Backaerobics at great risk of making things worse! How can it be otherwise? The fact that your back is bad makes it weaker, and that means you have to exercise even greater caution. Caution puts a crimp in your exercise style as far as spontaneity and enthusiasm go, but you can live with that. If you and your doctor think things like double ski poling and swing 'n' sway make sense for you, proceed slowly. That mostly means going easy with range of motion, increasing it only so long as movement is painless, and stopping on the slightest suggestion of discomfort. Stay away from groups if you tend to be competitive. Gradually increase range of motion, tempo, and duration. As your confidence builds, I recommend several short intervals of back work each day so as to push training without concentrations of movement that might be overdoing it.

Four-step double ski poling

sessions; it's a good dynamic stretcher (as opposed to the fixed static form) and will increase your core body temperature as part of your warmup. I often finish my Heavyhands workouts with DSP, which invariably leaves me more supple than when I began.

Muscles worked: DSP works a slew of muscles: the spinal muscles, of course, and to some extent those of the abdominal wall, and numerous groups about the shoulder girdle: the delts, traps, lats, and pecs. DSP is also an extraordinary quad, hamstring, and buttocks exercise, because of the flexions and extensions at both the knee and hip joints.

Variations: Increase the range of motion of the hips, knees, and spine; increase the cycle frequency; increase the size of your handweights (though I wouldn't hurry into that one).

Tempo: Remember, if you're counting complete cycles and doing the exercise in four counts, an increase of 5 cycles/minute—or a tempo increase of 20 beats/minute—is a *big* increase! Try 25 cycles (100 beats)/minute for starters, adjusting upward or downward after testing the waters for a few minutes.

Some Points to Consider with Four-Step DSP

A four-step DSP cycle is mechanically one-sided, because you always match the same leg with the same point in the arm cycle. While I've never seen injuries result, I do believe you would do well to learn early how to switch your *starting* foot from time to time. And while I don't usually make much of the matter of body symmetry, I can see some justification here, if only because of the massive work being done.

Once you're in shape, it shouldn't be long before you're swinging larger weights. Strength-oriented athletic types can become capable of performing DSP 30 to 35 cycles/minute with handweights that total as much as 25 to 30 percent of their bodyweight. Again, the weight should remain small until your technique is well established and you've experimented with various ranges of motion and cycle frequency.

Another thing to keep in mind is the knee-flexion, back-flexion choice. Actually, you'll be doing both. But you may wish to emphasize one or the other from time to time. Deeper knee flexions are terrific quad trainers, and will make you better able to handle hills, whether you're a runner or Heavyhands Walker. Indeed, DSP makes a perfect training adjunct for runners: It brings them the quad strength-endurance that running doesn't; it works back muscles that running doesn't; it imparts upper body strength-endurance that running doesn't. Now that we've been advised by Dr. Ken Cooper that more than 15 miles of running for exercise may be excessive, need I say more about the inclusion of a few minutes of DSP to buttress your aerobics sessions?

Take careful, immediate pulses after five minutes of DSP once you're able to hack it. Three months into your Heavyhands training, look back at your notations. While at the same old target heart rate, you will note that you're doing more work per heartbeat. That indicates an increase in your oxygen pulse, or the amount of oxygen you're delivering to your tissues with *each* heartbeat. That increase is fundamental to Heavyhands and, indeed, *all* aerobics.

Practice exhaling hard on the downstrokes. Going at a clip of 35 cycles/minute, that makes for a comfortable breathing pattern that will afford you as much air as you need. You can also accentuate the downstroke by consciously *snapping* the weights rather than waiting for gravity to assist you. That works the latissimus dorsi muscles, which are, as I've mentioned before, the body's most massive muscle-pair and a superlative bet for aerobic training. (That will, incidentally, make you a better rower or freestyle or butterfly swimmer, if you're aquatically inclined.)

A word of advice for those who will do much of their DSP outdoors: If you live in hilly terrain, do your DSP going *up* hills, not *down* them. Stumbling downhill is decidedly different, I learned to my acute discontent one day!

Backs: Underuse vs. Overuse

I have a lot of thoughts about the National Back Situation and its relation to aerobic exercise. I personally know of *no* chronic back sufferers with exceptional back-work capabilities. Orthopedic agonies, especially those of the back, seem to eradicate any fitness options. I think some of those people must believe the back is an inborn archfoe, a bad hunk of hardware loaded with vulnerabilities and demanding careful management if they're to avoid a lifetime of pain. *My* feeling is that 90 percent of back suffering represents simple lifelong disuse. So when I do a few consecutive minutes of DSP, I realize with some satisfaction that I'm giving my back as much to do in that small timeframe as most give their backs in a year!

Other Variations in DSP

One way to beat the balance problem we mentioned earlier is to go to a three- or five-step variation. That way, you can start each successive arm cycle with the alternate foot. It merely requires practice. The five-cycle variation is less demanding. You simply count five quickly executed steps while you execute one full, smooth, arm cycle.

When attempting the more difficult three-step variation, pull the weights down briskly during the first stride, finishing the return part of the arm cycle however it feels best to you while you take the next two strides. Going with small steps first will make it easier. Diligent practice will help to make it all happen smoothly, not jerkily. Three-step DSP is a fabulous producer of back strength-endurance, but should be embarked upon cautiously by folks with a shaky back history.

And the Beat Goes On

I read the other day that a Pittsburgh surgeon wrapped a piece of a patient's latissimus muscle around her failing heart, and then proceeded to "pace" the muscle by electrical stimulation, causing it to contract rhythmically in order to help the heart pump blood. I was ecstatic. That brilliant idea lends credibility to a favorite bit of physiological philosophy I once conjured: The best thing that could possibly happen to a given skeletal muscle would be to make it capable of the kind of "forever" behavior we count upon from cardiac muscle. The ultimate condition would be to have all of our skeletal muscles able to "rep" merrily for our entire lifetime—we'd be "all heart," in a manner of speaking! My ambitions with respect to our exercise future involve other odd alchemies, like making arms as work-capable as legs; making all the skeletal muscles function as one; making ordinarily "sedentary" muscles, like those of the lower back and abdomen, as tireless as conditioned legs; and making imaginative whole-body exercise commonplace. That should do for starters!

Body Flex—An Important Consideration

The depth and character of your body flexions will have enormous impact on your DSP workloads and, therefore, on the training effects and calorie losses you can realize. In a recent study at Pitt's Human Energy Lab, Tom Auble and a crew of graduate students measured the work of two kinds of in-place DSP: first with the handweights traveling past the legs at knee level; and then with the weights passing about 4 inches above the ankles. The energy cost of the second variation was about 40 percent greater!

The same applies to four-step "on-the-move" DSP, though at a given tempo the total work is greater when you're moving. Handweight differences also have a more significant effect upon upper torso work when on the move than when in place at the same tempo. This is probably because the forward-moving body must grapple with the opposing forces presented by the arms in their vigorous flight toward the rear. In this way, you can either take the full-flex route at slow tempos or the lesser body flex at higher tempos while remaining precisely at the same heart rate.

Swing 'n' Sway: An On-the-Move Variation

Originally introduced in my first book as an in-place exercise, swing 'n' sway has nonetheless become a favorite on-the-move exercise for many Heavyhanders. For those who aren't familiar with it, I'll present it in a stationary mode to begin with. Once you have the movement down pat, you'll have an easier time switching it to your walking repertoire. This exercise might be best considered as a lateral spine mover, just as DSP is one that flexes and extends the spine forward and backward.

Swing 'n' sway is also called "figure eights" by some, because the hand movements create a series of horizontal figure eights while the knees dip. Try it. Using tiny weights to gain the feel of the movement, stand with your feet at shoulder width. Keeping your weighted hands close together, begin to "swing" them. Start low on your right side, and move the weights upward and to your left; then arc them downward and start them again on a diagonal path upward to the right. As you move around and down to your right again, you'll notice you've inscribed a sideways figure eight in the space in front of you. Continue on smoothly without stopping.

Now pay attention! Your knees should dip a bit as you begin each upward movement. By the time the handweights are at the top of their climb your knees straighten. Totally confused? Consult the photos; they will help. Essentially, you're drawing this figure eight once, while dipping your knees twice.

Muscles worked: Quads, obliques, delts, pecs, lats, traps, arm muscles, and more.

Variations: Many range-of-motion increases are possible; knee dips will increase the workload significantly; or add side leans that go opposite the direction of the hand movements.

Tempo: Start modestly, at perhaps 80. When you become more accomplished, try it to music, going a full cycle to 4 beats of standard 120 pop music, for example.

To make a walk exercise out of it after you've mastered the in-place variety, all you need do is remember to stride with the leg on the side toward which the upward slanting hands are moving. Later, when you've really mastered the movement, you can deliver a side kick instead of the simple step. This movement is a suitable companion for DSP for making you totally "backaerobicised," to coin a term!

Another good partner for both in-place or walk versions of swing 'n' sway is the kick back, which mobilizes the hamstrings. Kick back the leg opposite the side toward which the hands are moving! When properly executed, the calf area

> **Swing 'n' Sway:**
> **A Simply Great Move**
> I love it. Others do, too, once they learn it. It's important at the top of the upswing to turn the hands over, then go "outside" rather than "inside" before starting the down slanted portion of this figure eight stroke. Refer to the photos below for the correct way. After you've got that mastered, you can use it in a variety of ways: sidestepping, forward-backward, just plain forward, and in place. Varying the depth of knee dips and side leans will allow you to fine-tune your ticker with swing 'n' sway. Given my druthers, I'd make it illegal for golfers and skiers not to practice swing 'n' sway variations!

Swing 'n' sway

Striding with swing 'n' sway

*Hamstring kickbacks
with swing 'n' sway*

of the kicked leg should touch the back of the opposite thigh. (Study the photos.) I don't imagine this combination will be your immediate favorite. Having done straight half-hours of it when I realize my hamstrings have been badly neglected, I've come to love it. You will, too.

Side and Back Leans While Striding

Here are two back movements included in pump 'n' walk that can be useful in a number of ways. You can do them separately, or employ simultaneous side and back leans while making longish, lunging strides. This move is especially enjoyable paired with sharp punches angled upward and a bit outward. For those with back vulnerabilities, DSP may seem a bit extreme for starters. I usually recommend these for people with back problems who might want to ease more gradually into Backaerobic exercise before tackling something as demanding as DSP or swing 'n' sway. These leans are good strengtheners, and include a range of spinal movements that are smaller departures from ordinary straight-up punch 'n' walk.

Side leans

Back leans

They can be performed at high tempos with light weights punched high; or with heavier weights at slower tempos pumping to Level 2. Side and back leans make great back trainers because you can manage them comfortably for miles early in your training. They're also effective tuners of your cardiorespiratory system because the hard work gets significantly harder as the leans become more enthusiastic. Your walking pace, using the lunging strides, may be quite slow—under 2.5 mph. But this vigorous punch-lean-lunge combo can get rid of 200 to 300 or more calories per mile, which can keep you slim without straying far from home! Using shorter strides will increase the tempo and overall upper torso contribution.

Another advantage of this movement comes from its complexity. The upper body moves both laterally and backward. So what it lacks in speed and subtlety it makes up for in terms of greater range of motion. And leans lend themselves to powerful armstrokes, which makes them ideal for the dry-land training of swimmers and rowers and other athletes.

At this moment you have a sizable Heavyhands Walking routine that works every major muscle into the business of cardiovascular training. (As you might notice, one area we haven't discussed yet is the belly. Never fear: There is a good bit of belly work embedded in all these movements, and in Chapter 15, I'll give you some specific "Bellyaerobic" additions to complement your program.)

Now to weave all these movements together into the fabric of good Heavyhands Walking sessions....

A Panaerobic "Dekinker" Combo

Tom Auble measured the O_2 uptake on this little in-place couplet, ideal for TV watching because everything moves about your fixed head like a good golf swing. You do 30 swoops, then 20 swing 'n' sways, then repeat the sequence. With 1-pounders at 80 cycles/minute, Tom rang up 10 easy METs. Now if everyone simply did a half-hour of this each day (less than 10 percent of the average total of TV watching), we'd be 100 percent fitter than we are.

Putting It Together: Heavyhands Medleys

There are a number of ways to utilize whichever of the movements in the last three chapters strikes your fancy. You can create an entire workout with almost any of them, or you can link several exercises together in what I call Medleys.

Heavyhands Medleys spice your workout with variety, because *many* movement ingredients can be woven into a prolonged aerobic workout. Medleys also provide an excellent means of bypassing small injuries. The hurts we feel while moving are usually highly specific. Most often they are tiny tears in muscles that simply don't hurt if you don't move them. The diversity of a Heavyhands Medley allows you to rest the ailing part while you continue to move in a very "total" sense. The more expert you become at a wide selection of moves, the more your Heavyhands Walk sessions will neatly elude whatever is uncomfortable.

Using Medleys, you may actually go through a 30-day exercise period without repeating a single workout! Try not to get mired in stereotyped rituals, something that happens readily to us exercisers. Mixing it up is what makes for Panaerobic fitness. Keep seeking movements that explore an angle or a muscle that hasn't gotten into the action yet. You'll know when you've hit something when you wake up the next day: There's a touch of pleasant soreness that tells you what you've discovered.

Imaginative people match their Medley selections with what's going on in their lives. If you play tennis, it's easy enough to make your Heavyhands Medleys stress the muscles that figure prominently in the game. Heart training proceeds nicely no matter which muscles you select to train with.

To ensure proper muscle endurance training, I recommend that each element in a Medley last at least 2 to 4 minutes. Sometimes I may string four or five movements together into a continuous half-hour. A good example might be: DSP, 5 minutes; pump 'n' walk to Level 2, 8 minutes; lateral flings, 5 minutes; cross-punches and cross-strides, 7 minutes; and then back to DSP for 5 minutes, for a 30-minute total that works

**Designing a
Heavyhands Medley**

Here are some things I like to consider when I'm formulating each workout:

- Training the heart
- Getting at a wide assortment of muscle groups
- Offering movement feasibility—in other words, making the exercises extensions of natural movements
- Getting to muscle groups largely neglected by other aerobic exercise
- Including belly and back training for those who are able
- Creating ensembles useful for special fitness purposes: strength, speed, fat loss, bypassing injured parts, practicing sports movements
- Making for balance, agility, coordination, etc.
- Allowing for space and time limitations
- Creating combinations that train without straining

more muscles than any single aerobic strategy without neglecting the heart.

Don't forget to go all the way occasionally, with 30 minutes or more of one movement you can manage for that long. Once you can hit the 30-minute mark, you're not as far from two hours as you might think! On beautiful cool days, when you're not cramped for time, try two hours just to discover what it feels like. Once trained, you may well be able to consume as much oxygen in brisk but comfortable two-hour Heavyhands Walk combos as most elite marathoners can within a similar timeframe!

Here are a few suggestions for Medleys that will make your Heavyhands Walk sessions more fruitful and interesting. They come from my personal experience, from that of other Heavyhands experts and instructors around the world, and from watching our group's spontaneous way of choreographing their Heavyhands workouts over the past four years.

Fifteen-Minute Medleys for Beginners

Do these combinations at your age-related target pulse if that's comfortable. If not, go at the highest comfortable pulse rate.

Your pre-workout warmup should include five minutes of pump 'n' walk to Level 2 using small weights at 110 stride-pumps/minute. You can cool down for a few minutes with a tempered version of what you had been doing. I don't make a ritual of cooling down, but by the end of a reasonably intense Heavyhands workout I'm usually more than willing to rest. In Heavyhands, the pooling of blood in the legs may not pose the big problem it does for leg-alone aerobicists. Still, a cooldown can't hurt and will add an edge of safety to your exercise.

Workout A (15 minutes)

- Just plain pump 'n' walk, all the way

This is the simplest Heavyhands Walk workout. It should be structured from your pretest (described in Chapter 4). Your test will tell you what your bodily response to that workload was—in other words, whether you fell short of, above, or within your calculated age-related target heart rate. Movements that feel fine while you're exercising may leave you with next-day soreness, especially if you're not accustomed to 15 minutes of continuous activity. Fact is, your original 5-minute test may have left you tender in spots. If it did, it might be a good idea to go a little easier when trying 15 minutes straight—perhaps at a slightly lower pulse rate, or simply ignoring the pulse rate in deference to pure comfort.

This introductory 15 minutes is more for giving beginning Panaerobicists their first feel of a prolonged, continuous exercise segment. It's practice. It's a time to locate and remove the inevitable flaws that plague any complex new movement. Remember to bring your pumping hands all the way down to full extension. How high you pump should be freely negotiable and is crucial in determining workloads; how far down you bring the weights isn't! As with your golf swing, it makes sense to groove the move properly from the first moment to avoid the displeasure that goes with undoing bad habits.

Workout B (15 minutes)

- Pump 'n' walk, Level 2, with small weights, at 120 strides/minute (popular music's typical tempo)—5 minutes
- Lateral flings with walk—2 minutes
- Pump 'n' walk, Level 3, with small weights, at 100 strides/minute—3 minutes
- Pump 'n' walk, Level 2, with small weights, at 120 strides/minute—3 minutes
- DSP, 30 cycles/minute (4 beats/cycle)—2 minutes

Once you're accustomed to it, you may wish to substitute DSP for the first five minutes of pump 'n' walk. Chances are good that this one will get you at least to target if you're truly a sedentary beginner. Go cautiously or eliminate DSP outright if you've a bad back history; speak with your orthopedist and perhaps even demonstrate the movement for him to get an opinion. Weights and tempos can be increased gradually. Level 3 pump 'n' walk can be increased to Level 3.5, and double ski poling can be substituted for other movements when you're in the mood. This routine works the legs reasonably, as well as the belly and back, and includes a generous share of activity for the little used lateral and anterior deltoids. It allows the beginner to work many adjacent muscle groups.

Workout C (15 minutes)

- DSP, 30 cycles/minute—3 minutes
- Punch 'n' walk with knuckles out, at 120 strides/minute (use weights you can comfortably punch and pull with strides)—5 minutes
- Pump 'n' walk, Level 3 to 3.5, with leans to side opposite your pump, 110 strides/minute—4 minutes
- DSP, 30 cycles/minute—3 minutes

Grace:
The Underestimated Fitness Factor

Grace implies added strength and suppleness. (Yet it is one of those things that defies rendition by still photos. When video cameras become cheap enough to become standard household equipment, the grace dimension will grab our attention.) When grace is added to any movement it signals that the psyche is dealing with that movement in better fettle: with less focused attention; with less self-consciousness and more confidence; and almost certainly, with more pleasure. Grace is to movement what beauty is to the body of the mover. Lots of people who didn't inherit beautiful bones can eclipse that deficit by liberal additions of grace. Grace is a form of body language; I don't know the derivation of the term "poetry in motion," but it makes good sense to me.

This sequence is great for those who have good backs and want to keep them! As you can see, there are six full minutes of DSP here. Remember range of motion in this exercise. While you shouldn't overdo, gradually inch your way toward pulling the weights higher during their backward sweep and increase the flexion of the back or the knees; then try both at the same time. I also like to pull the weights down sharply during the first of the four steps that form a complete single DSP cycle. One more good idea would be to start the first segment of DSP with your left foot; the last segment, then, should begin with the right foot to keep the work symmetrical. Pumps with leans done to Level 3.5 will mobilize your external oblique abdominals, and the punch segment will work the trapezius muscles, more delts, and the pectorals.

By this time you'll have decided about the warmup period. I don't usually warm up formally—that is, I don't designate any special exercise for it. I merely do whatever I intend to do for my workout at a slightly lower workload. For me, working at a 110 to 120 heart rate for a few minutes seems to appease my oxygen transport apparatus, and gets my body temperature high enough to allow me to move up comfortably.

While push-ups and sit-ups might seem rhythmic enough to qualify as good warmups, they are too strength-oriented to be ideal for that purpose. Light 'n' lively—plenty of range of motion and lots more muscle-group participation—is obviously better for getting the body machine prepared for work. Both push-ups and sit-ups lack those essentials. They mobilize few muscles and generate loud grunts, sounds that aren't consistent with good aerobics!

Whatever movement you favor for warmups, make sure it uses lots of muscle mass and is rhythmic (isotonic). Check your pulse after your warmup—at least early in your program. Unless you feel you're working too hard (uncomfortably breathless), give yourself a few minutes of exercise before you check it. Within a week or two you will make excellent guesses as to your heart rate, based on your breathing, mostly. Six months from now, you'll probably seldom count it unless you're sick or doing research!

Workout D (15 minutes)

- Pump 'n' walk, Level 3, 130 strides/minute—4 minutes
- Punch 'n' walk (use vigorous, snapping punches), 120 strides/minute—8 minutes
- DSP, 30 cycles/minute—3 minutes

Heavyhands Intervals

Interval training is not new to state-of-the-art exercise. It's used whenever exercisers need to push heart and muscle function to near their limits. Runners use intervals when they're interested in increasing their anaerobic capability (effort beyond the pay-as-you-go kind, where it comes to oxygen utilization) or to work on their speed, or both. So runners may run 200 meters, jog 200 meters, run another 200 meters, etc.

In Heavyhands Walk, we can add other dimensions to the concept of intervals. We can consider "regional" intervals, whose design is determined largely by which muscle combinations we wish to emphasize (for example, quads and lateral delts, alter-nating with hamstrings, anterior delts, traps, lats, and triceps). Or we could do "hard-easy" intervals: One move gets us to a relatively high heart rate, while its alternate allows the pulse to return gradually while the body readies itself for the next tough segment.

Intervals may vary in length and duration. I have experimented over the past few years with exceptionally long intervals, like 7 to 12 minutes, at relatively high workloads; and I've often found these to cause relatively dramatic lowerings of the heart rate at given workloads and at rest. Needless to say, hard intervals aren't for those whose health is impaired or even borderline.

Heavyhands Walk is a good place for experimenting with intervals. One of my favorites at the track is Level 3 pump 'n' walk for 220 yards alternating with 220 yards of pump 'n' jog to Level 2. Another variation alternates punch 'n' walk to Level 3 with faster paced pump 'n' walk to Level 2.

Double ski poling, alternated with pump 'n' walk to Level 3, is another favorite. Or 110 yards of pump 'n' run paired with 330 yards of hi-pump 'n' walk. Or fast lateral flings with DSP to work different pieces of the deltoid alternately. And so it goes. You'll never run out of them. Soon your responses to various movements will determine for you which of your Heavyhands movements will work best as intervals.

You may find the initial 130 tempo is pushing things a bit; any undue breathlessness should find you beating a hasty retreat to lower pump levels or tempos. These are all exercises in acquainting you with the most diverse and complex of all the aerobic systems. Technique here means, among other things, discovering in a few seconds what your bodily response to a taxing workload is, then moving to something more manageable. The more your experience grows, the easier those adjustments will inevitably become, and the less you will need to "bodywatch."

You'll notice that I sneakily inserted some "snap" into your punches. I believe these punching strides will become mainstays for you as they have for me. The snap is more than a biomechanical plus: It is a spirited move that will perk your mood. That snap is made for the upper torso; the legs either can't or don't do anything quite like it. It does for the arms what kicking 120 field goals per minute would do for the legs! You will also notice that these punches and strides are continued for eight minutes—the longest segment yet. Don't

Exercise:
Practice for Life

I pity those who don't practice anything. Not a craft or music or a language or dance or magicianship or a sports move. Practice as part of life makes you a different kind of person. Most runners and other exercisers I know just *do* it. There's no sense of practice about it. Practice implies tomorrow's performance and gives an upbeat, optimistic quality to ordinary activity. I must confess I carry this philosophy to extremes. I exercise just like I read. I read about yesterday and practice reading for tomorrow. There is always a conscious dual purpose. One is the present deed, its usefulness, and its pleasure. The other is always conscious or powerfully implied. I'm preparing for an improved performance tomorrow. That puts me in touch with the past and the future simultaneously while working in the present. And so it should be with exercise. When you work out, you're essentially doing your best with what you've become (past), and rehearsing for a better tomorrow.

be concerned if you can't continue snapping punches that rapidly for that long. Go easily and intermittently, allowing for rest. I can guarantee a time will come when a full hour of snappily performed punching strides will be easy!

Workout E (18 minutes)

- Punch or pump 'n' walk, Level 3 to 3.5 at 120 tempo—4 minutes
- Pump 'n' jog, Level 1 to 2, at 160 tempo—2 minutes
- Punch or pump 'n' walk, Level 3 to 3.5, at 120 tempo—4 minutes
- Pump 'n' jog, Level 1 to 2, at 160 tempo—2 minutes
- Punch or pump 'n' walk, Level 3 to 3.5, at 120 tempo—4 minutes
- Pump 'n' jog, Level 1 to 2, at 160 tempo—2 minutes

This 18-minute routine can serve as an introduction to interval work. Abandon it utterly if it seems too demanding or unpleasant for any one of a dozen reasons. It's placed in this series for those who are or have been runners and would like to include some running in their Heavyhands work. I purposely kept the jog segments half as long as the walk ones, because for most, the jogs will generate a higher pulse with any given weights. The pump height will figure prominently in determining the pump 'n' jog workload and thus the heart rate it will generate.

A good way to get to Level 2 is to barely touch your shoulder with the top weighted end in its arc upward. If it generates an uncomfortably fast pulse within a half-minute or so, settle in at a more realistic pump height like Level 1 or maybe 1.5. There's nothing sacred about our arbitrarily chosen levels. But *don't* jog pumping at Level 3 or higher. It's too ungainly, and though I included it in the original Heavyhands text, it should be avoided. If you're very fit, use heavier weights at lower pump heights or with a faster tempo—200 strides/minute is feasible for some! The alternating high-pumping walk will find you recovering very slowly from each two-minute jog, because its workload is too respectable to lend itself to much rest before your next jog alternate.

Workout F (20 minutes)

- Pump 'n' walk—5 minutes
- Punch 'n' walk—5 minutes
- Knuckle-up pumps while walking—5 minutes
- Pumps with kicks—5 minutes

You'll notice some differences in this workout menu. I've stopped dictating tempos and pump heights. By now I'd like to think you can select those yourself. Remember, the most important tempo is your pulse rate. All the other counting rituals are only ways of getting your heart going fast enough to train you without discomfort; a watch that keeps track of your ticker is really all you need.

But most of us are not our own drill sergeants, and for this reason timers are useful for a while. They give our oxygen transport devices a chance to learn what really continuous work feels like. It should be realized that even following a tempo precisely, one can inadvertently "relax" pump heights, punch velocities, and range of body flexions and extensions.

This workout also differs from the others in that we're including a stroke and stride variation. Suppose, for instance, your sore back precluded DSP for a while. Here are a couple of variations on the basic theme to make life interesting for 20 minutes at target. The knuckle-up pumps may be as easily regarded as punches when you snap 'em up there. And the kick-strides are just that. You may find 5 minutes of it more than you can handle at first, especially if you work with the briskness the move calls for. Practice it for a few minutes at a time, and studiously include it in routines on several consecutive days. That will enhance your technique and help you work out the quad soreness you may encounter in the beginning. Don't underestimate the amount of quad power these kicks require. They make ordinary striding seem tame, and they will absolutely increase the pace at which ordinary striding can be performed. They'll make you a faster walker.

Workout G (15 minutes)

- DSP, all the way

Contrary to what you might think, this isn't returning to square one where you simply pumped and walked all the way. It is truly an advanced workout. You may be doing Heavyhands Walk for weeks or longer before you can tackle it successfully. This 15-minute DSP session is perfect for preparing for ski season, and it's great for preparing for your workday as well. The variations of work intensity Heavyhanders can bring to this move are astonishing. Given the same weights and tempo, one individual can often outwork another by half again as much!

So much depends upon range of motion: how high you bring the arms up front; how far down the weights sweep past the legs on their passage backward; how much knee and back

Do Children Still Do "Chores"?

In my neighborhood I seldom hear the term. If kids did real chores, the work of exercise might seem like play by comparison. Kids probably don't enjoy brushing their teeth; they do it because they're supposed to. Does everything have to be defined as pure fun before it can enter the child's motor world? Maybe we should get the kids to exercise without seducing them with glittery promises. So long as the adult's best argument for exercise is that it's fun, the kids have the best excuse in the world for passing on it. I think kids quit exercise upon discovering that their parents, who profess love for exercise, are either exaggerating the truth or overselling.

My grandson works out with me. Neither of us experiences it as fun in the usual sense. Rather, we're enjoying ourselves together doing the necessary work that exercise is! Watching his face while hard at it, all determined with knit brows, he looks like a miniature working adult. Exercise can serve as a useful model for teaching kids the most important thing they can learn: the "love" of work. It's said that in every healthy adult there's a child that loves fun. Well, how about the flip-side of the idea: that in every child there should be the love of work? That work could come in the form of physical exercise.

The Game and Art of Fitness

Staying fit used to be a kind of anxiety-driven obsession with me. Perhaps because I'm older and a bit calmer, and hopefully because of new insights, fitness is a game for me now. This game encompasses my choices not only of how to exercise each day, but also, in the larger sense, of how to fit fitness into my life. In this game of staying fit and making those grudging gains that continue to be possible, the only opponents are your own fickleness and unevenness of purpose, and the environment, which poses a constant obstacle to your diligence. Once you've won the battle and have hewn a program that works for you, you've a chance to make the quantum leap that makes fitness an art. Why art? Because you've added a sensitivity, a touch, a certain class that makes you instantly extraordinary. The art of exercise is like other arts, characterized by the same special qualities.

flexion is involved; and how much snap goes into the downstroke. What's nice about it is that you can *gradually* increase these dimensions. There can't be any hurry. These increases are what I call upgrading dynamic flexibility. They are much more complicated than mere extensions of range of motion because they involve strength and work capacity as well. Try matching your breathing with the stroke, exhaling hard on the brisk downswing, inhaling as the weights are brought forward and upward.

This workout is also a prototype for single move sessions of any sort. There may be days when you'd like to treat your lateral deltoids to some strength-endurance training, which is best added through longer segments. Try lateral flinging for the entire 15 minutes. To go all the way, you may have to back off the weight or tempo, or both. So common sense dictates that when you go for long with single movements the workload has to be sacrificed somewhat at the beginning. Later, if you're like most, you'll be amazed at how long you can go with moves that previously had you in pain after a few seconds!

Workout H (30 minutes)

- DSP—5 minutes
- Punch 'n' walk—5 minutes
- Fast walk—5 minutes
- Lateral flings with kicks—5 minutes
- Pump 'n' walk—5 minutes
- DSP—5 minutes

This is the first half-hour Walk Medley. I think it's self-explanatory. You'll notice that I did something slightly different in the fourth segment. Here I've paired lateral flings with kick-strides, just as an example of the kind of thing you'll be doing to your heart's content, pun intended. While this is a

**How Many Calories
Can You Stuff
into a Mile Walk?**

Consider this. One day I calculated my calorie loss per mile of swing 'n' sway with kickbacks. With 8-pounders, stride-stroking at 80 paces/minute (slow by almost any standard), it would take me 132 minutes to cover a single mile! That's because the strides are somewhat to the side and only inch me forward about a foot every two steps. But the calorie cost per mile of that, even figuring modestly, would be about 1,980, or about 20 times what a mile of conventional walking would cost. Another way of thinking about this is that 1.76 miles doing my swing 'n' sways would lose me that heralded pound of fat, against .35 miles of less bizarre movement. The days of thinking 100 calories per mile are screeching rapidly to a halt. I should also point out that trained Heavyhanders can lose 1,000 calories per hour not only standing in one place, but without either foot ever leaving terra firma!

Medley, it could be used as a form of interval training. All you do is work harder—nearer your "max"—with some segments, and allow yourself to slow down a bit during the alternate ones. The other idea I want to emphasize here is the heavy-light option.

Once you've acquainted yourself with this workout, performed it a few times, and gotten rid of your next-day soreness from it, try a heavier version. Go from 1- to 2-pounders, for instance. Check your heart rate; you'll probably find one of two things: If you try to stick to the original tempo and range of motion, you might find the going too hard. It's also possible for you to find the work demanding locally—in your muscles—but at a lower heart rate! We see that constantly: people struggling with heavier weights but doing less aerobic work. Speeding up the stride and shortening the armstroke may get you to target with the heavier weights. One day you will be able to do with 3's what you originally could just manage with 1's—at the very least. That's what training is all about.

Again, remember these choices are mine. They reflect my experience; certainly they reflect my idiosyncrasies! So don't be afraid to experiment. The sequencing of this sample 30-minute Medley can be changed. I like to begin and end a long routine with DSP because it leaves most Heavyhanders more supple than when they started. But if you find, as many do, that your heart rate soars rapidly with DSP, don't use it either as a starting or finishing gambit. If you back off intelligently, DSP is quite usable both for warming up and cooling down. My experience suggests there may be some virtue in juggling the sequences liberally, because in the lab we've found differences in the response to a given exercise when it's performed early as opposed to late within a routine.

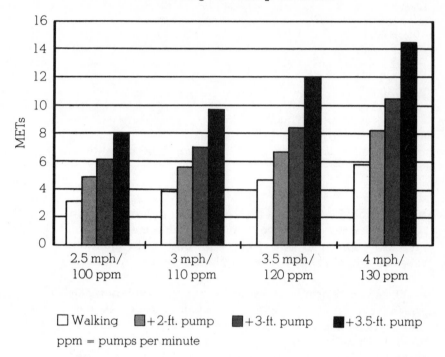

Aerobic Energy Costs of
Walking vs. Pump 'n' Walk

☐ Walking   ◼ +2-ft. pump   ◼ +3-ft. pump   ◼ +3.5-ft. pump

ppm = pumps per minute

Shadowbox—A Workout in Itself

Shadowboxing is an entire Heavyhands technique unto itself. In many ways it's my favorite "complex" of Heavyhands movements. Here's why: Since light weights suffice, it is portable; its lively format makes it suitable for music, and for me it feels like dance; it excludes almost nothing in the way of combined movements; given a sore heel or foot, high aerobic work levels can be achieved with both feet flat on the ground; it is a wonderful medium for those who like to improvise with movement; it is quite controllable, allowing for graceful changing of the work intensity on a moment-by-moment basis; and it can be accomplished effectively in the smallest space. I know of a few Heavyhanders who stay fit almost exclusively with variations on the theme of Heavyhands shadowboxing.

There are disadvantages, too. It's an exercise during which you can loaf if you wish. It may be understood best as a series of short, often very short, intervals, strung together. Not only is it demanding physical work, but you must learn to anticipate your next movement more so than in the simple repetitive types of aerobics—even more so than in dance, in which the routines are ultimately memorized and come spontaneously. You do this exercise uniquely each time, so there's a touch of creativity involved in shadowboxing. Some don't enjoy Heavyhands shadowboxing for these very reasons. But some have learned to prefer it, so I wouldn't dismiss it summarily at first clumsy blush if I were you! Shadowboxing is ideal for the no-fuss exerciser, who is diligent enough about investing time for exercise, but resents the extras, like getting to and from a spa or pool or track or ski trail. Varied Heavyhands Walking suits him fine. He starts and finishes at his house, without special dressing and traveling rituals. Shadowboxing can be the perfect indoor complement to his Heavyhands Walk.

There isn't room here for an in-depth treatment of Heavyhands shadowboxing. It's an open system: There's room for unlimited growth. Again, only one move would be sufficient to implement near-optimal aerobic training. But more moves do more for muscles and are cerebral stimulants, too. I'll leave you with a few suggestions and you can take it from there.

Basic Shadowbox

The basic move for shadowboxing is called "hand over hand." The hands rotate constantly, one over the other, when not specifically throwing punches. That generates a constant upper torso work level, to which the legwork is added. This hand rotation can amount to little or big circles, and follows the beat of whatever music you're listening to. Use little weights; with shadowboxing an additional pound can be instantly unwieldy!

Basically, you can either keep your feet stationary, or you can be airborne in a series of hops that roughly simulate the bobbing and weaving you see professional boxers do. When the feet are planted, the legwork comes from knee bending and hip motions; the upper body is thus lifted repeatedly and rapidly each minute to generate the workload and train an assortment of leg muscles.

The punch movements are thrown through almost endless angles. Part of the armwork comes from pulling the punch back. Hand speed—or how hard the punch is thrown—is a variable. As upper torso work capacity increases, the number of consecutive punches will increase spontaneously. At first, two at a time might be more than enough. Later, sequences of a dozen or more rapid-fire movements will become possible for many. Following punch combinations, the arms resume the hand-over-hand pattern.

A 10-MET Pump 'n' Walk Test

All you need is a yardstick or tape measure, a metronome or a piece of 130-beat music, and a pair of 3-pound handweights. Measure how high a 3-foot pump comes on your body (like to the top of your ear, top of your head, or bottom of your ear if you're quite tall). Then pump to that height striding simultaneously to the 130-beat tempo for four or five minutes. Count your pulse as soon as you stop.

This presumes you can continue for four minutes at about 10 METs moving both arms and legs. You might find that 10 METs of pump 'n' walk is about all you can handle—before training, that is. Keep at it for a while, and then watch your sparks fly! The quickest results occur in young, healthy, deconditioned people who train diligently, four hours weekly for 12 weeks, using varied Heavyhands stride-stroke combinations.

More Muscle with Fewer Exercises

As your Heavyhands training progresses, you will probably become a bargain hunter. By that I mean you will instinctively include more muscle in the time you slot for exercise. That is just as it should be, because of the extended benefits that gather as a result. As you add muscle—and that implies more joint action, of course—you'll also be wasting more calories per minute at given heart rates and enjoying more comfort at given workloads. As these moves evolve from simple basics to more complex forms, you will probably settle into fewer total movements to maintain your fitness.

Tips for Great Shadowbox

Use music when you can, and don't try to imitate exactly what you've seen in the ring. This should feel more like dance than warfare! For instance, you needn't stand at the conventional angle facing your imaginary foe. At times, at least, you can face him frontally, throwing punches symmetrically, abandoning the conventional left hand "lead" stance. I frequently toss in a sequence of lateral flings with hops to put some life into a lagging shadowbox routine.

It's a good idea to check your pulse frequently in the beginning. You'll doubtless be surprised by the high heart rates you reach quickly. Shadowboxing in the right "hands" can be a superlative heart trainer.

I've found that splitting my shadowboxing between some with feet planted and some while bobbing and weaving makes good sense. Even with good hip and knee dip work included, if you stick exclusively to the planted-feet version, your legs acquire a "heavy" feel. Interspersing some springy airborne moves (it needn't be much) erases that feeling. The workloads measured with each version, incidentally, turn out to be surprisingly similar in our lab. My division of the labor is more related to orthopedic subtleties than to oxygen transport.

Breathing at higher workloads presents a challenge with this exercise. Because of the irregularity of the punches, it's harder to adopt a rhythmic breathing pattern as you would do

Exercise Wave of the Future: Compound Panaerobics!

We're studying this idea in great detail at the lab. While combined movements are beneficial because of the inclusion of unusual amounts of muscle, there's a way, I believe, to further exploit that effect with compound movements. In a 12-count move, which is really three separate movements performed four times each, one combination of muscle groups rests while the other two are worked. It might be best thought of as chains of "mini-aerobic intervals": Instead of alternating work and rest, the workload merely shifts from one set of muscles to another without changing the level of intensity.

What astonished me about this idea is that its physiologic advantages never occurred to me until one day when I markedly underestimated my heart rate while doing a long 12-count interval. Then it all seemed to make sense. No exercise can use all muscle groups; but hooking a few combinations of them together can come close! Fatigue levels at given workloads drop, in part because oxygen transport becomes more efficient, and lactate levels should lower. This tactic should use more fat as fuel: Each muscle fiber works less hard and less often, while your whole body is doing more than you can do any other way! That should spell a lower per workload injury rate, too, and if my reasoning is on target, a lower blood pressure at any given work intensity. It takes training to get there, but it's well worth the investment.

spontaneously during running or swimming. I believe this could be a useful gimmick in the training of the respiratory muscles. In the laboratory, our shadowboxers have gone for prolonged periods at high workloads. The minute-by-minute volumes of air breathed and oxygen used are surprisingly stable despite apparent irregular movements and breathing.

Don't hesitate to improvise. Make up moves that are suitable so long as they don't reduce the workload unnecessarily. Shadowboxing or shadowbox dance is a "free-form" exercise and should be treated as such.

So there you have it: a repertoire of Heavyhands Walk with a few in-place supplements to keep you from being totally dependent on the outdoors, on-the-move program. It's more than you need for Panaerobic excellence. If you're the adventurous type, it may serve as a motivator for even more new movements.

The Basics for Indoor Heavyhands Training

Many of us find no suitable substitute for exercise in the great outdoors. I know some people whose exercise programs come to a dead halt during inclement weather. Many midsummer and winter days find them not only indoors but inert! For those who adhere to a program of three or four workouts per week, that can present problems: A few consecutive days of bad weather might mean a full week without exercise, which is about as detrimental to your exercise habit as a case of the flu!

When you live in a place where weather fronts move in and out frequently, it's good not to be too dependent upon fine weather for your fitness fix. The best way to defeat the outdoors-or-nothing trap is to become as expert at the game of exercise indoors as you are outside.

As you might have guessed, I believe Heavyhands is the way to accomplish precisely that. I could not have devised a system that didn't include that option. I am not one of those willing to nobly brave extremes of temperature, slick surfaces, and precipitation of one sort or another in the pursuit of fitness—surely not when I don't have to. I regard the complete exerciser as one who hasn't built a host of excuses into his or her intention to stay fit for a lifetime: not weather, nor time, nor convenience, nor expense, nor lack of companions, nor small injuries, nor boredom. In my obviously prejudiced view, Heavyhands comes closest to implementing my serious if not always gung-ho determination to remain fit as long as I can.

And once you've gotten the hang of indoor training, you may look for excuses to remain inside! There are many pluses that go with indoor Heavyhands exercise. An indoor track (you can find these at universities and private clubs or spas) goes a long way when you're doing Heavyhands Walk: A lot of physical work can be crammed into a short distance. And the temperature, humidity, and footing are more predictable. Miles cease to be an important consideration; work performed per minute at a useful heart rate is the more important question. To prove that point, I have pumped 360 calories into a single mile-long walk, where conventional walking or jogging would only have wasted the standard 100! Resorting to the ludicrous, using alternating, hard 5-pound punches and kickbacks at a snail's pace, I have spent more than 1,000 calories covering the same mile! Not for your first day of Heavyhanding, but certainly within probable range for most persistent adventurers with average bodily equipment.

There's No Place Like Home— or Anywhere Else—for Heavyhands

Indoor space needn't be spacious nor posh. My home is my favorite place for exercise. Any room suits me, but I must customize my movements for each. In our small den at home, I work out while I watch television. In the living room I move to the beat from the stereo, exploiting the soft carpeted floor for moves that get me airborne. There I do short marches of pump 'n' walk, planning my turns so as not to interrupt my cadence or aerobic work. I've checked my heart rates at thousands of little movement adventures and have failed to see any physiologic cramping of my exercise style while indoors.

The basic wisdom for indoor Heavyhands might be to make the best of private space when you've no choice in the matter! We all are inhibited to some extent. Forced indoors, we can take advantage of the release from self-consciousness. In

---

Aerobics vs. Aerobic Dance

To set things straight, I should mention that the term "aerobics" as Dr. Ken Cooper coined it originally had very little to do with its current meaning. Now the term almost always refers to *dance*. A number of splinter groups have arisen that use dance as a form of "aerobic" exercise. Now "low-impact" aerobics comes along and perpetuates this tendency to apply the word to dance techniques that are rhythmic, continuous, and produce "training" heart rates.

For me, "aerobics" means what it did when I first read Dr. Cooper's book. While it includes moves that resemble dance, it is hardly limited to dance. When Jacki Sorensen developed Aerobic Dance, and when successive aerobicisers came along, they developed what *now* is termed high-impact aerobic dance. No one called these moves "high-impact" in the beginning. My guess is that high-impact aerobics got its name from the physiologists and biomechanics experts who, after all, spent most of their time studying the most popular high-impact activity of all— running.

So I propose that the term "low-impact" aerobics and its cousins, "no-impact" and "controlled-impact," be freed from their chance connection with dance. All kinds of movements can be done with either one or both feet planted. And whether you decide that a given movement qualifies as dance or not seems as much a matter of taste and experience as anything else. If it works well with music and requires a modicum of grace, then as far as I'm concerned, it's dance.

time, the spatial requirements for good exercise will shrink to a mere 8 cubic feet and the best equipment, bought with just a few dollars, will occupy a small corner of your baggage when traveling.

A great deal of traveling in the last couple of years made me learn quickly how to keep in shape when both time and space were in short supply. Given my rather exorbitant eating habits, the fact that I gained no body weight over that period of time can only be attributed to the calorie cost of the exercise I was able to squeeze into my demanding, irregular schedule. I learned how to use a small hotel room full of furniture and with irregular patches of floor space. It became clear after a while which moves were right and which were impossible in a given situation. When the floors were hard, as with thinly carpeted concrete, I shadowboxed mostly, with both feet on the floor, utilizing movements at the hip and knee to work my legs. That pattern kept my eyes easily in command of the TV screen.

I also learned to divide exercise time during travel into short, high-intensity doses—perhaps 10 or 15 minutes at a stretch. News broadcasts became favorite times for workouts. Other considerations during travel taught me much about how to stay in shape when the situation was far less than ideal. An old back-pain sufferer, I never neglected a few minutes of Backaerobics like DSP and swing 'n' sway to keep limber without sacrificing aerobics. Pump 'n' run in place was easy to do in even the smallest quarters. I generally carried small weights on extended trips—perhaps 3- or 4-pounders at the most. I knew I could catch up on heavy weight work when I got home.

A radio provided music when TV programs weren't choice. Sometimes I carried a small cassette player with favorite selections to pace me pleasantly. A total of 7 pounds of my baggage was all I needed to tote my exercise equipment.

My Favorites for Indoors

In the following recommendations, I'll not go into details like range of motion, tempo, and weight size. By this time you know that these variables can be juggled dozens of ways with a given exercise, and combined to bring you to a comfortable target heart rate. Obviously, if you're at home, you'll have control of the music and will have an assortment of weights. If you're traveling, you'll doubtless have one pair of weights and one source of music; so range of motion will be what you vary most. I've tried to include every major muscle group in these exercises.

**Riddle:
How Much More Energy Is Used in High-Impact Than in Low-Impact Exercise?**

Answer: It's a meaningless question. I've noticed a cluster of articles devoted to that controversial topic lately. In some, it is presumed that low-impact aerobics *must* use less energy, *will* generate a slower heart rate, and *won't* cause injuries. The popular exercise literature, incidentally, is loaded with that kind of categorical information, eager to present the real "scoop" to the susceptible segment of the population. The confusion seems to stem from the false logic that equates low impact with low energy! High-impact exercise is only one technique for doing lots of work. Swimming or cross-country skiing can generate big workloads with little impact. Fact is, low-impact, even no-impact movements can be performed at as high or even higher energy costs, with equal or faster heart rates, than high-impact moves. You merely modify the movement design—use different hand-weights, different tempos, ranges of motion, etc. I'd like to be able to say that such low-impact exercise won't injure. You just can't guarantee that absolutely. Once people learn how to perform low-impact, high-energy movements, there are likely to be few injuries. You can't argue with physics!

Pumps with Side Kicks

Just kick to the side while pumping the same side arm.

Pumps with side kicks

The Injury Industry

While doing what we can to reduce exercise injury makes sense, some make *dollars* doing it! Some fitness-related magazines devote significant copy space to the injury dilemma, with articles discussing common injuries along with their prevention and treatment, and ads selling "safe" equipment, protective flooring and shoes, and an imaginative assortment of bandages, binders, blister kits, and warming ointments. What I find interesting from the public health standpoint is that all this is happening while we as a nation are chugging along at an average exercise intensity that's less than lots of cardiac patients can manage! It would be nice to see a rundown as to which subpopulations of exercisers are most hobbled by injury. One thing is sure: The 2 percent or so of us who consistently work at high levels couldn't account for all that cash flow! I'm suggesting that we get injured far more than we should, and at lower intensities than should cause it. I'm hinting that it may be because we're adhering stubbornly to techniques that injure. And I *know* I can teach most open-minded beginners to get hurt less while chasing more calories than that modest national average! What makes for a thriving injury industry are lots of exercisers whom I'd characterize as "fickle-rigid": They switch allegiances impulsively but not always wisely, and stay fixed too long without revising their game plan.

METs and Mls — Don't Read This!

Just ignore it unless numbers supply you with a sweet sense of certainty unequaled by anything else. Remember when I mentioned that a MET (metabolic equivalent) is a unit of work, and that 1 MET is the work required to do the body's work while at rest? And 2- or 5- or 10-MET workloads mean 2, 5, or 10 times the work of rest? A MET equals 3.5 mls of oxygen per kilogram of body weight per minute. Why? Because when they measured the oxygen consumption rates of a lot of people at rest, it averaged 3.5 mls of oxygen per kilogram of body weight each minute! So instead of describing a laboratory subject's labor in terms of METs, we can use "mls" language. In other words, instead of saying 1 MET, we can say 3.5 mls O_2/kilo/min. Here's how it breaks down:

METs	Mls of O_2/Kilo/Min
2	7.0
3	10.5
4	14.0
5	17.5
6	21.0
7	24.5
8	28.0
9	31.5
10	35.0
11	38.5
12	42.0
13	45.5
14	49.0
15	52.5
16	56.0
17	59.5
18	63.0
19	66.5
20	70.0

Keep these numbers around, just in case. I predict, because the popular literature is becoming progressively more laced with this kind of "talk," that everyone will be saying things like, "I ran at 10 METs for a half-hour this morning," or "Sam swims at 42 mls most of the time." After a while, when you hear "18 METs" the number 63 will pop into mind. The languages of work become interchangeable, just like you'd expect.

Cross-Punches with Kickbacks

Stand with your feet at least shoulder-width apart. The punch crosses the midline until well outside the opposite shoulder; the same-side leg kicks back so that the kicking ankle attempts to touch the opposite buttock. Side leans away from

Cross-punches with kickbacks

the punching side make it more interesting and useful for the obliques. (See Chapter 5 for more info on cross-punches, and Chapter 6 for kickbacks, or hamstring flexes.)

Folds

You can't omit these because you can do them anywhere. Experiment to find where in your workout you like to put them. Any bed is good equipment for folding (see Chapter 15 for more details on folds).

Folds

Heavyhands In-Place Moves and TV Watching

Our lab research shows that almost every walk-move has an in-place variation. We watch an average of six hours of TV daily; wouldn't these in-place Heavyhands Walk versions be wonderful for activating the body during normally inert TV-watching periods? The "no-impact" format allows the eyes to remain on the screen, while the body is muscle loading at a healthy heart rate. Exercise in front of the TV could help to stave off fitness deficiencies in adults and children alike.

Punch 'n' Dip

These are excellent when you're forced indoors and have sore feet; they give good knee-hip action without requiring your feet to leave the deck. The punches, thrown alternately, can vary endlessly—that includes, of course, the zeal with which you pull them back. The trick here is to both dip and straighten the knees by the time the punch reaches its destination. Put plenty of trunk leans into this; the more exaggerated the better.

Punch 'n' dip

The Case for 10-Minute Exercise

You can make an excellent argument for 10-minute modules of exercise; fitting as many of these into a day's time as your schedule and sense of enterprise will allow. Athletes who compete in events taking somewhere between 8 and 12 minutes—2- and 3-mile runs, 800-meter swims, etc.—seem to chalk up the highest work capacities. When we test people in the lab for VO_2 max, the test usually lasts between 9 and 13 minutes. Through our experience, we've learned why some athletes are able to predict their own record performances in long races (like a full marathon) by performing well in shorter races, like the 10-K. I guess what I'm saying is that for those who can't manage 30 or more continuous minutes of exercise, 10 minutes at different intervals will do fine. Fact is, for many people it may be a better way to improve the oxygen transport system. We automatically set our "ergostats" lower when we intend to go longer. And for young exercisers who are looking to lose fat and prepare for athletic competition simultaneously, I'd opt for several 10-minute, high-intensity intervals for best results. Ten minutes seem to pass quickly when you're accustomed to lengthy sessions. And if you're seeking a slower resting heart rate, these high-intensity modules provide a better shot at that. This sort of quality training should be a decided advantage to endurance athletes.

Double ski poling in place

Double Ski Poling

You already know the on-the-move version. Here's an in-place variation that can be nicely done indoors if you have four spare feet in front of you. You merely do four-step DSP, eight steps forward (accompanied by *two* complete arm cycles) and eight steps backward. To keep yourself confined to the small space available, you'll obviously have to take small steps! Starting with your left foot, take about an 8-inch step, then move the right foot so it's lined up with the left, and so on. Move the arms as usual during the forward and backward stepping.

Lateral Flings, Heel-Toe

With feet close together, pull your arms laterally, then back to the midline (about a foot or a little more in front of your breastbone). During the lateral pulls, allow your knees to dip and slide forward, while you move up to your toes. As the weights are moved back to the midline, move to your heels as your knees straighten and your backside protrudes. This is a great lower back/lateral delt combination.

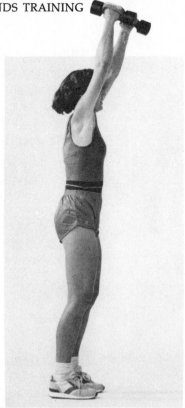

Heel-to-toe lateral flings

Pump 'n' run in place

Pump 'n' Run in Place

This version of pump 'n' run is usually done as a same-side move, as opposed to the on-the-move opposite pump-step pattern. Kickbacks can be thrown in as a variation here.

Swing 'n' Sway

I won't give you any additional explanation except to remind you that the range of motion here, and thus the muscle mass involvement, can vary enormously. That's good to keep in mind when you find yourself in a hotel room with smaller weights than you would typically use for swing 'n' sway; small weights needn't hold you back. The work increases rapidly as the knee dips deepen.

Dance

Here's a kind of free-form exercise thrown in for good measure, and for those who like dance and are good at improvising. I call it "dance" because it's the kind of thing that could make good use of music. Actually, you could call it a potpourri of other movements in this chapter, shifting as gracefully as you can from one to the next without missing a beat. It's a nice way to learn that the body doesn't care much what you're doing so long as you don't loaf, overdo, or injure. A continuous Medley fashioned from eight different movements, varying the sequencing and the music from session to session, could become a nifty indoor backup strategy.

Bringing Fitness to Sports
Mac Good teaches the Heavyhands technique at Ossining, New York, where he is director of the fitness programs at the Sports Learning Corporation. A renowned rower and skater in his youth, Mac has become interested in the training of athletes with an eye to adding fitness dimensions that relate simultaneously to health and the specifics of athletic prowess.

Mac Good

Shadowbox

It's more unwieldy than dance if you're off somewhere with large weights. If you're in a situation in which you don't have a large block of time available, use shadowboxing for several brief but brisk intervals, dividing the time between airborne bobbing patterns, and hard, fast shots with feet planted and rather widespread.

There are a lot of exercises here. You don't have to do all or even several. Each move can serve as an entire workout, because any one includes at least as many muscle fibers as any single aerobic exercise you could otherwise do. Let the spirit move you as it would in a restaurant, where everything on the menu is equally delicious!

Fast Walk with Heavyhands

A few months ago, while I was trudging pumpingly up and down the hilly streets of my neighborhood, it occurred to me that I ought to be working my legs faster. True, when I pump to high levels I do lots of legwork, especially when the weights are sizable and I'm moving at a tempo between 120 and 140. Then I thought of the racewalkers who may travel at stride paces approaching 180! I had tried that pace at the lab and found it reasonably comfortable as a pumping "sprint-walk" when using very light weights.

I dug into the literature and found to my surprise that the top competitive racewalkers raced at work levels below my training level! Since all were half my age or less, that got me thinking. My Heavyhands Walk training had apparently enabled me to walk *without weights* at a racewalker's stride pace, even though I never walk that rapidly during my ordinary pump 'n' walk sessions. That suggested that my slower pace accompanied by various light to heavy armstrokes had prepared my legs for something faster! And I discovered that at a racewalking pace (around 176 strides/minute) I had a surprisingly low pulse. Looked like my collection of Panaerobic Heavyhands Walk movements had, in fact, trained my legs and circulation for fast walk perhaps *better* than conventional walking would have. I couldn't turn back the clock and know for sure, but my high training work intensity and my slow pulse were presumptive evidence at least.

So I was reasonably sure that ordinary Heavyhands Walk could help me to walk faster than I usually do without weights and faster than most people can. I found the fast walk pace interesting and began experimenting with it with various weight sizes and pump heights. I learned that it doesn't take much handweight to bring you to "max" when you're pumping high at 160-plus pumps/minute! Experienced Heavyhanders with high work capabilities who wish to pump little weights at their usual training intensity have little choice but to walk quickly. Not quite as quickly if the pump heights reach Level 4, but still quickly.

Sedentary vs. Active

I have noticed a recent tendency on the part of the experts to divide people into those who are fit and those who are sedentary. On the other hand, I have always thought of fitness in terms of a continuum. There are sedentary people, extraordinarily fit people, and all grades in between. Those who push conventional walking as the best way to get and stay fit seem intent mostly upon rescuing us from the ravages of pure sloth! When 4.5-mph conventional walk is touted as being enough, that dismisses about 12 METs of fitness that may lie beyond 4.5 mph! If any educator suggested that a 200-word-per-minute reading speed was sufficient to data-process our way through life, they'd probably be tarred and feathered. The "sedentary versus active" polarity also presumes someone knows for sure how various fitness levels relate to health. I can't avoid feeling that the plea for modest levels of fitness has its origin in the fear of sudden death while overdoing it. While it's probably true that more runners die with their boots on than conventional walkers, I'd wager that more strollers die suddenly than fast runners!

Why Fast Conventional Walk Is So Hard

At the start of the book I made it clear that conventional strolling wouldn't be the best way of making us a fit nation. But did you know that after you reach a speed of 4.5 mph, walking becomes as hard as running? And that at faster paces walking gets harder faster? *Walking* magazine stated that walking 6 mph generates a workload of 6 to 7 METs. Not even close. At 6 mph (about 10-minute miles), walking is probably closer to 12 METs. While that's not an awesome workload, few can be coaxed to do it by walking. A recent study of fit young athletes found that few could *walk* to their target heart rates. After some training they were able to walk at an average of 5.3 mph! Mind you, these kids had enormous VO_2 maxes— between 52 and 75 mls, if my memory serves me.

Conventional walking has a built-in "governor" that keeps most of us from generating high workloads doing it. It's not a heart pump problem. There's simply too much friction involved when you abandon the option to go airborne! Good exercise needs to be accomplished in the airborne state. I never doubted it in the first place. The crucial question is "What's to fly?" The answer is that the whole body should remain on terra firma, and the pumping, weighted hands should wing it!

For example, if I want to train at my usual intensity with 3-pounders to Level 2, my walking pace must exceed 180 strides/minute! That provoked the next question: If a racewalker goes at full tilt at 176 paces/minute and you train him to pump weights at the same tempo, how fast can he walk *without weights?* I got a couple of racewalkers I know to try to pump weights at their race pace. As expected, they couldn't for more than a few seconds. Either the pumps lagged or their pace slowed, or both. And they ran up higher heart rates than they were used to.

I thought these were useful clues to upgrading the training of racewalkers. These athletes may be able to use Heavyhands Walk to advantage. Since they rely on a lot of vigorous arm assistance during their races, why not make the arms really efficient by working them harder than is necessary for their sport during training? Since walking slower while pumping heavy weights higher enabled me to walk faster, why not use that as a way to train racewalkers? If it works, it's another good example of how nonspecific training tactics can specifically help you to win!

The strange, fast striding of the racewalker got me to think seriously of including more fast stepping in Heavyhands programs. Just as slow striding using heavy weights can produce aerobic gains as well as new strength, stepping can also be pushed to fast paces. Then armwork can be added to make for an even higher training intensity.

When I've done extreme variations of pump 'n' walking, like using 15- or 20-pounders or moving at 200 strides/minute, I noticed that my legs usually fell behind the "beat" and usually ached more than my arms the next morning. It occurred to me that a good Heavyhands Walk program could get even better if you practiced at paces typical of racewalkers. There are not a lot of racewalkers; they are many times fewer than runners. Why should that be? My tentative theory is that at competitive walking speeds, it takes great perseverance to keep the walking momentum up, because of the supported stride that never leaves the ground. My own observations during pump 'n' walk bear this out: At fast tempos I have felt my legs struggling to keep up with my armstrokes.

Early in the development of the Heavyhands method, I was convinced that the best way to fitness nirvana was to pump weights high and reasonably quickly, so as to get much of the upper body muscle mass to work hard steadily. But the racewalkers got me to rethink in the direction of speeding up the supported strides of walk, and so lessening the tendency for the legs to fall behind trained arms. A few weeks of fast walk with lower but manageable fast pumps made a believer out of me. The result was a compromise: I began to do walk intervals—half with very fast low pumps (170 or more strides/minute), half with slower stride-strokes with high pumps (120 to 140 strides/minute). In that way, I got both lots of upper torso work and plenty of swift legwork in the course of a half-hour workout.

Why Fast Walk Works

Adding fast walk to your Heavyhands regimen makes sense when you consider that few Heavyhanders who actively pump weights turn out to be runners. Most of the runners who carry handweights these days literally "carry" them, I fear. Fast walk may be one way to get exceptional leg training without the difficulty and risk of injury posed by the fast airborne strides of running.

A word on fitness in relation to competition: My various Heavyhands training ploys, from shadowbox to dance to Medleys, have gotten me in excellent condition to walk fast, even competitively if I wished. I probably enjoy lower resting and working heart rates than 95 percent of racewalkers. My age is a bit of a disadvantage, mostly because my heart doesn't beat as fast as it used to (it slows approximately 1 beat/minute each year). But since I have a very low resting pulse rate, I continue to enjoy a large range of heartbeats available for accomplishing hard work. Working at a comfortable (for me) 140 pulse, I have 105 heartbeats—those between 35 and 140—to bring me to steady physical activity.

Fanny Wiggling and Heavyhands Walk

Some say that the total number of racewalkers stays small because many men don't relish the biomechanical necessity of wiggling their behinds to generate walking speed. Heavyhands Walkers don't need to do that. Of course they don't usually walk as fast as racewalkers, especially if they pump high and/or wield heavy weights, but they do more work!

Conventional walking can generate incredible workloads—if you can walk fast enough. Heavyhands Walk allows workload increases at much slower tempos.

Armwork in Conventional Fast Walk

Walking fast is almost impossible without arm assistance. Racewalkers pump their arms to pull themselves along. Fast Heavyhands pump 'n' walk creates a different movement pastiche. The arms act as facilitators for the legs, but they also create new legwork. You'd have trouble walking as fast pumping weights as you can without them, but you can't generate the workloads without weights that you can while pumping weights, once you're arm-trained. One thing seems certain: All the armwork you put into vigorous pump 'n' walk will not limit the leg training you can realize. Concentrating only on leg action during walk is of no particular advantage. Combining arms and legs vigorously doesn't limit training of either pair of limbs, in other words.

Pump 'n' Walk (120 strides/min at 3.5 mph)		Walk or Run Equivalents (no weights, no pumps)
Height	Weight	
2 ft	1 lb	Walk at 4 mph or walk up 2.5 percent grade
3 ft	3 lbs	Run at 5 mph or walk up 7.5 percent grade
3.5 ft	3 lbs	Walk up 15 percent grade

Walking Fast vs. Walking at Fast Workloads

Tom Auble tried pump 'n' walking at various speeds on the treadmill, doing each at the same tempo (120 beats/minute). To our surprise, he found that when going from 2.5 mph to 3 mph to 3.5 mph the workload varied hardly at all. When he worked at an assortment of tempos—110, 120, and 130—the story was quite different. The workload jumped promptly and significantly. This little experiment makes for a nice rule of thumb. If you'd like to increase the workload somewhat when walking with someone else, you can, of course, pump higher. Or you can take smaller, faster steps while still moving at the same speed as your partner. When you see a husband outdistancing his wife you know that either they don't know how to regulate the workload to maintain togetherness, or someone doesn't like the conversation!

Does that mean I'd be ready at present to racewalk competitively? Of course not. I'd need plenty of long, fast walks to immunize myself against the shinsplints I'd risk at first. I'd be likely to injure myself because my cardiorespiratory training would lead me to believe I could walk faster than my orthopedic equipment could tolerate. Starting from scratch, most walkers train the heart and the specifically involved muscles at the same time. Starting with higher work capability than the sport itself demands, ironically enough, can be risky!

If you read the "exerscience" literature, you'll discover a number of articles devoted to the subject of "anaerobic threshold," often referred to as "AT." That's the work level at which aerobic, pay-as-you-go oxygen usage begins to yield to so-called anaerobic metabolism. At that "threshold," lactic acid begins to build in the blood and the breathing mechanisms begin working disproportionately hard to maintain the high intensity of work. Some investigators have found it to be a decided advantage to have a high AT. Rowers and some other athletes who have to use high percentages of muscle mass at their sport are said to attain high ATs. My guess would be that racewalkers trained at Heavyhands would gain higher thresholds and that would also allow them to walk longer races at a higher percent of their maximal work capacity.

Fast Walk: No Cakewalk

Pumping little weights high in the air at tempos of 160 or better is not for newcomers to exercise, nor for vintage jocks just over a bout of flu. It is very difficult work—even elite runners will find these intensities of combined work impossi-

Don't Walk—Pump 'n' Walk!

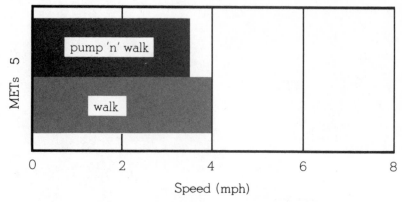

Speed (mph)

METs

Pump 'n' Walk: 120 strides/minute,
2-ft. pump height, no weights

ble at the beginning. But once you've become well trained at Heavyhands, fast walk presents a realistic challenge.

Many variations of strokes can be used with fast walk. I enjoy snapping punches best, using a variety of hand positions, from knuckle-up to knuckle-out, as well as variously angled armstrokes. Another favorite is fast walk with hard side leans and punches. I usually breathe at half the stride-stroke rate, so that at 160 tempo I'm breathing 80 times each minute.

I suspect one day a Heavyhands trainee will break a racewalk record. And I suspect Heavyhands training could substantially reduce the training time required by serious competitive walkers. More importantly, I'm suggesting that fast walk augmented by rapidly stroking arms makes an excellent addition to the complete Heavyhands program.

Fast Heavyhands Walk gives you more benefits than conventional fast walking because of the mobilization of the upper torso. And it's easy enough for children to learn.

Heavyhands Walk for Runners

11

I suspect that many vintage runners will look askance at that chapter heading. Since the advent of running with weights, some well-known runners have registered aversion in no uncertain terms. Mostly these negative remarks are related to what handweights do to their skill. "It knocks me off stride" is the cry I most commonly hear from them. Other competitive runners, however, have been more positive. Some have declared themselves frankly hooked after a few weeks of training, and a number of them swear their running times have improved since they began pumping while walking *or* jogging!

My first attempts at aerobic fitness came through running. I was almost 50 at the time. I didn't know it then but I was destined to become a mediocre runner. The spirit was willing enough; the body architecture simply wasn't designed to go very fast for very long. I have since learned that I am quite work-capable, probably in the top percentile for men my age. So I can work very hard at running, but not well according to the clock! For instance, there are runners who can equal any pace I can generate working about 70 percent as hard as I do! That means that running is a very good exercise for my legs and my heart, but would be a foolish choice as a competitive sport for me.

And there are many around like me. A quick scan of what's happening at almost any track tells the story. To be an elite runner you must have the body type that's right for it. The wrong body mechanics plus unshakable ambition to run well is a combination that often leads to both continued frustration and frequent injury.

As a heart and leg conditioner that can incinerate calories and firm up your self-image, running has proven itself millions of times. But I think Heavyhands training can make most of us *better* runners. And for those not utterly sold on running as their sole exercise, for those who seek plenty of variety, Heavyhands makes a logical complement.

Running as Sport and Running as Exercise

The more running is viewed as sport, the more it loses as ideal exercise, I think. Take elitist marathoners. If they log 100 miles each week, they'll probably do about 80 of those at 60 to 70 percent of their maximal work capability. If they run too fast for that 80 miles, their risk of injury shoots skyward. That means they spend the great bulk of their time nursing their bodies and mollifying their cardiorespiratory systems! These training patterns clearly exemplify the careful balance needed to tune the system while protecting it from injuries that scotch racing plans. The strategy is pointed at specific performance related to the sport, not fitness for life! Fitness for life would push diversity of movement and muscle, relatively high intensity, and less overall time investment. And I can't resist one final thrust: A decade of Heavyhands Walk has made me a better runner than I was after two solid years of just running!

Some orthopedists have asserted flatly that running while merely *carrying* handweights will injure elbows and shoulders. We simply haven't seen it. In our class of high pumpers, some of whom spend a good portion of their time jogging, there have been no arm injuries reported in well over four years. The smaller pumps associated with running, you'd assume, would be even less apt to injure arms than the high armstrokes of Heavyhands Walk. Neither high nor low pumps have been the cause of injury, in my experience.

While I realize that *any* movement can injure, I think some experts, when confronted by the press, are inclined to make unqualified statements that are long on hot opinion, short on cool experience! I've read quotes by orthopedic surgeons (presumably knowledgeable in sports medicine) declaring that pumping more than 3-pound handweights is simply out of the question. Thankfully, some physicians have learned the hard way that categorical, off-the-cuff remarks like that carry high risk of being pure nonsense. The longer I study the problem, the greater respect I gain for the human body. Given patience, common sense, practice, and respect for individual differences, it can perform all kinds of heroics—without injury.

Training the Runner's Arms— the Right Way

There has been a lot of talk about the usefulness of weight training for runners. I frankly don't understand, and no one has explained in logic that makes good sense to me, why *any runner* might need the upper body strength that conventional weight training offers.

It would behoove distance runners to be possessed of sinewy arms, stronger than most arms of similar size. Arms like these would bring: (1) the mechanical advantage that arms can bring to running; (2) greater overall aerobic capacity; (3) the ability to work continuously nearer max output. The distance runner needs arms that function as the legs' working partners, arms capable of hard work, not brute strength. Unfortunately, most runners' arms don't work very hard, on average.

So what's the best way to train the runner's arms? Not with heavy weight training; being able to bench press 250 pounds doesn't help much, I'm afraid. Instead, the best training would come from something that offers the rough *equivalent* of what the legs do while running: thousands of repetitions at something harder than untrained people can do for more than a few moments. Enter Heavyhands! However, you

Don't Run—Pump 'n' Walk!

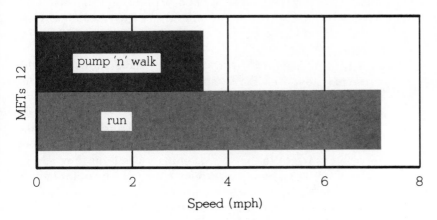

Pump 'n' Walk: 120 strides/minute,
3.5-ft. pump height, 3-lb. weights

may be wondering how you can improve your running by *walking* with handweights? Here are a few direct benefits.

1. Increased ability to work efficiently. Other things being equal, could it really be a disadvantage to you, as a runner, to be Panaerobically fit—having high degrees of work capability in *all* of your major muscle groups? Despite their apparent inactivity, arms perform *some* work during the running of a long race. That work, however minuscule, adds to the heart's total workload, inevitably elevating a runner's heart

---

Pump 'n' Run:
Not Just Pump + Run

I know I sound like I'm beating this theme into the ground but I can't help it. When a runner tells me he can't keep to his stride while carrying 3-pound hand-weights, I feel like asking: "Why on earth would you want to anyway?" There are dozens of things you could do to a runner that would destroy his stride: tie his arms behind his back, have him wear his tux, patch one of his eyes, clip a heavy earring to one ear,

stuff his mouth with a couple packs of bubblegum and have him chew vigorously, or give him running shorts hewn of sheet lead. You can't expect to dangle 3 pounds from each hand and stay true to your typical running stride! Something *has* to give when you add robust upper torso work to legitimate leg exercise.

Now, most runners I know are not great dancers. And that figures. People who like to do lots of interesting things with their legs aren't apt

to settle for simply picking them up and laying them down forever. So when runners grouse about something that seems to abolish their beloved stride patterns, you might guess that they only know one step, and running is it! The more confined an exerciser becomes to a single movement adventure, the louder the protestations of love for that activity are likely to be! Hungry newborns don't shriek for veal scallopine, either.

Fourteen-Minute Running Pace—Really?

We are indebted to Kenneth E. Powell, M.D., and associates for the numbers on how many runners are doing what. Consider those 45 percent of runners doing a 14-minute mile or slower; that would be about 5.4 million of a national total of 12 million runners. These folks are running at what is a reasonably brisk *walking* pace! Why bother? The airborne state surely adds to the risk of injury and the work rate could be upped considerably with arm action that almost anyone can accomplish untrained. Pumping little 1-pounders to Level 2 at 120 paces would get you there, and anything you can add comfortably to pump height, tempo, or weight load would all be training gravy.

rate. It is known that the less trained a given mass of working muscle, the *faster* the heart must beat to sustain that work. So having a well-trained upper torso could lower your running heart rate, or allow you to run *faster* at any heart rate you select!

2. Biomechanical benefit. Studies have shown that the runners whose arms move most run fastest. The sprinter, and to some extent the distance runner, actually *pulls* himself through space with vigorous arm motions. As a runner, you unwittingly experiment with these "assisting" movements. You may add "strokes" to your running until the strokes themselves begin to tax your stamina more than they add to your speed. Then you instinctively cut back. The point here is that the better work-adapted your arms, the more you can use them to enhance your running, short of tiring you.

3. Saved training time. There are a number of ways that you can save time by supplementing your running program with Heavyhands Walk. First off, once trained with Heavyhands, you will work at a higher average intensity than your counterpart who trains exclusively with running; that lessens the total training time needed to maintain a given level of fitness. Second, Heavyhands training allows you to add accessory training gambits—abdominal training, hillwork, weight training—all in one workout. Third, you can continue training and maintain your fitness level through an injury with Heavyhands Walk, saving you crucial sideline time. Fourth, Heavyhands training can increase the efficiency of your armwork without adding separate training time to do it. Finally, well-trained Heavyhanders enjoy slow heart rates on far less training time than most serious runners devoted to their exercise. To that extent, substituting Heavyhands for part of your running should cut total training time while preserving the advantage of a slow heart rate.

4. Superior cardiorespiratory training. With or without the addition of hillwork, pump 'n' walk can generate workloads that rival or surpass those attainable while running at similar heart rates. Subjects trained with Heavyhands—about two hours a week with equal time at DSP, pump 'n' walk to Level 3, and faster pump 'n' walk to Level 2—showed leg-alone gains when tested that were similar to those of a group only trained with running! Also, the Heavyhands group showed greater heart rate decreases at given workloads. That may happen in part because the heart's "stroke volume," or the amount of blood pumped per beat, increased more after Heavyhands training than following a running program.

5. Superior leg training. An imaginative assortment of Heavyhands Walk moves included in your training schedule will produce leg benefits not available to those who simply run. Quad, abductor and adductor groups, hip flexors and extensors, and hamstrings can be emphasized during brisk walk routines, while the upper torso is trained simultaneously, with minimal addition of muscle bulk. The same applies to abdominal-wall training.

6. Injury prevention. Since the longer you run the more apt you are to get injured, Heavyhands training should lessen injuries by lessening running time. Heavyhands can also actively prevent injuries by (1) distributing the workload more evenly among more muscles with shorter, higher intensity workouts; (2) augmenting leg strength in ways that conventional running can't; (3) introducing a variety of complex movements that provide some relief for overused muscles and tendons.

By stressing certain movement elements through intelligent choices of Heavyhands Walk Medleys and intervals, runners can protect their knees and backs. Because of varied training needs and anatomical and functional differences between individuals, it's difficult to be specific here; but those moves that strengthen the quads—various kicks and DSP in particular—could help prevent runner's knee. At the very least, Heavyhands Walk training, through its orthopedic and cardiac effects, can reduce the risk of overuse injury by lessening the tendency toward overtraining. The time-honored training specificity doctrine in sports can be pushed too far, I believe. While it makes sense to practice the things you do that help you win, many of the injuries sustained in sports are related to movements that hadn't been rehearsed! Varied, nonspecific training strategies may keep more athletes whole longer. And that's quite specific!

7. Help for the overweight runner. Many people love to run despite the fact that their physique is not ideal for the sport. The reason you've never seen a 220-pound winner of the Boston or New York City marathons is because that amount of body mass and repeated 5-minute miles aren't compatible. The extra weight can be fat *or* muscle. A weightlifter's beefy torso is only somewhat more suited to long fast runs than is a body lugging 50 extra pounds of fat. Nonetheless, some folks with those generous proportions will continue to run, albeit poorly and at high risk of injury. I'd prescribe a larger portion of Heavyhands Walk with high pumping for these runners. It will usually become a more effective calorie waster for them

Weight Load Limits for Pump 'n' Run

How can people wax categorical about things they don't know about? A couple of years ago someone published the statement that more than 3 pounds pumped while running is apt to be too hard or too dangerous. I called the author and asked him questions. He hadn't, in fact, tried it, but felt ''strongly'' about it, he said. Since he was respected in the fitness community, the quote spread like the plague to many magazines, no one wishing apparently to question the source.

We go through this negative prophesying in sports all the time. Nobody will ever better the 4-minute mile, the 2:10 marathon, the 7-foot high jump, the 70-foot shotput, the 18-foot pole vault, the 60-yard field goal, the 300-foot javelin...one could go on and on. But this is different. Those predictions are legitimate enough; they simply prove to be wrong! But blind remarks about pumping 3-pound handweights while jogging enjoy a fundamental stupidity because the author really has no data points to reference. Like the knowing axiom that more than 2 pounds can't be used with impunity in aerobics. If we as humans didn't differ more than that suggests, we'd never have anything to say to each other!

Running Speed and Pump 'n' Run

Tom Auble measured his oxygen uptake while pump 'n' running with 3's to Level 2. He ran at 5, 6, and 7 mph. Then he ran without weights to determine how much faster he had to go to do a corresponding amount of work. The results are presented below.

With 3-Pounders	Conventional Run
5 mph	7.3 mph
6 mph	8.3 mph
7 mph	9.3 mph

Tom's heart rates were about 6 beats faster while running without weights. That is of more than casual interest to any Heavyhander, because Tom devoted at least a decade to running. These data are also important in terms of injuries. For many exercisers, the slow, weighted format would be much less likely to produce injuries while producing considerable armwork capacity. Walking is even more exciting, simply because as the pumps get higher, the muscle mass inclusion makes the ratio of workload to miles per hour more impressive. To give you an inkling, a trained Heavyhander pumping 7's high can generate 50 mls O_2/kilo/minute—a huge workload—walking at less than 3 mph! Some physiologists have a tough time believing that. But you need only two things to verify it: the usual lab setting and someone with enough *unusual* training to make it happen!

How Much Practice Should Running Require?

There's been some new research that strongly suggests that swimmers who swim 25,000 yards a day don't need to do that to win. How does that apply to running? Tom Auble ran a 10-K a year ago after not running for a year. His time was about a minute slower than his finish a decade earlier, when he was training at the rate of 50 miles/week. So it does make you wonder. It would be nice to know what would have happened had he split his training time, allowing for some pump 'n' run (which he hadn't done) or even a few miles of weightless running. His training that year had been mostly Heavyhands calisthenics to music and pump 'n' walk, slow and high.

(higher possible workloads) and will reduce the chance of bad knees that might eventually make running impossible.

The Proof Is in the Running

Since the publication of the first book on Heavyhands, I have received dozens of letters from serious runners discussing their inclusion of Heavyhands movements in their training programs. I have met personally with many while traveling about the United States. Their anecdotes have been encouraging; in most instances, the improvement they experienced in their running was greater than I would have predicted. What makes it even more exciting is that most of these runners had been at it long enough to have reached fixed plateaus in their performance. We are planning some studies to help determine the "mechanisms" by which these improvements are brought about.

I and many other Heavyhanders have been able to sustain or improve our running times on nearly zero running mileage! While I wouldn't predict such a happy outcome for *every* serious recreational runner, I can predict unabashedly that Heavyhands training for those of us who run will make most of us better, more durable runners overall.

Naturally, I have to be more cautious in prescribing Heavyhands training for the serious running athlete. It's not

Competitive runners can get many benefits—most notably increased strength and endurance—from supplementing their training with Heavyhands Walk.

that I've a smidgen of doubt about the good effects proper Heavyhands Walk can have upon running ability. Rather, individuals differ enough that I can't be certain in a given case just which moves and how much Heavyhands would optimize the runner's chances of winning. I suspect the future will see coaches familiar with this method who will be able to individualize Heavyhands training for various runners.

It is vital that a runner seeking greater Panaerobic fitness and better performance through Heavyhands training understand the dynamics of the exercise sufficiently to avoid trouble. Arm pumping action during either walking or running increases the total intensity of the work *enormously*. Pump 'n' walk and pump 'n' run are *not* the same as ordinary walking and running movements. They feel different and are demanding in different ways. But just as the addition of a second dance step doesn't confuse the average dancer, we've rarely seen four-limbed exercise ruin an athlete's performance in leg-alone movements like running. The human motor cortex seldom finds a simple movement addition a major challenge!

Injury per Unit of Work— That's What Counts!

I must admit I'm proud of my decade of injury-free exercise. Does that mean I've never felt pain? Most certainly not. I've had dozens of little ones. The worst happened five years ago when, not paying attention, I got clipped in the left biceps tendon by the nose of a forcefully thrown, spiraling football. My left arm's never been the same, and hurts plenty sometimes when I've got one of my grandchildren tucked under that wing. Thankfully, my pumping ability's been preserved. Not only have I never missed a day's workout because of injury, but I've never worked out while in pain. I simply find a movement combo that doesn't hurt, no matter how ungainly.

I'm even prouder because my injury status was maintained at workload averages which, considering my age, must be in the 99th percentile. Runners of any age who work out at my average oxygen uptake rate per kilo have a high incidence of injury. The comparison, again, isn't exactly fair because they're accomplishing it all with a few leg muscles while I'm studiously dividing the work among lots of muscles. But I think future students of exercise will more closely monitor how much of a certain exercise does what to whom, where, and when! Their observations should make pump 'n' walk more attractive.

Many Heavyhanders have improved their 10-K personal bests following Heavyhands training that included little actual running. One Heavyhander did as well at the 10-K as he had 10 years earlier when he had logged 50-plus miles weekly. He logged zero running mileage during the two years preceding the race! Virtually all of his Heavyhanding was done either walking or in dancelike calisthenics. We have found alternating Heavyhands Walk and Jog to be an extremely beneficial training tactic. It can be done literally dozens of ways. Pitt's Tom Auble recorded his heart rates over a half-hour workout during which he alternately walked and jogged: He walked 4 minutes at 130 paces/minute pumping 5-pounders 42 inches high, and then jogged 2 minutes at 170 paces/minute pumping the same weights to a height of 24 inches. His heart rates during the entire 30 minutes remained remarkably constant. Similarly, when he repeated the same exercise in the laboratory, his oxygen uptake remained consistent throughout.

Implementing Heavyhands in Your Training

You can jog a lap and walk a lap alternately, or use any one of many combinations. While it would be naive to try to maintain a pace or even a stridelength identical with your ordinary jogging pattern, the combined workload, after training, turns out to be higher than those you would spontaneously select for running without weights. Using the alternating "interval" method, many runners can improve their ordinary running while logging less total training mileage.

I seldom run without weights anymore. Most of my ambulatory Heavyhands comes in the form of walking that ranges from sedate strides and strokes to frankly outrageous movements. My ability to run long or to sprint has only improved. It appears the body's "memory" for running can be nicely preserved with brief, intermittent "reminders" accompanied by pumping handweights. As many runners decide to lessen their mileage, the addition of carefully selected Heavyhands movements may reduce their training requirements even further. This is particularly true of those for whom running is merely another way of staying fit.

To this day, I have not seen a runner whose pace slowed once he devoted 50 percent or more of his training time to aggressive pump 'n' walk variations. I have spoken to dozens who indicated that substituting Heavyhands Walk and jog for part of their total running mileage made running feel easier and actually *quickened* their times.

The distinction between running as exercise and running as sport is a crucial one. The concerns voiced by some that running with handweights disturbs the strider's form or interferes with the pleasure of running or produces a "consciousness of the armwork" usually come from those who simply haven't practiced pumping the weights. My years at this have taught me that most bodily movements seemingly impossible today become second nature sooner than we expect. Runners overwed to their sport should try dancing with handweights! In 20/20 retrospect, I realize I should never have discussed "running with weights"; the *real* exercise is pump 'n' run, and that's about as similar to ordinary running as swimming is to kicking a board across a pool!

Once you understand that, you'll realize that the handweights aren't merely adjuncts to running. Running is not the central theme in pump 'n' run. Nor are the arm pumps. The exercise is a *total* experience in its own right. Given that, the pump 'n' runner's attention doesn't drift to his arms' spirited activity any more than a runner is preoccupied with his legs. In developing pump 'n' run, I was attempting to include the legwork of running in a *combined* exercise, not to preserve correct *running* form, whatever that means, during the exercise. It was only later that I learned from others and through my own experience that this exercise, properly practiced, left most runners better at running!

I'm not discouraged by the declining running numbers. If fitness is the issue, there are dozens of rhythmic movements that can condition our hearts and muscles at least as well. If we consider exercise a psychic stimulant, we'd have to agree that we can upgrade all of the conventional aerobic forms.

Weightlifting and Running

Which runners should lift heavy weights? Those who aren't set upon winning long races. A few heavy lifts might help a competitive sprinter because of the powerful armstrokes that literally help pull him through space. Distance runners don't want the upper body muscle mass that conventional weight training would add. In competitive distance running, even an ounce or two of added shoe weight is often seen to be critical. I'm more convinced that weightlifters could run to their own betterment than the reverse of that proposition! For those who run strictly for conditioning, a bit of weight training may add welcome poundage to the upper body. I would prescribe Heavyhands Walk first, to allow for some of the physiologic changes that make for armwork capability, and then add the heavy lifting purely to gain whatever "pure" strength is necessary.

Heavyhands Strength Walk

12

One evening I met a young man whose huge, bare arms and humps of trapezius muscle told me he was an experienced iron pumper. He knew about Heavyhands but never identified tiny handweights with the kind of hefty chore that interested him. At 21, he was able to bench press 420 pounds—several reps worth. When I asked if he thought he could walk pumping 15-pound weights, he expressed quiet confidence. When tested, the young weightlifter had a surprisingly high oxygen uptake capacity for one so bulky (short stature at 200 pounds). But 15-pound pumps at 100 strides/minute, not quite to Level 2 (just shy of 2 feet), had him completely worn out in less than two minutes.

That's not an unusual story. If you ask an assortment of fit people—including athletes—to pump heavier than usual handweights while walking for several minutes, they don't do as well as either their proven strength or their aerobic fitness might predict. Lifters simply can't handle several hundred reps (say, 100 pump-strides/minute for six minutes), and runners aren't built to grapple with the sheer strength involved, though their leg-alone tests show they've aerobic power to spare.

Heavyhands Walkers, especially those who spend some time with heavier than typical handweights—which we call Strength Walking—outdo others. I have seen some pump 'n' walk with 15 to 20 pounds on a level treadmill and come within 90 percent or more of their maximal leg-alone capacity! The significance of that is hard to appreciate if you haven't tried doing something "heavy and fast" for five or more consecutive minutes. Estimating from our experience, I doubt that one-hundredth of 1 percent of the population could pump and stride with 15 pounds to a 42-inch pump height at 100 strides/minute for five full minutes!

Let's back up for a moment and start at the beginning. What is this special quality of fitness I'm getting at here? I call it strength-endurance, though I have called it "strength-aerobics," and more recently "slowaerobics," because of the

The Best Way to Sculpture Your Body

If that Greek look is what you're after, I have the recipe: Learn to pump the heaviest handweights you can to your target heart rate. That's it. Why does it work? It's elementary. When you sculpt your body, you're aiming to make muscle and lose fat. You want to bring your muscle tissue as close to your thin skin as you can. You want a high index of aerobic power (better, Panaerobic power) because that squanders energy—and burns fat—faster. How about the muscle in your sculptured finished product? Well, you want muscle with lots of ability to work, because that burns the fat fastest and makes more muscle simultaneously. How much muscle will you want? Not too much, because too much will cut into your work capacity and therefore your ability to burn fat. What's wrong with a hulking sculptured effect? Again, low work capacity, as well as a horrible requirement to starve too much in order to expose rips and cuts. A lean and mean statue is really the happiest statue—and Heavyhands Walk provides the means to build that statue properly!

The Special Body of a Heavyhands Strength-Walker

Strength-Walkers may end up looking like bodybuilders but that's deceiving. They're less bulky, of course. They know that too much beef would probably lower their work capacity. Since they need the work capacity to burn fat—which they prefer to dieting—and since they didn't intend to become professional bodybuilders anyhow, that sinewy rather than massive look suits them just fine. What's most important about these lean-physique types is that if they do 30 minutes of the right stuff a few times a week, they won't even have to think about body maintenance. Then there are a lot of subtle differences that are not as easy to describe, though they're every bit as real: things like the effects of combined exercise that pull together a lot of muscle into graceful movements—something few bodybuilders may have time for.

Working with heavy weights

cardiovascular training that can be achieved at slow movement tempos. I believe strength-endurance acquired during combined exercise is a unique fitness factor, not obtainable in quite the same way with any other exercise or sport.

What makes this factor so exciting for me is that it simultaneously accomplishes two of the things people seem to want most from exercise. According to the pollsters, we exercise for health and beauty. Strength-endurance may be the royal road to both! Let me explain. The body sculptors among us know that great physiques are carved by losing fat and making muscle. It's as simple as that. By universal consent, the best way to lose fat isn't by diet or by suction lipectomy! It's by killing two birds with one stone: incinerating fat and training the cardiorespiratory system with good exercise.

The other sculpture medium is muscle. To make ourselves shapely as well as slim we have to manufacture some of it with a special kind of activity, one that employs strength—which in its purest form is the measure of how much weight (or resistance) we can handle at one time. Lifting a weight a few times, probably under 10 "reps," is thought to be the best way to produce bigger muscles. As the number of repetitions increases, the exerciser gains a bit more endurance (cardiovascular training).

Circuit Training: Why It Doesn't Quite Work

In recent years some have properly sought to wed aerobics with weight training. The technique is called circuit training, and it has gained popularity in this country during the past decade. Circuit training involves doing a few reps (about 12 usually) at one "station" of a weightlifting machine, quickly moving to another station, working another set of muscles, then to another, and so on. Observers found that these exercisers had generated respectable heart rates at the end of 20 minutes of circuit. So they presumed that this was indeed good aerobic exercise, conferring cardiovascular benefits that rivaled other forms of aerobics. To take it a step farther, a few researchers measured the endurance levels before and after on circuit trainees. Surprisingly for them, the findings were somewhat disappointing. So there was a bit of an enigma: Why did circuit training, performed at target heart rates, not produce significant increases in aerobic capacity?

A couple of years ago at least part of that question was answered. Two respected researchers conducted independent studies in which they measured oxygen consumption of circuit trainers. I needn't go into details here, but both studies showed pretty much the same thing. The circuiters were working at about 35 percent of their maximum oxygen consumption rate. That's far less than the 60 to 90 percent usually recommended. Their heart rates evidently were being raised not by the hard work performed, but by the elevated blood pressures that typically come from weight training.

On the other hand, Heavyhands Strength Walkers pumping weights of 5 to 15 pounds generate very high oxygen consumption rates. Why? Because walking while pumping heavy handweights differs sharply from circuit training tactics in several respects: (1) circuit training works just one or two muscle groups at a time, while Heavyhands mobilizes lots of muscle mass; (2) in circuit training you do 10 to 15 reps and then pause, but with Heavyhands there are no rests—you may perform hundreds of consecutive reps; (3) whereas you work

---

Heavy Heavyhands and Injuries

I have seen few injuries from this Heavyhands technique over the past five years. At this moment I recall two, but neither were sidelining injuries. I have heard of some, but most of them have been blurry comments from orthopedic surgeons. One I read recently referred to "a rash of injuries around the time Heavyhands became popular." I've always been surprised that there aren't *more* injuries, simply because in some ways new exercisers are like enthusiastic dieters: They like to do it all the first day. That's the best way to get hurt. And heavy weights, used at full throttle before good technique has been established, increase the odds for injury.

But it's hard for a doctor to tell you precisely what or what not to do. Medical expertise notwithstanding, everyone should exercise caution early. Boldness and versatility should grow along with better technique. In some respects heavy weights are safer because we wield them more slowly; on the other hand, it only takes one movement to tear something. A hard, jerky hi-pump first time out with a heavy weight could pull a trapezius, for sure.

Running Strong vs. Walking Strong

Running does not promote strength-endurance with handweights as well as walking. The grounded foot during walking makes the difference. It makes you able to do all sorts of things with heavier handweights and to use the resistance provided by the body's weight more than you can when you're airborne. The airborne condition of running makes lower pumps obligatory, which also cuts into the potential workload. The slow strength mode of Heavyhands Walk is another way of ensuring a high workload/low injury ratio.

Why the Lure of Muscle Definition?

It's because the grooves move! Muscles, in fact, do ripple. Get a limb going and the visible cords of developed muscle fibers shift from place to place as the movement proceeds: The lines of highlight and shadow actually travel. Catch a well-defined body when the sun is low in the sky and the effect is quite remarkable, because even at a casual stroll the entire body surface seems to wriggle under its skin. My guess is that observers attribute a special dynamic quality to these people whose bodies seem to ripple effortlessly. It reminds me of the spooky ease with which a concert pianist tosses off a spectacular cadenza. It's perpetual motion that smacks of magic.

Circuit Training	Heavyhands Strength Walk
One muscle group at a time: small muscle mass.	Multiple muscle groups: large muscle mass.
10–15 reps, then pause.	No pause, 80–110 reps/min for several minutes.
Moderately heavy weights (barbells or machine resistance).	5- to 15-lb handweights.
Modest range of motion.	Moderate to great range of motion of four limbs, trunk.
Slow, deep breathing pattern.	Rhythmic breathing of modest depth.

in a modest range of motion in circuit, Heavyhands allows you to increase range of motion dramatically, thus making the work harder.

What's even more exciting is that Heavyhands Strength Walk also makes people purely strong—able to lift substantial weight without prior heavy training. Interestingly, the opposite doesn't hold true: Being purely strong, as our young behemoth proved, doesn't predict good strength-endurance on the Strength Walk test. Sometimes it works the other way around. Strength and bulk acquired through conventional weight machines or free weights predicts a modest or poor performance at Strength Walk. Actually, two kinds of athletes—at the extremes—fail my test: the strongest lifters and the runners. Obviously, they fail for quite different reasons.

You can realize *some* strength-endurance with cross-country skiing or rowing, but there are some important differences. Muscular strength requirements in both are limited by the nature of the sport. And the movements are more stereotyped. For example, the proportion of armwork to legwork in both is rather fixed. And the strength element is limited as well, by the body weight of the skier and the terrain he's skiing, and by the length of the oars and viscosity of the water for the rower. Where it comes to this intriguing "compound" fitness factor, Heavyhands has no equal. Nothing you can do will as effectively combine cardiovascular training *and* muscular strength—and Heavyhands Walk does it with a practically endless assortment of movements.

A Heavyhands Pioneer

My friend John McKean is probably the most ardent and successful proponent of Heavyhands among the strength athletes of the world. John's list of feats in strength is hard to believe. He held state records in the squat in two weight divisions for many years—555 pounds in the 165-pound division, and 530 pounds in the 148-pound division. Now over 40, John continues to compete, performing lifts more than triple his body weight in the squat and dead lift (400 pounds each). He has competed in more than 100 powerlifting meets over the past 20 years and has won every major powerlifting event conducted in western Pennsylvania. He has established 12 state records and 20 local and district records.

A high school teacher by profession, John is also an accomplished free-lance writer. He has contributed many articles dealing with weightlifting and powerlifting to numerous publications. His current interest has to do with combining Heavyhands training with strength training for high school athletes. Beyond the use of standard Heavyhands movements, John has already devised modified movements for strength athletes. Soon after the publication of *Heavyhands*, John recognized the wisdom of including Panaerobics in the typically one-sided training habits of strength athletes. His courage, leadership, and ingenuity will doubtless inspire the strength athletes of the future to embrace activities that will not only bring superior performance, but better overall health.

Will Strength Walk make you as strong as you might get through conventional weightlifting? No. But unless you're talking about interior linemen or wrestlers, my guess is that most of us don't need to train for bulk and strength. Few of us encounter life situations demanding great "pure" strength. In contrast, strength-endurance is something most of us could put to practical application every day of our active lives. Furthermore, the piling up of muscle bulk can become excessive. Too much muscle can erode our capacity for work, because a heavy body causes excessive "drag" in our gravitational field. We're overworked just lugging our "equipment" about, you might say. That's why striding and pumping 15-pounders can be tougher on a 250-pound noseguard than on a sinewy lightweight. The latter has less "pure" strength, but strength-endurance to spare!

John McKean

Suggestions for Strength Walk Specialists

You can actually build an entire exercise program from Heavyhands Strength Walk if you want. I lean strongly toward workouts that mix plenty of light and lively moves, some with moderate-size weights, and perhaps 10 percent executed with the heaviest weights you can manage. So if you exercise a total of three hours a week, 20 minutes or so of Strength Walk

The Strength-Endurance Potential of Women Bodybuilders

I'm eager to work with a group of women bodybuilders willing to train with Heavy-hands Walk. Their bodies are theoretically ideal for com-bined work: low percentage of fat and strength that doesn't quit! It could be an interesting training study, because body-builders train their muscles "single file," one muscle group at a time. My guess is their combined efforts at the outset—such as pump 'n' walking up a sloped tread-mill—would be fantastic, be-cause many are aerobics in-structors and thus have great work capacity in addition to strength. And if you haven't noticed, women bodybuilders have extraordinary flexibility. Many are gymnasts or are dance-trained. All in all, women bodybuilders possess the makings of great athletes who can bring metabolic he-roics to exercise as well as sport.

distributed among your workouts should keep you strong. By your heaviest usable weights, I mean the heaviest ones that you can use in combined exercise for *at least* 4 minutes (preferably more) at something approaching your normal exercise heart rate.

I tend to discourage heavy Heavyhanding in those older than 50 who have been sedentary or have any cardiovascular problems including high blood pressure. If "heavy" weight work makes you dizzy or headachy, stop until your doctor gets a look at you. He can simply take your blood pressure immedi-ately following a "sample" of your heavy walking about the office or on a treadmill for a few minutes. That will tell the doctor how your cardiovascular system responds to this sort of exertion and enable him to help you decide whether it's safe for you.

Heavy additions to Heavyhands Walk can be made several ways:

1. Take a heavier weight through a movement with which you are already familiar, only at a slower tempo. Example: If you've been walking at 120 paces/minute with 2's pumped to Level 3 (3-foot pumps), try Level 3 with 3's. Start at about a 110 pace. If that seems too hard (suggested by a faster pulse, excessive muscle fatigue, or a combination of those), cut the tempo until you reach a comfortable pace. Then check your pulse after three minutes of steady work. You might also experiment with 4's at 100 strides/minute. Even 5's may well be within your capacity once you slow the pace appropriately. I can't be precise about my recommendations here, because individual differences, things like body weight and composi-tion (fat versus muscle of the arms themselves, for instance), make for varied responses among individuals. Using heavy

Muscle Mass, Strength, and Aerobic Workload

I've talked ad nauseum about the relationship be-tween strength and endur-ance. "Excess muscle" means more than the optimal amount for good aerobic perfor-mance. The body's mass literally becomes too big to do lots of reps. And bulking up may inhibit the production of

mitochondria and loads of nourishing capillaries. The shape of your muscles seems to be important, too. A muscle that's long and slender is apt to be less strong than a com-pact yet bulky one, and more trainable with respect to aer-obic (continuous) work. Like-wise, a short, chunky individ-

ual will probably be more able to bench-press a ton than his slender (linear type) counter-part. A 240-pounder may be a world-class rower, especially if he's about 6 feet 7; the same mass compacted into about 5 feet 10 makes a better full-back, and I'd not choose him first for my rowing team.

weights with lower pumps is good leg-strength exercise, too. I've watched petite women in our Heavyhands group do vigorous side leans toting 10-pounders. In that instance there is no actual armstroke, though much work is being done by many trunk and upper torso muscles and legs.

2. Try pumping heavier weights to a lower level. You may need to up the tempo to remain at target. As your training proceeds at a particular heavy weight, you will find yourself gradually able to increase either pump height, tempo, or both. As you feel those changes occurring, add another pound to the original pattern. That way you'll constantly be working strength-endurance increments into your program.

3. Work toward strength by pushing speed. Consciously "snap" the weight to increase the speed of your strokes, whether pumps or punches or lateral flings; utilize various hand orientations—knuckles up or out, for instance. Do this for only a minute or two at a time (interval work, actually), gradually smoothing it into longer sessions. You'll find this facilitates your use of heavier weights.

4. Do some outlandish range-of-motion work with weights you usually pump less extravagantly. Briefly push to Level 3 or 3.5 if you can reach it; the workload increases tremendously when you add three inches to the top of a pump. Adding this increment intermittently at normal tempos will bring speed and "recruit" more muscle fibers for your usual steady exercise.

5. Do the same stroke/stride combinations but with exaggerated trunk moves. This really amounts to increasing strength by doing something while balanced more precariously. Throwing a walking punch during a vigorous side lean is an example. The stroking arm is less supported and must work harder to accomplish its move. This sort of thing is very useful for athletes called upon to move powerfully without the benefit of solid support—like a scrambling right-armed quarterback throwing deep while moving to his left. I've a sneaky feeling that this strategy—depriving yourself progressively of the easy way of doing something—might even help protect against injury. The reasoning here is fairly obvious. Making things harder decreases the vulnerability of those body parts likely to get injured. For example, adding twisting trunk movements to walking is a good idea because this sort of movement so often causes injury—mostly, I think, because it's not rehearsed enough in ordinary training.

6. Try heavy Heavyhands intervals. Using a heavier-than-normal weight, alternate fast pumps to Level 2 with slower ones to Level 3 or higher. Pumping a heavy weight

Ginny Miller

> **Bodybuilding the Heavyhands Way**
> Ginny Miller is a well-known bodybuilder in the Atlanta area. She has won more awards than I can list here. She has taught Heavyhands for years and is a pioneer in the long-term project of making strength and endurance entirely compatible virtues. She is modest to a fault, but I am told by spies that no one can keep up with Ginny when she's "going after it," Pan-aerobically speaking.

Should Your Children Be Training with Weights?

A controversial matter, as you know. Experts for years have been concerned that heavy lifting might endanger the growth plates at the ends of a child's long bones. They're softening a bit nowadays on that subject, but still warning against really heavy lifts. I can't help feeling that a Panaerobic introduction to exercise would be best for kids. The child's musculature should have a liberal share of mitochondria and capillaries. Heart training is easy, and there's usually no hurry to achieve outsized strength. But it's the psychological penchant for movement that grabs my main interest. Given the motivation that makes for the development of skill, functional growth is all but guaranteed. Many children, however, become phobic of movement at a very early age, which I think is probably an outgrowth of garden-variety awkwardness. When a kid retreats, embarrassed, from movement in general, physical training suddenly becomes rather academic. If our educators could concentrate on studying the fun of movement in our children, there's no telling how much the total expense of teaching the three R's could be reduced. That's worth a pilot study, surely!

high at 100 strokes/minute, I end up achieving a heart rate similar to what I might work at while pumping to Level 2 at perhaps 140 strokes/minute. That's me; your combinations will probably be different. Try to select a weight/range of motion/tempo combination that you can handle continuously for at least 4 minutes. By the time you can comfortably do 10 minutes of each, you'll be ready for more weight.

Without nagging at you, I must reiterate: I've known some people who've used heavy weights as a defense against working! They can trudge along swinging these monsters in long, lazy, sweeping arcs that just don't amount to much work when we measure it in the laboratory. In order to couple strength gains with the aerobic quality that loses calories and makes all kinds of muscle work harder, your heart rate or your practiced guesses as to how hard you're working are the best gauges. Don't trust messages like local muscle effort and ache. Working at a higher clip, you may actually feel neither of those.

Your heaviest usable handweights will *not* produce your highest aerobic levels. That's another way of saying that you can't work at your highest steady work rates pumping your biggest steadily pumpable weights. But for those in search of strength-endurance, the trade-off appears to be justified. I have long felt that working with "heavies" ultimately translates itself into more effective work with *smaller* weights. Your small-weight performance may be bumped up substantially by devoting 10 percent of your workout time to strength-dominated Heavyhands.

Anyone who does anything in the way of weight training will instinctively understand this tactic. Using this logic, you could move to the ridiculous and write longhand with a 2-pound ballpoint pen, having discovered that a few minutes of "training" with it makes the rest of your writing a piece of cake. Bat weights do the same for ballplayers. Some say the sense of ease you feel with little weights after using the large ones is strictly psychological, but my 10 years of training dictate otherwise.

A Few Words on Definition

I must remind heavy weight users that in Heavyhands Strength Walk we shun like the plague the notion that muscle discomfort is the goal. We don't even count repetitions, and in any case we wouldn't place added value on that last agonized pump. While Heavyhands strength work will surely increase visible qualities like "rips" or "vascularity," rhythmic isotonic exercise is not the best way to pump up for your physique

Heavyhands Walk and Leg Strength-Endurance

Many of you still might not understand how Heavyhands Walk can give you strong legs. Here's how it works. Pumping handweights increases the work of walk so much that you can't possibly continue at your fastest walking pace while pumping. If you slow the pace to accommodate the upper torso "add," the leg training is probably going to be modest. The legs are underworked, actually, while the whole body is doing more. So how do you add work to the slow leg pace? Merely by knee dipping to various depths. In the lab we have learned how much an inch or two of added knee-dip depth increases legwork, especially at rapid stride-stroke paces. The quadriceps muscles do tremendous work in pulling you out of a dip. These extensions of the knee may be likened to the hillwork of running, and indeed a full workout involving these maneuvers will leave you feeling as though you'd been hill climbing throughout.

Does this form of leg strengthening produce the strongest possible legs? Of course not. Leg presses and heavy squats will do that for you. The question is, do you want pure strength in your legs? Pure strength usually means massive muscles, and suggests some reduction of work capacity—fewer muscle mitochondria, enzymes, and capillaries. What's purely wonderful about leg strength-endurance is that it enables the legs to do greater work without a significant increase in leg mass—a physiologic bargain for sure.

photographer! That's because the cardiovascular effects of this kind of exercise are quite different from those that accompany a few heavy repetitions, and blood pressure elevations are far smaller.

If you're looking for more definition, diverse movements and plenty of reps will help, partly because they'll incinerate more effectively the fat that covers the normal "striations" that are the essence of visible muscularity. With Heavyhands Walk you can move in more ways than any barbell or machine work will allow. So if you're a diehard heavy weight aficionado, throwing in a couple of hours of fast, hard, ranging movements will apply a new sort of polish to your muscular texture!

Heavyhands Walkdance

All of the Heavyhands Walk movements described in this book can become part of a Heavyhands Walkdance routine. The variations possible and the muscle groups worked are practically endless. The moves lend themselves to an assortment of tempos from the slowest "largos" to the most brisk "prestos" and anything in between. If you use nothing more than the typical modern music with a good beat that comes in at about 120 to 130/minute, you'll have no trouble choreographing Heavyhands Walk movements.

Music + Rhythmic Exercise = Dance. What that broad definition lacks as an art form is made up for by the fun and good health it can promote. Studies show that most of us can work at exercise longer and harder when we're motivated by musical accompaniment. Over the course of a lifetime of exercise, that could mean we can eat a little more without getting fat because of the addition of music! I find that a most tempting justification for Walkdance.

Heavyhands Walk is a good way to introduce yourself simultaneously to the worlds of fitness and dance, if you've been avoiding both until now. True enough, strutting while

Why I'm High on Heavyhands Walkdance

My excitement about this activity really ignited once it became utterly clear that no fitness factor would be sacrificed in a program consisting of nothing but Walkdance! There are those among us who will never become fit doing conventional exercise, which often demands a Spartan sort of personality. Walkdance adds the necessary flair that may spell the difference for millions of people. I've often thought that the fittest members of our population are a bit masochistic; they seem to need to bear various crosses to make their successes complete. Wouldn't it be nice to see a new breed of exercisers in whom fun is not only a vital component of their activity, but an important ingredient in its overall success? Instead of pride in remaining fit despite all sorts of impediments—the yes-I'm-fit-but-do-you-realize-the-personal-cost syndrome— it would go more like, "One of the things I like about being fit is the joy I derive from the whole process!"

Heavyhands Walk: Great Low-Impact Aerobics

Walking while pumping handweights is, of course, low-impact aerobics. During walking, the foot strikes the ground with 1.5 times the force of the body's weight. That's quite tolerable considering runners hit the ground with a force of about 3 times the force of gravity. In order to make low-impact aerobics "measure up" to the loads generated by jumping aerobics—without the shinsplints—several things can be done:

1. Abandon the 2-pound limit for aerobic handweights. That's a highly individual proposition. I know gals who handle 7's in long sessions handily!

2. Use the depth of knee dips during flat-footed movements as another useful variable in determining workloads. Three inches deeper can throw you quickly into the anaerobic "red" at a given tempo.

3. If even 2 pounds are actually too heavy, really work on the range of motion. Consider this: Doing snappy punches with 1-pounders while knee dipping at 120 beats/minute (slower than most aerobic music), most exercisers will be exceeding the national high average for aerobic work.

4. Use all of the above for variation and better training of skeletal muscle group combinations.

Low-Impact Aerobics, One More Time

The glut of articles on this subject all tussle with the issue of its fundamental legitimacy, its safety, and the question of how best to do it. Recently, at the Human Energy Lab, Tom Auble performed a simple trio of Walkdance movements. Working with 3-pounders at a frequency of 120 beats/minute with both feet planted, his workload was 18 METs. So without lifting a foot he was able to generate *twice* the work that the most demanding high-impact aerobics classes can manage. With that in mind, let me make a few predictions about low-impact aerobics, which, incidentally, I have both practiced and preached for a decade:

- While low-impact aerobics embraces many variations now (things like yoga and martial arts movements), when the dust settles, handweights will be the way to go.
- The warning that 2-pound handweights are an absolute limit is balderdash. During the next decade, 90 percent of the most petite low-impact aerobicisers will be pumping 5 pounds with neither strain nor injury.

- Weight-toting aerobics, once properly entrenched, will raise the national fitness level. Women will gain a new kind of fitness, and men will join in by the millions.
- The injury stats will plummet.
- The diet industry will suffer appropriately once low-impact programs like Heavyhands Walk and Walkdance demonstrate their effectiveness as fat burners.
- Kids will take to exercise more readily.

When Does Heavyhands Walk Become Walkdance?

When that extra little movement is added: a hint of strutting; an exaggerated move or offbeat angle of movement of any limb; a nod or wag of the head; a twist or lean of the trunk; a flick of the wrist or a pointing of the toes. More importantly, you're Walkdancing Heavyhandedly when it feels good and makes "instinctive sense" with the music. When it feels free and spontaneous and is accomplished with a mild sense of intoxication without the benefit of wine, you've arrived.

pumping and punching handweights is not likely to evoke the admiration of most dance experts. But it shouldn't make any difference. The dancelike quality of Heavyhands Walk serves as a vehicle for the substantial physiological and psychological gains that come from combined exercise. And the chances are good that these fitness improvements will occur with fewer injuries than would be incurred with conventional dance exercise at identical workloads.

Many in our group have gone from tentative Heavyhands Walkers to brazen Walkdancers in a few short weeks. I have predicted that four-limbed walk and dance will become the favorite forms of exercise before the end of the 1980s. So perhaps there is a sort of poetic wisdom in attempting to wed the two in Walkdance. Most dance looks like outrageous extensions of normal walk. By the time a pump 'n' walker is strutting to a thumping beat, a wonderful metamorphosis, good for a lifetime of sweaty fun, will have taken place.

I think four-limbed dance will eventually lure more men to exercise with music. Since the publication of *Heavyhands*, there has already been considerable movement in that direction. There are hundreds of coed Heavyhands classes in the United States already, and we haven't scratched the surface.

From what I read, the average intensity of the aerobic-dance classes around the United States is about 6 METs. You'll recall that means six times the work of doing *nothing*! One MET is the energy requirement of rest. Six METs would be about the same energy output as walking 15-minute miles (4 mph). Almost all of our young Heavyhanders work at least at 10 to 12 METs, and usually more. To my knowledge, no one has felt deprived of the pleasure of conventional aerobic dance as a result of the upper torso "add." A few young people I know have gained the courage to try social dancing after they cut their eyeteeth on Heavyhands Walkdance!

Walkdance is suitable for working a number of fitness factors—using slow tempos for strength work, faster ones to bring speed and exaggerated ranges of motion into play. In the lab, we have measured oxygen uptakes with movements like shadowboxing, done with a dancelike quality, to musical accompaniment. And four-limbed dance is at least as intense an exercise as any other form of Heavyhands. We discovered that during "free-form" movements—in which things are constantly changing to the whim of the exerciser, as in Walk-dance—the workloads remained, surprisingly, about as constant as they do with continuous walking or jogging on the

The Unique Contribution of Heavyhands to Dance Exercise

You'll surely note that many dance forms are already chock full of arm movement. Indeed they are, but not the ambitious armwork I'm talking about. In Heavyhands Walk-dance I always follow a 1:1 ratio of arm to leg movement so that, just as in Heavyhands Walk, no leg move occurs without an arm doing something. In ballet or modern dance forms, the arms add balance and grace and beauty, things that enhance the effectiveness of dance as an art form. In Heavyhands Walk-dance, I shoot for a bit of that, but the overriding motives are enjoyable hard work, inclusion of as much muscle as possible, and keeping injuries to the barest minimum—the essence of Panaerobics. As the movement toward controlled, low-, or no-impact aerobics gathers momentum, you will see more and more aggressive use of the upper body and trunk and more generous knee dipping to make use of the energy formerly utilized to get the dancer airborne. As those techniques develop, the movement patterns of dance exercise will surely change. But handweights will become essential equipment, because it's so easy to include them and so hard to get the job done without them!

Heavyhands Back 'n' Forth Walkdance: A Heavyhander's Staple

A while back, while working on some Heavyhands movements for a video, I realized that a back-and-forth Heavyhands Walk routine might be just the ticket for generating respectable exercise in the small space in front of a TV. My initial trials elicited some surprises. Working at 110 to 120 paces/minute, I found myself at higher heart rates than I had predicted. The routine involved pump 'n' walk, four steps forward, then four back. Closer inspection of my responses to long segments of this, compared to those generated by forward walking alone, indicated I was working 15 to 20 percent harder at the back-and-forth routine at the same tempos! We tried it at the lab, measuring oxygen consumptions to verify our findings. It was true. Everything else, like pump height, tempo, and range of motion, being equal, going back and forth was harder work! Moreover, depending on the subject, some went as much as 25 percent higher than when doing the same thing on a one-way treadmill. What's astounding about all this is that there is literally no ceiling on the work levels that can be generated. We've seen some trained Heavyhanders work harder at this (with little 3-pounders), without getting airborne, than if they were to run 5-minute miles. And you can throw in embellishments just like you can dress up a plain pizza!

A basic 12-count (perform each "pair" twice)

**A Low-Impact Workout:
The Shadowbox Trio
12-Count**

Here is a movement combo that could become your entire exercise program. It's really 12 moves; you merely repeat each "pair" (see photos). Go easy at first! Use tiny weights. You will soon see how many ways you can "move up" using this exercise. One-pounders used with generous ranges of motion and plenty of knee, hip, and side-leaning action at 100 beats/minute will get many exercisers to 12 METs! What's best of all is that even if you can't run at 12 METs to save your life, you will, within three months or so, be able to cruise at that level with this combination.

treadmill! It appears that the trained Heavyhander will "self-select" a workload for Walkdance that is remarkably constant from moment to moment.

The secret in Walkdance is including—and as a result, training—as much muscle as possible. Walkdance can make aerobic drivers of many muscle groups not often used repeatedly in sport and conventional aerobic dance. I'm thinking of the abdominals, hamstrings, hip flexors, lats, traps, pecs, and the small groups of muscles that rotate the shoulder blades and mobilize the hip joints. I can't think of a single sport requiring a variety of fitness factors and multiple skills for which Heavyhands Walkdance wouldn't provide excellent training.

Heavyhands Walkdance can be performed many ways. A single stride-stroke combination matched to the lively music of a radio headset can serve as an entire workout. Or a number of combinations can be strung together as Medleys. For intervals, you can choose hard versus easy alternates for a few minutes each. Most walk moves can be done in place; and almost all of the in-place variations can be done on the move as

Bringing the Heavyhands Message to School

Bonnie Voss must be considered a Heavyhanding pioneer. For nearly five years she has taught Heavyhands technique to the students of Highland Park High School in Highland Park, Illinois. Starting with a single section, she now teaches five elective classes. During the 1984-1985 school year, Bonnie was chosen as Illinois's Physical Education Teacher of the Year. In 1985-1986, she earned the honor of Midwest P.E. teacher of the year, and that same year was one of six finalists chosen for the National P.E. Teacher of the Year, an award presented by the National Association for Sports and Physical Education. Bonnie's spirit and know-how have made her a perfect role model for her students. My conversations with Bonnie over the years have always left me a little smarter.

Bonnie Voss

well. Once you discover you've been spending a lot of your exercise time dancing without an iota of detraining, you're apt to become addicted to Heavyhands Walkdance.

A Sample Walkdance Routine for Use Anywhere, Anytime

A short time ago, I found myself trying to put together some Heavyhands basics for a video. One problem was space. Could you perform a lively step in the small confines that typically lie between you and your television set? Trying to stay as elemental as possible, I fashioned a four-step-forward, four-step-backward eight-count routine, just to see how well I could perform it in a 4- to 6-foot stretch of floor if need be. It worked just fine. Pump-striding "opposite side," I'd go four steps, then start back with the foot that landed last. Thus my right arm was pumping while my right leg was back-tracking. It took a few minutes to get used to, but then felt "right" and even graceful.

This movement can form a useful basic to which lots of action can be added. Side leans while pumping or punching add appreciably to the energy cost of Walkdance. The strides and strokes can be substituted endlessly, so that you can mix and match moves to suit various tempos and weights. The total muscle mass involved in Walkdance is extraordinary. The task posed by the back-tracking activates the hamstrings and but-tocks; and a touch of side soreness the day after your first try will indicate the mobilization of trunk muscles. The overall biomechanical chore created by changing directions 25 to 40 times each minute makes it a challenging exercise even at modest tempos.

Once you master the slightly tricky direction reversing tactic, your eight-counts can include a lot of exercise and skill. The next logical addition is a lateral move. That can go side-close-side or step-cross-close, the crosses accomplished with one foot passing either in front of or behind the other. All this, of course, is accompanied by pumps or punches or lateral flings—strokes of one sort or another—and you can just wing it as you go. Now you have the makings of a complete Heavyhands Walkdance routine you can do within viewing distance of your TV screen!

I also suggest you add these moves, especially the for-ward-backward version, to those described in Chapter 9, for indoor workouts. Walkdance versions are also excellent as three- to five-minute warmups for any aerobic session.

"Slowaerobics"

Some publications list the current popular music best suited for exercise. Those spe-cifically labeled for aerobics are typically high tempo, mostly 150 and faster. Why? Simply because the typical movements in aerobic sessions need to be done that fast to scare up a target heart rate among the average class members. The advent of "low-impact aerobics" will change things a bit. Without as much of the jumping that makes for high-impact exercise, some aerobicisers may find it diffi-cult to generate their target pulses without using hand-weights. With handweights it will be easy. In the lab, we've recently experimented with the other end of the tempo spectrum, going extra slow (tempos of 80 or less!) using relatively heavy handweights. We discovered to our delight that both heart rates and oxy-gen uptakes were just what the doctor ordered—right on target and between 55 and 85 percent of maximal oxygen uptake, respectively!

Heavyhands Walk Techniques for Athletes

For a long time I have puzzled over the dilemma presented by the elite athlete who, when tested, proves to be in no better condition than his less athletic but more health-minded neighbor down the block. The sad fact is that many sports can be managed superbly without high levels of cardiac or muscle conditioning. Some athletes slide into a fitness level that is simply *enough* to ensure performance at their sport. Many seem to psychologically shelve the ideals of fitness *because* they are athletes. They may find training dreary when compared with the adventure of play and competition. And while that's easily understood, it may create problems for younger people, who may feel the need to identify either with the athlete or the fitness seeker.

One of the blatant problems with any sport is that, by itself, it often doesn't serve as an ideal training device. So when a tennis player tells you he stays in shape by merely playing tennis, it should be clear that in doing that he's settled for a less than optimal fitness level. Even distance racing, which promotes high levels of cardiovascular conditioning, may omit other fitness essentials like strength and flexibility. Fitness is a health-related virtue for everyone. While athletes need not be the fittest members of the community, it would seem that for them fitness could be doubly important.

Heavyhands Walk and Training Specificity

Our experience in the lab with athletes whose heart rates had plateaued after prolonged regular running indicates that Panaerobic workouts result in the most efficient heart function: slower heart rates per workload and generally lower blood pressures at given work levels, as well as at rest. A very slow resting heart rate derived from training usually predicts a fast heart rate "return" following peak levels of activity. Interestingly, this quick recovery from bursts of activity cannot be had in the absence of substantial aerobic fitness. That's a good example of how the doctrine of training specificity can be

Is Being a Super Athlete a Good Excuse for Being Unfit?

Of course, I'm being as cynical as I sound. For me it just never made much sense for an athlete not to be at least as fit as the guy down the block who gets an exercise prescription from his doctor after his exam finds him healthy but out of shape. Two kinds of reasoning prompt my strong feelings. One is that fitness is part of health and wellness, and athletes deserve both as much as the rest of us. The other kind of reasoning relates to some specifically athletic advantages to fitness, particularly the kind relating to aerobic power, or work capability. Let's say you decide to vacation in Rome or London or Philadelphia. Your time and your pocketbook impose limits. You've got to do as much as you can within a short time-frame. Your aerobic capacity is crucial. It will determine how hard you can ''work'' at it, how fatigued you'll be at the day's end, whether a glass of wine will have you snoozing before dessert arrives, how eagerly you'll attack the next day of laborious sightseeing, and probably how soon you'll plan a similar caper elsewhere.

With athletes, the same logic fits. Given two soccer players with identical talents and athletic physical specs, I'll take the one with the higher fitness quotient every time.

He'll always have just a little extra to add about the time his counterpart is wilting. His thinking should be clearer during competitive play when he's working as hard, or just as clear when he's working harder, because he does everything at a lower percentage of his maximal capability. In other words, the strain or effort for given tasks is less. That gives him the edge that coaches love to see.

Of course, there are other contributions to that complicated ensemble that make a great athlete. What I'm saying here is that the best Pan-aerobic fitness the athlete can spawn *has* to be an advantage, whether he's a steeplechaser or a bowler. One reason this simple wisdom seldom surfaces is that, in general, athletes don't seek fitness beyond what's essential for doing their sport.

misleading: Sports that do not require great endurance for prolonged activity may make specific use of that capability indirectly. The rigid adherence to the doctrine of "training specificity" could be a near-sighted disadvantage to some potentially great athletes.

Beyond its cardiovascular benefits, Heavyhands Walk offers an endless variety of combined movements, some of which can duplicate those of the sport itself. It is a fast calorie loser for athletes who need to "make the weight." Heavyhands Walk lends itself to the development of limb speed and strength-endurance training because of the supporting foot, and it probably reduces the risk of training-related injuries at high workloads because of the variable distribution of the workload among many muscle groups. And in this age of expensive training aids, Heavyhands Walk is economical: Its equipment is inexpensive and compact.

Heavyhands and the Sport of Rowing

As you may have guessed already, it's my belief that Heavyhands is the best supplemental training for athletes of every persuasion. My own trials and tribulations with rowing bear this out.

A couple of years ago, my wife Millie surprised me on my birthday with a boat. I couldn't help wondering nervously why she'd bought it. Then I remembered a particular morning when the lake was glassy and rippleless, every reed and housetop mirrored impeccably along its edges. The air was cold. The warmish water was covered with irregular flowing patches of mist. The sun had just shot its first gold streamers across the water.

Then I saw it. Coming past us from left to right, silently, was a scull, two rowers skimming in and out of the mist patches. I think I merely said, "Wow." Millie heard it, and I guess that was enough. She must have known the intense envy and admiration I felt at the moment; besides, it's hard to choose birthday gifts for aging men who continue to perceive themselves as active if not youthful. Anyhow, here was my one-man shell, and there was no turning back!

My experiences during visits to Florida with my rowing shell provided me with useful insights about the relationship between fitness and skill. My initial clumsiness with the stroke limited the work I could bring to it. To work well at rowing you have to be able to put many successive strokes together relatively quickly. The interruptions that come from a faulty stroke often scotch the process and don't allow the rower to "steady out" at a high heart rate. But it was fun to watch my steady rowing heart rate rise as practice brought me an improved technique. Soon my confidence and enjoyment were escalating rapidly as well.

Once I began to think of myself as a serious rower, an interesting thing happened to my Heavyhands exercise. I began to include moves I knew would make me a stronger rower. Lateral flings took on a new meaning, for example. During the rowing stroke, the rower exerts a slight outward pressure to keep the oars fixed in their locks. The lateral delts facilitate it. My "new'" lateral flings facilitated the facilitation! What had been vaguely "good" for my delts now became a conscious, purposeful ploy. My abdominal folds and other Bellyaerobic and Backaerobic moves also took on new meaning, inspired by my rowing addiction. I knew how to prepare for Florida rowing by including it in my thoughts during Pittsburgh Heavyhands workouts.

My rowing example shows that what might seem to be nonspecific training can actually be quite specific to a particular sport. I believe you can get similar positive results from Heavyhands workouts to benefit your own sporting interests. Merely choreographing Heavyhands Walk routines that make best use of those muscle groups mobilized in your sport will put you ahead of your game.

And if you go beyond muscle specificity to movement specifics, you're really in business! It sounds confusing, but the point is that *muscle* specificity and *movement* specificity aren't necessarily identical. The latissimus dorsi are great swimming muscles. They're also climbing muscles. Get most elite swim-

Reasons to Train Athletes Panaerobically with Heavyhands Walk

1. Training lots of muscles is a physiologic benediction that has special effects upon work capacity and the circulation. Athletes, as well as nonathletic types, can use those advantages.

2. Upper torso training can be a biomechanical advantage to lower body function, because in almost any sport the two work together.

3. Panaerobic fitness can enable an injured athlete to remain conditioned. He has enough skeletal muscle "backup" to continue to heart-train while resting the injured area.

4. Athletes get at least as bored with exercise as the rest of us do. Heavyhands Walk is diverse enough to be interesting for many.

5. Some sports, especially the team variety, are not good training. They are often inconvenient and, expectably, involve high injury rates.

mers to spend 10 minutes climbing a rope and their lats may be
so sore they can't do anything for a week!

A Sampling of Heavyhands Moves
for Specific Sports

What follows is a variety of moves that help implement
athletic prowess while training heart and muscle. Sounds like
a large order, but I believe Heavyhands Walk is better able to
deliver it than is any single conventional aerobic strategy.
These exercises are offered with the foregone conclusion that
total fitness *cannot* be a liability for any athlete; optimal work
capacity plus an assortment of other fitness factors is a must for
health *and* athletic performance, and should be a lifelong goal
that transcends the need to win.

I have chosen a series of popular representative sports.
With each my aim is twofold: to describe a series of movements
which *in themselves* can produce high-level fitness, and to
enhance athletic performance. Heavyhands movements are
such that *both* aims can be accomplished simultaneously in
most cases.

With each sport I'll briefly discuss the sport's major
muscular requirements as I see them, and then list a series of
movements that accomplish those ends. Most of the basic
exercises I've chosen will probably feel quite unusual for
non-Heavyhanders.

Baseball

- High pump 'n' walk, three minutes, alternating with
  pump 'n' jog sprint, 30 seconds to one minute
- Double ski poling
- Bellyaerobics
- Punch 'n' walk and variations
- Swing 'n' sway
- Shadowboxing
- Punches and kickbacks
- Forehand-backhand alternates

Because of its low aerobic requirement, most baseball
players do not show high aerobic capability when tested
unless they're into some form of accessory aerobic training.
Therefore, almost *any* Heavyhands Walk move will enhance
that dimension of the player's fitness. Many shadowboxing
moves roughly duplicate the fielder's movements in bending
and scooping grounders and getting the jump on fly balls in
every direction. Pump 'n' run interval work helps with the

extra base hits. Ballplayers need "fast hands" in a variety of circumstances, so I include punching strokes with plenty of snap.

Heavyhanders with a good grasp of the system are quickly able to customize moves that are "position-specific." Catchers and pitchers have vastly different requirements, but the exercise of a second baseman and a shortstop would be similar. A first baseman needs exceptional flexibility in the hamstrings, groin, and back, along with general fitness. I included the kickbacks because ballplayers tend to experience a fair number of hamstring pulls, and because combined exercise delivers a respectable aerobic workload.

Basketball

- Fast, high pump 'n' walk
- Interval work: pump 'n' jog (Level 2), three minutes, alternating with pump 'n' walk (Level 3-plus), three minutes
- Swing 'n' sway
- Double ski poling
- Swoops

This game calls for brief running sprints, jumping capacity, and arm strength and speed, as well as good general aerobic capacity (the higher the better). Good trunk strength and mobility are assets, and help avoid twisting-type injuries. I've added pump 'n' run simply because running makes up a large part of the total playing time of basketball. Topflight basketball players typically have the aerobic power of good sprinters. A couple of hours of Heavyhands training weekly will surely raise that level and give players a decided advantage in the last quarter of play.

Bicycling

- Pump 'n' walk variations
- Swing 'n' sway
- Double ski poling
- Shadowboxing

Cycling is somewhat demanding on the arms during long races because of the isometric strain, but you clearly don't need to have the arm-aerobic capacity of a boxer or a swimmer. I'm prescribing a bit of vigorous pump 'n' walk for two main reasons: You may need upper torso effectiveness for other activities; and since cycling isn't a weight-bearing sport, walk will help make you fitter for those activities that demand good

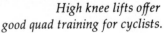

High knee lifts offer
good quad training for cyclists.

leg function. Double ski poling and swing 'n' sway are added simply because cycling doesn't do anything for the back muscles; and I've included shadowboxing because of my perverse need to see the cyclist do something diametrically opposed in every way to his normal preoccupation.

Boxing

- Shadowboxing
- Punch 'n' walk variations with side leans
- Bellyaerobics variations
- Swing 'n' sway

I find boxing immensely interesting, but, frankly, I think its traditional training methods are outmoded. Judging from my own experiences, elite boxers—even the small ones—don't have enormous aerobic capacities. The ones I have known, surprisingly, haven't had heroic upper torso ability. Some are tremendously strong but can't work continuously with their arms at high intensities. I've never been exactly sure of the purpose of their "roadwork," which is anything but training specific. The leg moves of boxing, be they the shuffling or bobbing variety, are all they need for leg training. Hitting the timing bag must be mostly for the benefit of spectators who happen by the gym. Skipping rope is also very "nonspecific" training; one could think of dozens of things that might work as well or better. As I see it, boxing has become more walled off from the fundamentals of modern physiology than are many other sports.

My theory is that the rhythmic moves with the light bag and rope were inspirations of the old trainers. They knew instinctively that the boxer's sharp "reflexes," or reaction times, more accurately, were the functions likely to be lost dismayingly early in a fighter's career, though few spoke of brain damage back then. I'll keep my recommendations simple here, though I have to add that I don't believe in the intermittent kind of conditioning we often see among the pro ranks. Staying in shape year round has to be as easy and certainly as important for a pugilist as it is for his accountant or mailman.

Decathlon

- High pump 'n' walk
- Shadowboxing
- Pump 'n' walk, pump 'n' run intervals
- Double ski poling
- Swing 'n' sway

Since decathletes are the acknowledged aristocrats of sport, there would seem to be little need to add to their already sublethal regimen. I have always wondered, though, why the founding fathers of Olympic sport decided to omit armwork from decathlon events. A single powerful explosion is required in the shot put, discus, javelin, high jump, and pole vault, but not one event requires repetitive action (read: work) of the decathlete's uppers. So I'm offering Heavyhands Walk out of sheer pity for this elite group whose careers are short and who continue to wear their arms for a lifetime!

Fact is, decathletes are not really consummate athletes because they don't do anything that requires more prolonged endurance than a 1,500-meter run. My fantasy is that one day they will do an "eleventhlon," which will include some event that requires four limbs and trunk for a full half-hour (length of a very good 10-K race). And just to keep the athletes interested, the scoring of that event will be multiplied by three! I do think, however, that any decathlete could do better at a given event just as it is, once consummately trained on Heavyhands Walk. It would also help in the 1,500-meter run, in which few decathletes are heroic. Swing 'n' sway and DSP are added because of the cooperative movements between arms and trunk involved in the throws.

Football

- Pump 'n' walk variations
- Double ski poling
- Pump 'n' walk, pump 'n' jog intervals
- Swing 'n' sway
- Strength Walk

I included football mostly because I didn't want to omit it. You could classify it with soccer, though purists will surely object to such an insensitive generalization. Football, generally speaking, is played by big, strong, fast people. Strength and sprint speed fit nicely together in the same physical package. That's why sprinters are well muscled, and distance runners had better not be! But I'm dismayed by the fact that pro football players don't on average enjoy good longevity. While I think I understand the primal joy of competing and winning, it would be nice to see athletes living longer to reminisce over those days of glory!

Maybe in the future, when people become more aware of the conflict between the chemistry of strength and that of endurance, smaller, fitter people will play an even faster game of football. Meanwhile, big football players would be better off with Heavyhands Walk than with their exhausting, sometimes abortive attempts at running. So I'll simply serve up some Heavyhands staples to ballplayers who aspire to more comprehensive fitness. By the way, I'd drop at least 60 percent of their heavy weightlifting time for Strength Walk a la Heavyhands, and wager that they'd gain more in endurance than they'd sacrifice in "pure" strength.

Golf

- Pump 'n' walk variations
- Swing 'n' sway
- Punch 'n' walk with side leans
- Double ski poling

Almost anything in the Heavyhands repertoire works well as training for this sport. Golfers must do supplemental training to remain in even reasonable aerobic condition. In sports as low in continuous energy cost as golf, much of the value of Heavyhands Walk exercises comes from its aerobic effects and its prevention of the injuries that occasionally occur

Swing 'n' sway simulates the "swing" action of golf.

when deconditioned muscles perform acts as violent as a hard golf swing.

I would exclude running as preferred training for golfers, simply because possible injuries could make playing difficult if not impossible, and golfers don't have to run unless they have dysentery or need to avoid lightning! Equal or better aerobic gains can be had using Heavyhands Walk as a training staple, with far less risk of orthopedic injury. Golf is a good example of a sport in which you derive precious little aerobic benefit from a lifetime of doing lots of it. If golfers did a half-hour a day of swing 'n' sway properly, they'd all enjoy a slower resting pulse, would hit the ball farther, and many could drop six inches from their waistlines. The double ski poling is added because golfers can use extra back strength and suppleness.

Gymnastics
- Pump 'n' walk, with extra use of heavy weights because of the strength required for the sport
- Double ski poling, in place and on the move
- Swing 'n' sway

More Variety, Please

Perhaps you've wondered why my suggestions for such varied sports vary so little! Many of the sports listed don't, in themselves, make their players awfully fit. What I tried to do is give players a liberal dose of Panaerobics to cover their sport and their wellness needs simultaneously without boring them to distraction. So I used a lot of exercises I'd prescribe for anyone seeking our kind of fitness. And when the sport lent itself to it, I got more specific. I've a feeling that many athletes, after some basic Heavyhands indoctrination, will choreograph movements even more specifically based on what they perceive as special needs and deficiencies in themselves.

Oddly enough, I tend to compare the fitness potential of gymnasts with that of female bodybuilders and lightweight boxers and wrestlers. Some, if not all, of these athletes have a problem in common. For either aesthetic or biomechanical reasons—or simply to comply with the rules—they need to control their body weight. A Heavyhands Walk staple would give them the best handle on that problem, allowing them to avoid the always uncomfortable, sometimes dangerous starvation-dehydration ritual. I like pump 'n' walk because gymnasts can do a variety of movements that rely upon the supported foot. Double ski poling and swing 'n' sway could supply additional strength-endurance. For obvious reasons, I'd see running as a waste of precious training time that carries a higher risk of injury than walking.

Martial Arts

- Shadowboxing
- Punch 'n' walk with karate kicks
- Bellyaerobics
- Pump 'n' walk variations with side kicks

Martial arts practitioners around the United States have already begun to add Heavyhands to their training. It simply makes sense. Karate and other martial arts routines could become even greater aerobic advantages with the addition of handweights. Both strength-endurance and hand and foot speed can be increased by working at the kicks and punches while using an assortment of handweights. The specific exercises I suggest will bring additional muscle power to the explosive movements associated with the martial arts.

Skiing

- Double ski poling
- Fast walk with light weights, Level 3.5 pumps
- Bellyaerobic variations
- Pump 'n' walk with cross-punches and cross-strides
- Swing 'n' sway

Both Nordic (cross-country) or Alpine (downhill) skiing call for great quad strength, good armwork capability, and a powerful and flexible trunk. Heavyhands provides an endless variety of movements for the off-season to make for both muscular fitness and maximal heart training. Heavyhanders from around the United States have reported no soreness after the first day of skiing for the first time in their recollection.

Double ski poling is an excellent trainer for cross-country skiing.

General endurance training and good strength and dynamic flexibility will help skiers.

I included the cross-punches and cross-strides to work in twisting movements of the trunk, which are so much a part of both slalom and cross-country skiing. Some of the country's top ski teams have already adopted Heavyhands as a standard training tactic. Fast walk with high pumps will be an advantage to Nordic and Alpine skiers alike, but the armwork makes it a must for cross-country. Likewise, great abdominal strength-endurance is useful for both. Fast walking (a pace of 150 strides or better) combined with vigorous high pumps will prepare the legs for the fast, gliding strides of Nordic skiing and produce high degrees of cardiovascular training.

Soccer

- Pump 'n' walk, pump 'n' run intervals
- Double ski poling
- Punches with karate kicks
- Shadowboxing

The Sports/Fitness Split: A Fascinating Dichotomy

A recent magazine article included a graphic detailing the ways our population stays fit. They are listed below as they appeared.

Fitness and sports seem to be tossed into a common receptacle. But if you pared this list down to those who really get fit doing whatever, I'd have to bet there are no more than 2 to 3 million who'd qualify. First off, those who do any of the "game" sports exclusively for their exercise would have to be eliminated. And I excluded from that number basketball's 42 million because of the reasonable aerobic capacity it may confer. Gymnastics and weight training are questionable commodities. The runners and walkers' numbers contain a huge scattering where it comes to fitness, as do those representing exercise to music. Next, I would divide sports activities between those that can and those that can't confer minimal fitness. Sports like golf, baseball, softball, and probably football are best cataloged as recreational activities that qualify as sufficient exercise only for those who are at present, and are content to remain, unfit! The sports that *can* constitute good exercise in their basic form (running, racewalking, swimming) need to be wrestled down to the individual case, to see just what each delivers as typically performed. I don't know why they didn't include cross-country skiing and real rowing. Guess what I'm saying is that articles of this sort project an optimistic note with virtually zero useful information!

Activity	Number of Participants (millions)
Exercising with aerobic equipment	44
Basketball	42
Fitness walking	40
Exercising to music	39
Fitness swimming	39
Volleyball	36
Weight training	36
Running, jogging	33
Fitness cycling	32
Football (tackle or touch)	32
Softball	28
Tennis	27
Baseball	26
Backpacking	25
Golf	21
Gymnastics	17

I'm including soccer because it's one of the world's most popular sports and because soccer does little to train the upper body. I watch my TV screen carefully to gather good excuses for making Heavyhands Walk the basic trainer for soccer players. The heads of most players are more active than their arms! But soccer players also don't post exceptionally high aerobic capacities, probably because there is lots of down time. It's difficult in a game like soccer to know how you would function given aerobic capacity that the game doesn't explicitly require. You might fatigue less rapidly during the game; you might be more proficient in subtle ways.

If you watch soccer players carefully—study them in action—you begin to see that "standard" moves are few. Most of the moment-to-moment moves can't be trained. They're kaleidoscopic, infinitely variable. Just tie a soccer player's hands behind his back and watch him flounder miserably as a player. Yes, the leg kicks the goal. But the whole body is steering that leg, and the arms, trapezius muscles, lats, obliques, and others all have a role in shaping the player's ultimate success.

Swimming

- Punch 'n' walk variations with hard leans
- Swing 'n' sway
- Lateral fling crossovers
- Double ski poling
- Lateral fling variation (for breast strokers)
- Bellyaerobics variations

Swimmers can get extra upper-body work with this lateral fling variation.

Creating Heavyhands Sports Medleys

It's really a pleasurable challenge. And you needn't limit it to one sport or even to sports, period. I free-associate as I work out. If I see somebody doing something that intrigues me, I stuff it into my routine. Or if I think of a move that I haven't done since Hector was a pup, I toss it in just to kind of touch base with it. What's nice about improvisation is that you can depend upon your by now delicately balanced Heavyhander instincts to bring you in at target heart rate and around anaerobic threshold. The more experience you gain, the more you'll use your physiologic wherewithal to satisfy your motor whim of the moment! If that varies every few minutes, either by impulse or by design, you'll be doing Medleys.

Swimmers train about as hard as any athletes I know of without registering the kinds of laboratory numbers I would expect. Heavyhands should be a natural for them, because they bring a huge amount of armwork to their sport. It would certainly be a more logical exercise choice for a swimmer than heavy weightlifting. Running is another part of the swimmer's typical dry land training that could be reduced if not dispensed with in my opinion, especially if vigorous and demanding pump 'n' walk—both heavy and light style—were substituted.

I learned recently that a good deal of the swimmer's time in the water is spent doing the freestyle or "crawl" stroke—regardless of which stroke happens to be his or her specialty. Which leads me to believe that most swimmers could swim less and do great things out of the water to enhance their specific strokes. This is not the place for an in-depth discussion, but I have experimented with punch 'n' walk variations that do a fair job of duplicating the biomechanical specifics of a given stroke. These studies are continuing.

I've listed Heavyhands moves that could bring more essential power to the swimmer's body and heart than four or more hours of each swimming training day. It's a kind of meat-and-potatoes exercise menu, you'll notice. If you're a swimmer, you don't need the agility of a basketball player or a boxer. And you don't need the explosive leg power of a defensive tackle, except when you're diving or turning. Some of the exercises are aimed at increasing local muscular power and protecting from typical swimming injuries, such as swimmer's shoulder and swimmer's back (thought to be caused by prolonged hyperextension of the back).

Tennis

- Swing 'n' sway
- Pump 'n' jog, in place and on the move
- Punch 'n' walk with side leans
- Double ski poling, on the move and in place
- Lateral fling crossovers
- Shadowboxing

This game calls for quickness and agility generated from an endless variety of body positions and postures. To be a good tennis player, you must also possess superb balance and the ability to move with power and precision while off balance. Your deltoid and pectoral muscles must generate power for the backhand and forehand strokes. Accordingly, I suggest a variety of movements that call for unusual arm and trunk motion, and quad power to make you light on your feet. All these moves should be performed at target heart rates; some interval work and Medleys help maximize training effects.

The high-intensity training should lower your resting heart rate, resulting in a fast heart rate return after long and difficult rallies, and reduce heart rate peaks that often result from flurries of arm effort with untrained arms. I'd use these exercises for other court sports, too, like squash, handball, racquetball, and badminton. As you move from the wrist stroke of badminton through the elbow dominance in racquetball to the shoulder stroke of tennis, you should include those particular characteristics of the armstroke in your Heavyhands Walking stroke patterns. Again, don't be a purist. Adding other strokes will help you in subtle ways with the basic ones. With its combination of quick hands and light footedness, shadowboxing should make a good training supplement, too—especially where your volley is concerned.

Weightlifting

- Pump 'n' walk and variations; 20 percent or more of total workout time should include the heaviest weights
- Double ski poling
- Bellyaerobics
- Shadowboxing

One of my top priorities is to squeeze Panaerobics into the training strategies of weightlifters, powerlifters, and bodybuilders. It will not be easy. The psychology of many men, in particular, makes "bigger" equivalent to "better," and so it won't be easy to separate them from that dedication when it comes to physical training. But consider this: Women bodybuilders, many of whom are aerobic instructors, are better paragons of total fitness than are their male counterparts. The difference is simple: Too much muscle bulk kills aerobic vitality. Women bodybuilders are ripped, cut, and blasted the way men are, but are more work-capable. The more massive male musculature usurps that form of energy we call "aerobic." Once that simple fact reaches male consciousness, men will be less content to have bulk without function. Go back and read Chapter 12 for a more detailed harangue.

For now, I'm content to plead the case for Heavyhands Walk for strength athletes. Panaerobic training will do at least three things that single file "isolation" tactics can't. (1) It will train those muscles for which exercises and machines have not been invented, the ones that integrate arm and leg movements.

The Evolution of Your Heavyhands Walking Pattern

As time goes on, you will probably become a bargain hunter. By that I mean you will instinctively include more muscle in your Heavyhands exercise. That's good, because the benefits multiply. As you add muscle, and that implies more joint action, you'll get more calorie loss per minute at given heart rates, and more comfort at given workloads. As your movements evolve from simple ones to more complex forms, you'll probably settle into fewer total movements to maintain your fitness.

(2) It will waste calories (fat) far faster than even high rep lifting in the conventional or "circuit" modes, and will reduce the need for the starving ritual that is part of the life of competitive bodybuilders. (3) It will do good things for the cardiovascular system that big weights can't. Naturally, I'll include pump 'n' walk because of its mobilization of all that beef, and would emphasize pumping high; double ski poling to aerobicize and protect the lower back; Bellyaerobics to get more calorie loss into "ab" work; and shadowboxing to bring dynamic spirit to training.

Wrestling

- Shadowboxing
- Pump 'n' walk variations
- Swing 'n' sway
- Strength Walk

I include wrestling because it's a good example of a sport that's demanding in terms of strength and flexibility but excludes many other fitness elements that might give a wrestler the subtle advantage in the ring. Elite wrestlers don't have extraordinarily high aerobic capacity when compared to cross-country skiiers, runners, or swimmers. Panaerobic training, with its great emphasis on both strength and endurance, would be a natural for the wrestler, whose primary objective is locating and exploiting weaknesses in an opponent's muscular armor.

I'm not sure it's necessary to use heavy weights ever, unless you want to move up to a higher weight classification. I would then use them about 10 percent or less of total training time. You'll notice the absence of pump 'n' run. Why risk injury when you can have higher aerobic capacity than you ordinarily enjoy simply by doing variations of pump 'n' walk?

While the advantages of aerobic fitness may not be immediately obvious, many college level wrestlers enjoy relatively high aerobic capacity just from doing their sport. The sport and its training must demand it. Good wrestling is an example of strength-endurance. The sport calls for a rapid succession of agile moves combined with fierce capability in terms of isometric strength.

———

It would be nice if some studies showed that total fitness would make for excellence in multiple sports while diminishing the investment of time spent training for any one sport. Sport tends to make some of us specialists in ways that could be unfortunate. I've heard kayakers say they won't row because they believe rowing would tend to spoil their paddling stroke.

Training specificity, the doctrine that says if you want to be a good pole vaulter you must pole vault, is actually a complicated idea. Perhaps it would be more useful to think of several *kinds* of specificity, each of which needs to be addressed in the training of the hypothetical consummate athlete. For example, some training specifics could make for skill; others might yield general fitness; others would protect against injury, work on certain body parts, emphasize specific fitness factors, or stimulate sundry improvements in the psyche of the athlete that make for a generally healthy athletic perspective.

Athletic interest makes training for fitness potentially more rewarding psychologically. Weaving specific sports skills into an assortment of fitness factors adds a practical and exciting dimension to exercise. It brings new meaning, goals, and rewards to the chorelike aspect of exercise. Perhaps it's redundant to say it, but exercise without interest enjoys poor staying power; interest cannot be sustained without some hoped-for reward; and people's ideas of what is rewarding often change. Bottom line: Only *you* can design a combination of fitness and sport important and interesting enough to include in your life plan. That's the challenge, and that's the charm.

Heavyhands Bellyaerobics

I initially wanted to introduce abdominal exercise after Chapter 7, in which we dealt with aerobics for the back. But I changed my mind because I wanted you to get acquainted with Heavyhands training before I heaped this chore upon you. Most people are wary of belly exercises; they do them with painful reluctance because the abdomen is a constant problem for most of us concerned about our bodies.

Folds:
The Heavyhands Answer to the Sit-up

Those readers familiar with the first Heavyhands book already know about the fold. I consider it the prototype for a new exercise species that will take care of the belly wall—the "abs"—and many muscles of the arms and legs, all without neglecting the cardiorespiratory system—thus the term "Bellyaerobic." I've said that Heavyhands Walk will work every major muscle group, covering those that running or conventional walking don't begin to train. That goes for the abdomen, too. But for those of you who want additional abdominal work and are not particularly enamored of the sit-up, the fold will bring all the advantages of that household ritual and then some.

The sit-up does strengthen the abdomen, but it doesn't heart-train much because the small muscle mass of the belly wall doesn't make a fitting partnership with the heart pump's delivery capacity: The belly gives out after a few fast reps; and even thousands of reps won't generate a useful cardiovascular response if performed too slowly. So Bellyaerobics includes lots of limb muscles to train the heart while keeping things going for the abdominals, which can't manage it on their own for long. You'll get as much belly-strength as you would with sit-ups, and you can combine any number of folds with other Heavyhands Walk movements to make a calorie-losing aerobic workout of whatever length you wish.

**Spot Reducing:
Does It Work?**

After all these years, two ideas still make me uncertain about the issue of spot reducing. I'd like to be able to make a clean statement about it, but I can't. For two reasons. One is that the legs, which do most of our movement for us, have the least amount of skinfold fat. Second, our bellies, that move least, have the largest share of adipose tissue. I know some studies have shown that a lot of sit-ups haven't changed our outlines significantly. Problem there is that no number of sit-ups that you can exact from an experimental subject during a typical training study will eradicate the huge movement inequality that exists between the legs and abdomen. All said, I think I believe in the theory of spot reduction. I also know we don't have enough Heavyhands Walking side leaners to prove it—yet.

Caution! Don't do a lot of folds the first time you try, or your next attempt will be painfully delayed a week! Just work several seconds at first, adding a couple more folds each day until a few minutes are possible. Don't worry about your target heart rate in the beginning for a couple of reasons. One is that the exercise is new and different and therefore "locally" demanding; the other is that all the circulatory reflex "signals" switch when you do rhythmic exercise while on your back. That's because the blood flow back to the heart pump isn't impeded by gravity as it is when we exercise in the erect posture.

Also, your abdominal muscles will not tolerate the prolonged work at fast tempos required to generate anything resembling a target pulse. The exercise is aerobic from the start. But working at your usual exercise target rate should be postponed until the muscles involved have had a go at it for a few weeks.

Do your folds on something soft to prevent your pelvic bones from being forced into an unyielding hard surface, which can hurt. A padded bench 12 inches wide and 4 to 4.5 feet long is ideal; a pad or cushion on the floor under your lower back is okay for starters. The fold is simply that: folding of your body. Use light weights. Starting with your arms and legs fully extended, bring your knees toward your chest as you bring your weighted hands forward, elbows extended, past your folding legs and past the bench or to the floor at about midthigh. Then "unfold" and stretch out straight again.

Some of you may be concerned that folding might injure your back. I respectfully admit that those worries are justified. In a world where almost everyone is vulnerable to a bad back syndrome of some sort, an ounce of prevention can't be ignored. If you're concerned that the stretching out part of the fold might place undue strain on your lower back, or if your initial efforts tell you that it already does, simply do it all with knees bent. If that hurts, abandon folds, for the time being at least, and retreat to other Heavyhands exercises like double ski poling and side leans during pump 'n' walk; these will work the belly without jeopardizing your lower back as much.

I would be suspicious of any movement prescription accompanied by the suggestion that it simply *can't* hurt your back; most strenuous exercise involves the risk of injury to that area. But I can also say with absolute certainty that the stronger your back becomes in the course of doing hundreds or thousands of difficult movements, the lower the overall risk of injury will be. What we'd really like, of course, we can't have. The risk can never be reduced to zero!

Folds

Modifications of the Fold

If the fold seems a bit too much initially—but not so hard on your lower back to keep you from doing Bellyaerobics altogether—you might want to try what I call the "prefold-sit-up-with-upper-torso-add!" Simply keep your feet planted near your butt, your bent knees pointed at the ceiling. That will take a bit of the strain off unused abdominal hardware. This way you can work your way up to folds in small installments, and even its ambitious V-sit extension. With the outstretched weighted hands you'll merely be working the upper torso into the belly act before finally adding the lower body.

Try to work up to three full minutes of the fold or prefold at 50/minute; if you work at it diligently, it should take you about four weeks. If at that point you feel you'd like to extend the exercise, make a "V-sit" out of it, so that your upper body comes up to greet your approaching knees. That extension will require you to lower the tempo somewhat, but since you'll

Rounding Out Your Bellyaerobic Repertoire: The Spread

I have a passion for discovering arcane moves that include weird muscle combinations. The spread was one of these. It's just what it sounds like: You lie on a bench (preferably padded, of course) and simply spread arms and legs simultaneously. The legs are raised somewhat during the spreading act, depending upon how your body tolerates that. The arms do what they do with lateral thrusts. A bit of a V-sit can advance the exercise, so that you sit up during the spreading phase, back down during the "closing" phase. What I like about this exercise is that it works the thigh abductors and adductors better than possibly anything you can manage while on your feet. You also work buttocks muscles and delts.

Prefolds

have added a new element of difficulty to the exercise, the work will be just as hard.

You'll probably notice that your breathing is surprisingly labored at a relatively slow heart rate. That happens almost universally, but it's related to why you needn't concern yourself about heart rate with the fold. If you know you have high blood pressure, *go easy* with this exercise and with the other Bellyaerobic exercises. That means using small weights to lessen the grunting strain typical for beginners, and purposely remaining at a low heart rate. Regardless of your condition, your abdominal training should proceed in intervals; a few reps, rest, a few more, rest, and so on. Your limitations at this juncture are purely muscular. Your heart is quite willing and able.

The fold and its modifications essentially put the abdominal muscles where they belong—in concert with the heart and

V-sits

orchestrated with the rest of the muscles. These exercises will ultimately allow you to give up sit-ups.

Diagonal Opposites

I'll leave you with one more move from the Bellyaerobic repertoire. It is, I believe, an excellent complement to the fold and makes a good companion for that exercise in "benchaerobic" Medleys. This exercise works more ordinarily underused muscles than any other I know of. Properly executed (it does take practice), diagonal opposites mobilize the inner and outer thighs, the buttocks muscles, the hip flexors, the abdominal recti *plus* the obliques, pecs, delts, lats, traps—and I could go on listing minor contributors!

The photos will describe this move better than I could with words. Essentially, while lying on your back, you pull

Exercise: Work or Play?

The more I think about the problem of mobilizing kids toward regular exercise, the more I look for hitches in our approach. One that always comes back to me is that we might be trying to lure kids into exercise by disguising it as play. But is that logical? I was once a kid myself, and some of the images of play are still fresh in my mind. Play never felt like running a 10-K, that's for sure. Most of it was short, panting, sprinting stuff. When we were kids, we didn't realize we were running; it was simply the best way to get away from someone, to overtake someone, or to hide quickly. It was reflex: Like breathing, we did it to survive in a child's world of continual play. In our own zeal to be fit, we're trying to force this passion upon our kids and call it play. And we're frustrated because they respond a bit reluctantly. Why shouldn't they?

Belly Sprint Medley

Here's a good movement combination that won't neglect your cardiorespiratory equipment while working belly, low back, and an assortment of limb muscles. Work toward three full minutes of these three exercises, pacing yourself slowly enough to finish. Once you can do that, work on tempo, pushing gradually toward something close to 60 moves/minute. That number isn't inscribed in stone, incidentally, and you will not offend the fitness gods if you never get there! The three moves are:

- Folds (or V-sits)
- Diagonal opposites
- Spreads

Start with a few of each done as a Medley sequence, like 10 or 15, gradually inching toward 50 or 60 of each. This should get you to a total of three minutes or more. Most will find their hearts at target (at least) at the end of this Belly Sprint Medley. Actually, once you're able to do that without much immediate or next-day discomfort, I predict you'll go for more. You can turn this into a super TV-watching interval workout, by doing the Medley intermittently.

Diagonal opposites

one arm over and somewhat outward. Lift the opposite leg and foot from the floor, knee bent, so that your foot passes across your body until it's in line with the pumped hand of the other side. Then immediately repeat the sequence to the opposite side. Your body kind of twists or rolls from side to side to allow these contortions.

Beyond its purely aerobic and muscular benefits, this move may improve your flexibility in ways that conventional static stretch doesn't. It improved mine and thus became one of my favorites. As I mentioned before, it works well in combination with the fold, the two together allowing you a longer Bellyaerobics stint, once you've practiced a bit and aren't getting a sore belly any longer. And as usual, you will learn the hard way about the new muscles you have called into action after performing your first few diagonal opposites. The fold/

Flexibility: Two Kinds?

This fitness business is in a constant state of flux. Nothing ever gets settled permanently! Just when static stretch was becoming an accepted ritual, we learned that it doesn't work for everybody, doesn't always magically prevent injuries, and is sometimes hurtful in itself. A few years ago everyone stretched before doing anything else. Now we're told that warming up—actually increasing the temperature of the muscles—is wise before attempting to stretch anything. Warmed elastic tissue stretches better and more safely.

But what about "dynamic flexibility?" At press conferences and TV appearances I usually demonstrated some moves, and the comment I heard most frequently related to my unusual "flexibility." Since it's the fitness factor in which I've always gotten the lowest grades, I tried to figure out how I'd fooled everyone. I think it's simply the range of motion I achieve during movement. People may think that can readily be converted to the heroic pretzel bends that Jane Fonda does. Wrong—those would surely cripple me! As I see it, my flexibility is actually a combination of strength, muscle endurance, and a bit of grace. Hers is the real article, which I'll never achieve. When I plotted my grudging improvement after some months of diligent static stretching, I decided hair and static flexibility were two items I'd better forgo with good humor.

diagonal opposite combo will help increase abdominal definition as long as you're not adding poundage at mealtime.

One last idea: If you find these exercises more abominable than abdominal, don't worry. There are other ways of skinning this cat. You can get plenty of respectable belly exercise from Heavyhands Walk movements. Side leans and double ski poling will do wonders for your belly. Just keep your belly in mind as you pump and punch. That way you'll twist and bend in ways that won't neglect your middle.

Heavyhands Walk and Weight Control

Weight loss is like the weather—everybody talks about it. I used to tell young doctors during teaching rounds that a good understanding of obesity probably suggests you understand plenty about the human condition in general! I was always delighted when cases of obesity were presented because the material was always multifaceted. It becomes clearer and clearer that the number of heavy people increases even as we learn more and more about the reasons for it. A most frustrating state of affairs for health professionals. The arguments rage on as to how inherited or "learned" obesity is, and when strategies ranging from starvation to exercise extremes should be prescribed. The field is becoming cluttered with the expectable cliches, having to do with adopting new ways of eating or changing lifestyle. I think we suffer here from the usual tendency to shoot for sweeping statements in an area where the differences between victims outstrip the similarities.

My purpose in this chapter is to convince the reader that Heavyhands Walk is the most practical way to make exercise a lifetime habit that will help avoid obesity while it's doing good things for health and beauty, and therefore, I suppose, happiness.

A Quick Review of Fat Basics

A human body can be too large in three ways: It can have too much fat, too much muscle, or too much of both. We can dispense with the last one first. If a large muscled man, say a retired football player, deconditions without dieting, he'll predictably be left with a body with too much muscle for what he's doing, which will proceed to gain surplus fat. The second category refers to a condition called "excess muscle," in which there's so much of it that it actually impedes the individual's work capacity. These overmuscled people can't do much work because they've more than enough to do just moving their body around! The first category is by far the largest: Most of the too-big people of this world are simply too fat for their own good.

Fat Loss vs. Fitness

One of the unspoken complications of obesity is that it tends to eclipse the issue of *fitness*. After people lose weight, they must walk faster to keep the workload up to snuff if they want to continue to train the heart muscle. If they don't, they're actually dogging it more as time passes and their fat gradually incinerates. Lots of people don't pay much attention to the intensity factor in their exercise. Instead, they tend to go longer in order to lose more total calories. That is a perfectly legitimate tactic, by the way, if all you want to do is lose fat. But too many obese people tend to look for "outside" fitness, the visible sort, to the exclusion of "inside" fitness, the invisible sort that is more associated with function and well-being. So most obese people in exercise programs get on the scale to see how they're progressing: They seldom are spontaneously curious about their pulse count.

What Is Setpoint?

Everyone is said to have one. It's best thought of as a weight to which your body has learned to gravitate. If you lose or gain, the changes become more grudging as you move further from your setpoint. That's what keeps us from enormous obesity on the one hand and perfect proportions on the other. If you're heavier than ideal, the trick is to lower your setpoint; a few of us may need to raise it a bit, though that's a rarer problem. Dr. Gilbert A. Leveille, who wrote *The Setpoint Diet*, says exercise is the way to lower your setpoint. And I'm saying that Heavyhands Walk is *the* setpoint exercise!

Here's my reasoning. You can do *more* exercise, for one thing. Once trained as a Heavyhander, you can go longer and at a higher intensity than you can any other way. The heart doesn't have to work harder when it delivers to more working muscles. In fact, we have reason to believe that the heart works less delivering to lots of *trained* working muscles. Exercise produces lots of capillaries that tend to reduce so-called peripheral resistance to blood flow, perhaps one of the reasons that exercisers frequently show lowered blood pressures.

More muscles contributing mean less fatigue and usually fewer injuries; that adds to the total work possible. And our research suggests that as the amount of trained muscle mass increases, the tendency to use fat as fuel creeps upward. I can pump 'n' walk steadily at 15 METs or more using more fat and at a far lower heart rate than if I try to work that hard simply running. Of course, more studies must be done, but other research unrelated to ours has echoed what we believe to be true: The more trained muscle recruited for exercise, the more fat is burned while carbohydrate is "spared."

The plot thickens. We can't readily isolate fat from muscle, because the most popular way of losing fat—starvation of some sort—also decreases muscle in the process. Exercise is better than dieting in that sense, because you tend to keep more body protein (muscle) while you're shedding fat. And so we already know the cure for that enormous population of too-big people: enough exercise and not too much food for the activity of each day. It's that simple. Get everybody slim through lots of exercise, then get them to eat only enough to just cover the body's total daily heat production.

Oh, there are special cases when that dictum doesn't quite work. There are some people who are such efficient metabolic machines that they conserve energy too well and store it as fat even when they don't eat much. But these don't begin to make up the garden variety of fat people who are stretching the statistics from generation to generation. And few experts would try to explain the mounting incidence of childhood obesity we're experiencing now with notions of some metabolic abnormality.

Panaerobics: Why It's a Smart Choice for Heavyweights

I believe Panaerobic training may be at least as wise for the obese as for sleeker people. A fat arm will tend to become an inert arm. It only makes sense. In fact, all manner of body movements become statistically less probable, or require a higher degree of motivation, when the body is heavy. Let's presume you want to keep it that way, or at least all your efforts toward change haven't been very rewarding. Why not, then, train all your muscles to simply make *any* movement feel easier? Then your plan to lose weight through exercise will be easier to launch, and will enjoy a better chance of success. I'm suggesting that some people might be better off getting Panaerobically fit *before* they decide to lose weight. I ask my overweight patients to avoid concern about their weight until their working and resting pulses are significantly slower.

Why Is Heavyhands Walk the Best Fat Antidote?

So now we all realize that the best way to shave unwanted fat away from wanted muscle is through exercise. The new question is: which exercise? First off, it must be an aerobic exercise because for burning fat anything else is plainly impractical. Rhythmic, continuous work that gets you to an appropriate heart rate is what the doctors order. So which of the standard aerobic exercises are useful? It depends in part on how overweight you might be. Very heavy people—30 percent too heavy or more—can't run comfortably, if at all, and may injure themselves even more frequently than do skinny runners. I'd rule out rope skipping for similar reasons: For most heavyweights, airborne exercise usually is not feasible. What's left? Bicycling, walking, swimming, cross-country skiing, rowing, and aerobic dance would make up 95 percent of what's left to choose from.

Bicycling, rowing, and swimming have one thing in common: Not one is a weight-bearing activity. These exercises may be somewhat easier than the others for those who are overweight. Being heavy tends to make a given pedal frequency at a given wheel tension on a bike easier, because of the body's added heft. Many heavy people do use cycling, either stationary or on the move, for exercise. I would suspect, however, that most fat people who cycle outdoors don't do it long enough or hard enough to produce any lasting training effects; and many people (not just fat ones) find exercise bikes boring.

I like rowing better than cycling because of the additional muscle mass involved. And I prefer rowing to swimming, too, because the legwork in rowing is brisker than in most swimming strokes. But the great body flexion promoted by the moving seat on most rowing machines can cause back problems. Many rather obese people are good swimmers because of their great buoyancy. But for that same reason, fat swimmers can drift into slack workloads; some of them have swum the English Channel in respectable time despite the fact that their treadmill tests are not apt to break records.

What about the martial arts and aerobic dance? Both can be excellent calorie losers. I put them together because they're often done in groups and would appeal to those with a flair for graceful movement and such. Unfortunately, the groups are seldom formed by putting people of similar weight together. In aerobic dance, heavy people naturally will have a discouragingly difficult time with airborne routines. And I don't think martial arts instructors are getting rich teaching tae

Diet Books and the Crusade against Fatness

The way I see it, the number of diet books published annually is proportional to the worsening of the problem the diet books were written to combat! This is just a hunch, but I believe buying a diet book (maybe reading it) is a psychic substitute for conquering the problem once and for all. It proves to our conscience that, damn it, we're trying! The best diet books I know of are rather sedate reading that say it like it is. The more a book comes on with fanfare and promise, the more I predict it will do "well" without doing any real "good!" Here's why. Those of us who've literally spent years being depressed over our body specs need fanfare more than solid information. And that's what we buy. The book provides needed hope. Most of the chronically obese, deep down in their hearts, don't expect long-term cures. The best way to sell a book is to create fantasy by way of its title. If the title paints promise—extended life, fitness (which, I'm afraid, translates as "beauty"), wealth, perpetual love—and doesn't have a jacket that makes the customer vomit, it's got a chance. If beyond that it's written by a celebrity, it's on its way.

The Calorie Game

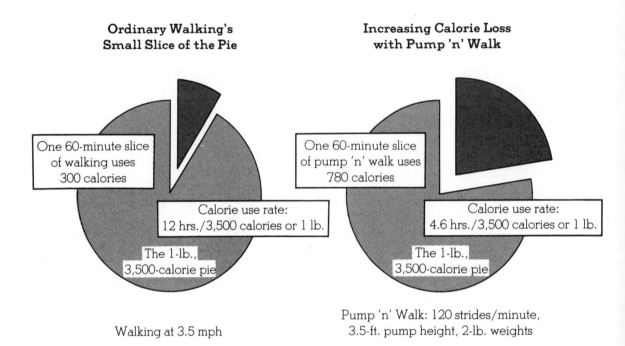

Ordinary Walking's Small Slice of the Pie

One 60-minute slice of walking uses 300 calories

Calorie use rate: 12 hrs./3,500 calories or 1 lb.

The 1-lb., 3,500-calorie pie

Walking at 3.5 mph

Increasing Calorie Loss with Pump 'n' Walk

One 60-minute slice of pump 'n' walk uses 780 calories

Calorie use rate: 4.6 hrs./3,500 calories or 1 lb.

The 1-lb., 3,500-calorie pie

Pump 'n' Walk: 120 strides/minute, 3.5-ft. pump height, 2-lb. weights

Knocking the 2-Pound Limit Axiom

All you have to do is scan the obvious differences between people to realize that a 2-pound limit on handweights for continuous exercise is arbitrary and dead wrong! Lyle Alzado might have more trouble manipulating 2-pounders than a sinewy little aerobics instructor weighing about 95 pounds, especially going at 150 tempo for four minutes! It's because Lyle's arms are far larger than the girl's legs, and are the biggest resistance to fast pumps or punches. For him the 2-pound "add" is merely the last straw!

kwon do to fat people. Both martial arts and aerobic dance are apt to be somewhat riskier for obese people, who may get injured trying to keep up with slimmer classmates.

So how about walking? Walking is certainly advocated by most experts as the right exercise for obese people. Is it good enough to burn calories and help you lose weight? Of course. But you must walk *enough*. The number of calories lost, and therefore fat metabolized, in walking depends on two factors: how *long* you walk, and how *fast* you walk. The best way is to walk long *and* fast. Not many obese people are willing to walk a 12-minute mile, however, and some, frankly, aren't able. If you walk more slowly, and do enough of it to lose significant poundage, you should soon become able to walk faster.

My belief is that Heavyhands Walk is the best aerobic exercise for heavy people—for many reasons. No matter how slow their stride pace, if they pump even tiny weights to a respectable height they will lose as many or more calories per minute than they could if one could persuade them to walk those impossible 5 miles per hour! If they can increase their armwork (which they surely can do) while their walking pace remains the same or increases only slightly, they can more

Fat and the Counting Game

Counting often turns out to be a symptom. Sometimes we count when we don't want to "look at" something else. The more insistent the counting ritual, the more I think of some sort of cover-up. We've all done it. We count what's "in" at the moment: calories, carbohydrates, percentages of various dietary nutrients, milligrams of added vitamins and minerals, skinfold-fat thicknesses, pounds, percentages of lean body mass, body mass to height ratios, clothing sizes, movement reps, minutes or calorie totals of weekly exercise, point systems—just to scan a sampling. It's like exchanging one kind of focus or interest for another. But while looking hard at numbers, we may ignore *images* that are more important. There's nothing wrong with counting itself, but it often signals some avoidance. Body management is such a complicated and individual proposition that it can't be right when we're just looking at *part* of the information. What I'm struggling awkwardly to say here is that the more we ritualize counting, the better the chance that we're losing the battle. What we tend to believe is, the more we *count* the better we're doing. But I suspect there are more *fatter* people counting more things now than ever!

How Heavyhands Walk Beats Obesity

Let me count the ways:

1. More total exercise. Heavy people often have joint problems relating simply to excessive weight bearing. Easy things become harder when you're obese. Spreading the work out among lots of muscles gets both more muscle mass and more joints to share in the action. The result is less trauma and higher workload, a practically unbeatable combination. It means you can go both longer and more vigorously, again a combination that serves doubly to lose calories and train the oxygen transport mechanism to do even more.

2. More fat used as fuel. The better Panaerobically trained you are (more muscles participating, that is), the more fat you use to fuel your activity even at higher levels of intensity. We all use fat as fuel when we're merely ambling along. As work gets brisker, carbohydrate mechanisms kick in. Fat fueling delays that. We say, "fat spares carbohydrate." We have reason to believe that happens most effectively when plenty of trained muscle is orchestrated. Lots of muscle fibers working at 50 percent of their capacity may be far better than a few working at 70 to 90 percent of theirs.

3. Lower setpoint. Physical training is the premier way of lowering the standard body weight that your body seems to gravitate toward. It happens presumably by increasing the body's general metabolic enthusiasm somewhat. Since muscle tissue is, by its nature, highly metabolically active, and since it can be trained to be more so, Heavyhands Walk is doubtless the preferred setpoint exercise because it works so many muscles.

4. Higher intensity in workouts. Big bodies doing many conventional exercise programs, especially those that are leg-dominated, just can't generate respectable workloads in most cases. It's like asking a petite, deconditioned woman to pump 'n' walk 5-pounders high and fast for 10 full minutes. Her encumbered arms become too heavy to be work-capable. An obese body suffers from precisely the same problem in moving itself about. To go long it must go slowly, simply because there's too much of it to "rep" rapidly for more than a few seconds. So fast-moving aerobics is essentially out; but slow movements involving as much beef as possible are what the doctor orders for health and looks. As training effects gather, the whole body can include faster moves with light weights to expend greater numbers of calories and train heart and muscle even more.

than double their initial calorie loss: Their healthy hearts will readily accommodate the larger workloads. At three hours of exercise per week, each additional calorie of heat loss per minute amounts to nearly three additional pounds of fat loss per year!

Muscularity as a Body Style

You've doubtless guessed that combined fitness—fitness of the heart and the muscles—is, in my view, one key to lasting success at the weight control game. It involves gradually converting your emphasis from *outside* (surface, silhouette) to *inside* (muscles, functions). Given a group of fat exercisers whom I knew nothing about, I'd bet that those whose heart rates—at rest and at given work intensities—had lowered most during their training would be more successful at losing weight. I'd also bet that those who had experienced visible muscle gains would stand better chances of keeping the weight off in the long run.

Another way of saying this is that the wish for general muscularity acquired aerobically makes the prognosis for weight loss better. The mere obsession with *losing fat* ignores the wealth of structures beneath the skin and the function they can generate. A body slimmed through starvation is seldom what most dieters fantasize about. The high rate of recurrent weight gain may suggest that the new body is responded to with something like, "This ain't no big deal—eating's better!"

Part of the puzzle is that weight loss is thought of as a kind of total effect. While looks seem to be the main motivator, the anticipated appearance is often a blurry slimness, tied to a selected number of pounds overweight people have committed themselves to lose. Most dieters never do reach the real payoff, spelled out in idealized contours. If fat isn't beautiful, less fat isn't much better.

When I developed Heavyhands Walk, I really didn't intend it to be a method for weight control. But the obese person is precisely the one who has most to gain by it. Heavyhands Walk is a most effective, physiologically rational means of losing calories rapidly for big people who can't move easily. And through its endless varieties of movement combinations, it's a great way for heavy people to become interested in their body once again. An obsessive preoccupation with body weight actually creates a form of disinterest in many things—including, ironically, the body itself.

Combined aerobics gives you the best shot at muscularity and performance, which wed heart and muscle and mind, and make eating what it should be in the first place—an anxiety-free pleasure! The cures that call merely for "changed eating habits" I regard as empty rhetoric: another example of an isolated idea that neatly avoids the average whole person.

To Diet or Not to Diet: Is That the Question?

Unfortunately, too often it is. Diets have become so commonplace that you get the feeling that many if not most of us are either starting, following, or straying from a diet. The overweight condition has become part of our national character! Here's a quick look at fat, and why I think we're ever-fattening.

1. Generally speaking, there's plenty of food around (there are some appalling exceptions to that, of course).

2. Feeding is probably the most unequivocal pleasure most of us know.

3. Eating satisfies more than "real" physiologic hunger. Modern man has learned other reasons for resorting to feeding. The stocked fridge has become a kind of universal antidote for what ails us at a given moment.

4. Being slim is touted highly but turns out not to be such a big deal. Slim silhouettes are abandoned by the millions once achieved.

5. There are numerous unconscious reasons for becoming and remaining stout. Some of us get fat "at" somebody, usually someone important who would like us not to be fat. Sometimes fat is a self-inflicted punishment that is related to assorted guilts. A few fatten up to avoid the "dangers" that lurk behind attractiveness. I could go on. Some of us never really outdistance the notion that "fat is beautiful!"

6. Studies show that men don't worry as much about their overweight condition as do women. I think this apparent immunity from concern in men is related to macho fantasies that often equate physical size, however wrought, with manliness.

7. We don't enjoy enough those processes which squander large amounts of body energy. That's why our language sags with words like laziness, inhibition, lassitude, and relaxation.

8. Sloth precludes heavy investment in the joy of motion, and lack of practice makes us awkward. Awkwardness makes movement an anxiety producer, and all of these help make us both gluttonous and immobile.

9. The diet industry has helped "program" us to scan each other's silhouettes—mostly to discover how wide we are. Being in shape has come to mean being narrow, especially around the middle. That's why it's quite possible to have a functionally deficient body that's reasonably slim, though surprisingly too fat.

10. The great emphasis on structure, or what we look like, tends to rob fitness programs of imagination and skill. We tend to think of *how much* we do rather than what we do. That leads to what I call "overstable" routines with a chore-like quality that makes quitting even more likely.

11. Patterns that lead to obesity may receive subtle sanction from all of us—parents, teachers, insurance actuaries, health-care professionals, journalists—who are weary of losing the battle. If we can't beat obesity, in a certain sense, we join and justify it!

Given these predisposing conditions, it should be clear that body control is a big job. It requires constant vigil, wisdom, psychic and bodily skills, the capacity to delay gratification, honesty to a fault, flexibility of spirit, knowledge of one's inner motives, marvelous humor; and after that, generous padding with extra motives to ensure success. The diet philosophy is an attempt to suppress the complexity of carving and keeping a proper body. It is oversimplified, and millions of man-years' worth of the practice prove that it can't work. The question isn't whose diet we're trying or whether we're following it. The question is, do we understand how tough a problem the body is, and can we do what's necessary to solve the problem? In my book, any repetitive dieter has probably learned the art of self-deception too well!

Heavyhands Walk for Groups

We really don't know as much as we should about the great penchant we have for working out together. A vintage psychiatrist might give some of the following explanations:

1. Companionship. Exercise is lonely business at best, and the old saying suggests that misery looks for company. Besides, some of us are honest enough to know we depend heavily on the "human" environment to keep us doing anything that requires discipline.

2. Example. On a more positive note, we learn nicely during group experiences in which we have plenty of examples of good and bad performance to observe.

3. Safety. Some of us are terrified of the possible consequences of vigorous movement, so it's cozier knowing a few people in the vicinity can administer CPR if necessary.

4. Exhibitionism. We're all fundamentally exhibitionists—there's a bit of showbiz in all of us. Groups basically consist of ourselves on stage, and the rest as audience.

5. Teamwork. The lure of the group involved together at the old college try is quite strong. It's like nationalism or other forms of competitiveness: "Our group's better'n your group."

6. Sex. Many of us are scouting for things other than lowered heart rates and muscle definition.

7. Escape. Some of us are intent upon getting away from the spouse or the kids or the house and into a social situation. The exercise is a secondary rationalization that's acceptable.

8. Power. This may motivate the beautiful, the well coordinated, and the very fit among us to torment our fellow exercisers with electric evidence of our physical superiority.

9. Sympathy. Pity is a form of love. Strange as it may seem, some of us may join exercise groups to get a bit of pity-love. The long suffering, audibly complaining exercisers who come up with more than their fair share of aches and pains, and never seem to lose an ounce, might alert one's suspicion as to what's really being sought.

10. Conversation. The gab gambit, so to speak. Those who work at low intensities in group exercise often turn out to be the talkers. Talking with others, in fact, may be their prime motivation for joining an exercise class.

Togetherness!
Think of it. Couples no longer have viable excuses for escaping from each other during exercise! If there's a desire to work out together, Heavyhands Walk provides many opportunities. My wife happens to suffer from bronchial asthma. That means some mornings breathing comes hard. But I can always slip nicely into her slower pace by going heavy and/or high with my strokes. Her problem increases the gap between our work capabilities for the moment; but at the same time there is no degree of her slowing that I can't accommodate through some added leg- and armwork that keeps me just as slow. And I can add strength to my strides with duck walking, double ski poling, or swing 'n' sway on the move. This same principle applies to larger groups. Essentially, we're saying that the group can remain together because at *any* stride pace all Heavyhanders can generate workloads that get them to target heart rates! That's a revolutionary idea in exercise, and probably can't be accomplished without the benefit of the combined format.

Fun in Groups!

The group experience makes exercise fun for many, apart from choreographic considerations. When new movements—a bit different, perhaps more difficult—are accomplished by the group, there is a bonus sense of shared success that may be likened to a team win. I think it's a good idea to always have something new, if only a subtle movement "twist," for the group to work on. It lends an additional motive for attendance. The kind of thing that actors in a play, a troupe of dancers, or those lucky enough to play in orchestras or string quartets enjoy uniquely. Obviously, the difficulty of the technique is not nearly as important as the "togetherness." When we learn skills in a group situation, we also learn lots about nonverbal kinds of communication, and feel the joy of communal pride—a form of love we all can use.

If any or all of the above have anything to do with why you like your exercise in groups, you're certainly not alone. Physiologically speaking, Heavyhands Walk and its variations have no peer when it comes to group exercise. The four-limbed and trunk muscle option is what makes this so. Because everyone in a group can juggle the workload at a given musical tempo by varying the weight and range of motion, the fittest in the bunch could be doing seven or more times the work of the least fit. That can't happen with clustered people at the track or on the road without Heavyhands unless everyone totes an appropriately weighted backpack! By juggling weights and ranges of motion, each member of the group is following precisely the right exercise prescription. In our experience, those awesome workload differences haven't spawned a bit of competitiveness that becomes dangerous or embarrassing.

In the original Heavyhands text, I explained my avoidance of issues like fun and "feeling better" by saying they didn't lend themselves to the precision of numbers. As I enter my seventh decade, however, I'm prepared to say that fun makes exercise better. It's why music is a good catalyst of strenuous physiologic work, and why the whoops and hollers of groups of hard-working exercisers make the sweaty action even more delicious. Good moods, however generated, make exercise better; and spirited action improves moods.

While groups are good catalysts for continuing an exercise program, I must add a soft word of caution about them. Having gotten reasonably skilled at calculating workloads at a distance, I've found that those who "socialize" most during our group sessions may be sacrificing a part of what they're there for. It's not that talk itself requires enormous amounts of oxygen; it's probably that sensible conversation isn't easily sustainable when you're going at 60 to 90 percent of your maximum intensity. I've tried making good sense with an exercising partner while breathing 60 to 80 times a minute, and I usually end up deciding to make my point during a water break. There's a special kind of concentration required to maintain a steady aerobic state.

For long group sessions, I often recommend at least 20 solid minutes of "asocial" Heavyhands sandwiched somewhere in the middle of an hour, for example. That gives you good warmup and cooldown periods done at a more recreational intensity that goes well with good conversation and whatever. Another idea is to decide with a partner to go the interval route, in which you agree to cut the gab and really work for a certain amount of time, and switch to conversation when you both drop the workload. Like talking when you're at Level 3 pumps, then lapsing into a speechless pant at Level 3.5!

Choreographing an Indoor Group Workout

It's actually pretty easy to construct Heavyhands Walk workouts for indoor settings so long as there's adequate space for each participant. I recommend starting with pump 'n' walk around the room's perimeter, initially without music so that everyone can get used to the movement. You can almost always anticipate, especially in groups larger than 5 or 10 people, that some people will experience initial difficulty doing basic pump 'n' walk. When that happens, it's almost always one of two problems: They're either pumping too high or they can't avoid a same-side, stride-stroke pattern. If this is happening, reduce the arm pumps to the point that they're almost imperceptible. Just an inch or two is quite enough to establish the sense of the movement. If they start losing the opposite stride-stroke pattern, advise them to stop and restart. When the intervals between errors begin to lengthen, tell them they're in business.

Once you start the music, which should be slow (100 beats/minute or slower), those who have seemingly mastered pump 'n' walk may have trouble. Then the instructor should demonstrate the movement, again with very low pump heights, to help convey the way the move "fits" the beat. Sometimes the class should simply walk to the beat first to avoid confusion, adding little armstrokes gradually.

Finding Heavyhands Walk Groups

As of this writing, the great bulk of Heavyhands groups in the United States are found indoors. That's because Heavyhands Walking has not been fully established. That will take some organizing. As of now, some aerobics groups are just beginning to experiment with walking to musical routines. It will prove to be a winning format for good reason: It avoids the injury risk inherent in some dance routines (regardless of floor construction), and will produce more doable work for most. I know of a few groups of women who hit some lovely Pittsburgh park trails each morning. They've been at it for years.

A Few Added Tips on Structuring Heavyhands Classes

1. Watch for "dangerous" Heavyhanders. Occasionally, you may encounter individuals who seem to overestimate the distance between themselves and their classmates. They may pump extravagantly and a bit erratically and have too many near misses. Some of these folks have visual/perceptual problems and just don't read space well. Whatever the reason, do something about it early if you don't want a painful collision down the line.

2. Vary the music. New music makes the "bread-and-butter" moves seem pleasantly different. Allowing everyone to suggest favorites may add to the fun. Working grooved moves to new music is an adventure in improvisation that many never experience outside their exercise class.

3. Suggest periodic pulse checks. This is especially important for any exercisers who seem to be breathing unusually hard or whose faces seem strained. Be sure everyone has a medical okay before entering the class. Almost every class with middle-aged members will contain some with chronic back problems. Preach some caution where it comes to DSP or Bellyaerobic moves for back sufferers.

4. Include periodic chat sessions. Get members' notions on how the class seems to be going and what seems to be lacking. Every class should be unique, and that specialness should evolve as a result of shared goals, so long as the rudiments of good exercise are kept in mind.

5. Invite class participation in instruction. Make a bulletin board available to which anyone can tack anything from a magazine article to a cartoon that makes a point. This exercise is an open system, and that means intelligence about exercise and health should blossom, too.

Heavyhands Walkdance classes can be of three types where it comes to organization. Each type has advantages and disadvantages. Classes can be well structured, led by an instructor. Or they can be free-form, all participants doing pretty much what they wish to the music. A third, quite viable possibility would be a combination of the two: an instructed portion followed by a freewheeling time to do one's own thing. Our class—utterly free-form—has continued for nearly five years now without the benefit of five total minutes of formal instruction. There is a good bit of friendly advice doled out informally to newcomers. It's just a group of consenting adults exercising with variations of Heavyhands Walk four to five times weekly, to music ranging from Brahms' *Lullaby* to Zulu folk songs with a good beat.

This is not to say that I prefer unstructured classes across the board. Beginners need to learn the basic moves in an organized fashion so they don't pick up an assortment of bad habits. I also like to spend a few minutes up front during the first few sessions, simply chatting about some rudiments of exercise physiology. This adds a few ideas to their goals as exercisers: what they can and can't expect from exercise; how long it takes; how much it takes to retain fitness, once acquired; how to avoid initial "traps."

Good humor and plenty of encouragement help to dilute embarrassment, which tends to be greater when the group members are strangers (a good thing to consider when putting classes together). One of the great pleasures I've realized from my class participation with Heavyhands Walk has come from watching how well these astoundingly different people function together. Their shapes and sizes, work capabilities, ages, personality types, knowledge about exercise, and needs are all over the chart, so to speak. But there is an unmistakable sense of cohesion in the group, as though we're working for a common cause. Most wonderful of all, and frankly, kind of surprising to me, is the apparent pride each person takes in the accomplishments of the *others*. Imagine how that model could translate into corporate effectiveness! I describe it as the opposite of competitiveness.

Outdoor Workouts

Group activities, however well constructed, don't fully satisfy all exercisers. Once you achieve a high level of conditioning, you may need to do some exercise alone in order to work at the pace that will train you optimally. Working alone outdoors also allows special nuances you can't get in the gym:

hillwork, training on varied surfaces, the dubious joy of tilting with the weather, etc. I've found I learn from my group experience what I like best about exercising alone—and vice versa!

Which isn't to say that group Heavyhands Walk isn't perfect for outdoor exercise. As technique improves, shyness naturally recedes, and many groups become creatively adventurous. All to the good. The perimeter walk pattern can be retained while in-place movements in the center of the space can be added. Members can opt to move from the outside walk group to an indoor facility at will.

We began seeing these Heavyhands Walk groups sprouting spontaneously around the Pittsburgh area a couple of years ago. Mostly women, the groups meet and walk through fair and foul weather. I predict this sort of thing will become increasingly popular among all age groups.

Forewarned Is Forearmed

Now the most important warning in the book: *Always* guard against the possibility of striking someone with a handweight or being struck by one yourself. You just can't be too careful. In hundreds of hours of Heavyhands exercise at our gym, I recall only one traumatic event: My nephew received a glancing blow on the wrist from my son-in-law! But that event was enough to make me an absolute nag on the subject. Given its unyielding surface, a 3-pounder traveling at high velocity could crack a skull. The strapped weight is an advantage, and allowing 100 square feet per person is a good rule of thumb. But nothing is as important as keeping your eyes open! No level of fitness, no movement adventure, justifies an unnecessary injury. The danger of trauma looms largest in nonstructured classes, of course, and least where everyone has a place and remains in it.

In large rooms where the perimeter is utilized for walking, the danger increases when faster walkers or joggers attempt to pass others. It's wise to designate fast and slow lanes, keeping the fast lane closest to the walls. Our group works without a leader. The center of the gym is usually occupied by people doing in-place moves, and the periphery by those doing a variety of stride-stroke combinations. That has provided plenty of space for freewheeling activity with maximal safety.

The Dangers of Handweights in Aerobics Classes

There is no question in the world that putting iron into the hands of fast-moving people within limited spatial confines will pose additional risk. Risk of various collisions between body parts and iron are real and the most important of the dangers to be addressed. Then comes risk of injury: to bones, joints, muscles, tendons, ligaments, and more superficially, to the eyes and skin. Heart attacks and strokes have occurred and will continue to occur when motley groups exercise at various intensities, whether they are monitored or not (though monitoring may help reduce the likelihood, obviously). It was always safer to walk than to run, and we always knew it. But, then, people have always been willing to take on calculated risk in the process of achieving something better.

Sometimes the articles I read sound as though the author is on some mission to protect readers from these bad people who have a bizarre love for watching misfortune strike exercisers! When the multiple benefits of combined exercise are well entrenched, we'll grouse about the dangers less and sensibly plot obvious ways of reducing the risks to near zero. If that sort of thing weren't true, there'd be no airplanes or autos or appendectomies—or any exercise, for that matter.

For Those Over 50

18

I spend considerable time in Florida. Since so many come here to retire, I get plenty of opportunity to watch carefully the walk patterns of older citizens, ambling about in shopping malls or around the neighborhood or on the golf courses. The stiff walking I see is an absolute stereotype. My guess would be that a lifetime of ordinary walking can't protect against it. The arms hang, the shoulders are drooping, the stride is short and ungraceful, the body is often too heavy for the energy available to transport it powerfully and easily. It seems as though a large percentage of the combined reserves of the heart and the muscles is being invested in the belabored act of barely getting about.

It's pretty clear that this shrunken motor function is not a primary loss of heart power, in most instances. As a gerontologist, I have watched too many of those admitted to nursing homes decline in a matter of weeks from good walkers to inhabitants of wheelchairs—even though their hearts were healthy. Rather, this resiliency of the body has been lost gradually by a shrinking motivation to push the system to do more than *merely survive*. I think this notion runs parallel to the one about unfit athletes, whose overall conditioning is too often determined by what the game requires of them. Their orientation seems locked into the present. But physical training, by its nature, is oriented toward the future. Overkill tactics in the world of movement are simply rational: If you don't do more than life requires of you at the moment, you're probably headed toward a time when your functional level will only just make it.

The demographers tell us that fully one-quarter of the people in this country will be 65 or older by the year 2020. The energy transmitted by that huge segment of our population will determine to a large degree how we come across as a nation. If we're characteristically unwell and inert, passive rather than involved, we'll become an expensive drain on the country's youth and vitality. If you spend any time in a good nursing home, you'll see that fact in stark exaggeration—how many strong youngsters it takes to care for the older residents.

Fat and 50-Plus

It's wise to become lean and mobile *before* you hit 50! It's harder to lose weight once you've adopted the sedentary life, and if you wait until you're 50, you lessen the odds for your success. But I believe Heavyhands Walk is the best way to handle extra fat even if you begin to exercise at 50. Again, heart and muscle training deserve the highest initial priority. Being 50 and a beginning exerciser would make fast fat loss through exercise an unwise, perhaps dangerous proposition. Gradually work toward a training base before you consider losing perhaps a pound per week!

You're Only as Old as You Feel!

The fitness texts tell us that by age 17 or so we're about as work capable, on average, as we're destined to be. After that, things fall off very gradually. But this, again, is the average. At 62, I'm about 30-plus percent more work capable than the average 17-year-old. Now pass that adage by me again. How old am I supposed to feel?

The Inevitable Aging Process

After middle age, the human animal's fitness profile tends to spread across the chart of extremes. Our lifestyles continue stubbornly, now in exaggerated versions of what we were during our younger years. Weight may be put on faster as food intake and lessened activity combine to cause more fat to be stored. Muscle atrophies and becomes more laced with fat cells. It is said that people in their middle years lose a quarter-pound of muscle and gain a pound of fat each year. Depression, hardly the ideal emotional state for launching and maintaining a good exercise regimen, is more common among the elderly.

Genetic factors begin to surface in exaggerated form. These may be present in the form of degenerative diseases, such as atherosclerosis, that have their onset earlier in some than in others. And the effect of rigidly pursued lifestyles becomes caricatured in later years. Changes in the body's elastic tissues, evidenced by markedly reduced suppleness, may occur. When depression, bad luck, or major losses in social supports happen at the same time, these bodily changes may speed up at an alarming rate.

The story is quite different for those in whom regular activity has been a lifelong pursuit. They typically move gracefully through the decades with almost imperceptible motor losses. And what is most encouraging in this area is the mounting evidence that good fitness achieved early can be preserved well on a small time investment, i.e., ideally on two hours per week or less.

As sedentary types become more so, so, too, do active types remain active. The fitness revolution has probably generated more physiologic disparity among senior citizens than among any other age group. We have created a new subspecies, many of whom at age 70 are entirely capable of running a marathon: Literally hundreds of thousands in retirement are regular runners who log respectable mileages at respectable paces; or they swim, lift weights, dance aerobically, look well, remain trim, and think young.

Exercise: The Fountain of Youth?

For a long time the question of exercise and its effect on longevity has been debated. This year the *New England Journal of Medicine* published another of Dr. Ralph Paffenbarger's studies. This one shows convincing though not absolute proof that good exercise makes us live longer.

I and many others believe that, other things being equal, those who remain in a chronically deconditioned state are more vulnerable to the ravages of the aging process. And those exercisers who continue to experiment with movement adventures seem to be best preserved in their advancing years. Those things are hard to prove quickly, but waiting for proof might be foolish. Personally, I would rather risk the energy investment now than be regretful later. My belief in general conditioning of the entire body is rooted in the facts gathered in the laboratory: More trained muscles can do more work and tend to remain functional longer than untrained ones—the "use it or lose it" axiom applies quite specifically. During the last couple of years I have been most interested to read that people like Drs. Ken Cooper and David Costill had recently recorded their highest yet oxygen uptake values! I'm not surprised. Studies show that healthy hearts and muscles need not deteriorate as quickly as we had supposed. In one recent study, 13 male exercisers were studied closely over an 18-year period. On average, no functions had deteriorated significantly, and some had actually improved!

Heavyhands Walk: What the Doctor Ordered

My prescription of Heavyhands Walk variations for our seniors runs parallel to my reasoning in the case of obesity.

Weight Sizes for Heavyhanding Seniors

My experience dictates that if you keep everything moving, you're not likely to lose muscle mass, no matter what handweight sizes you use. A slightly heavier weight may add muscle, but don't go that route until your doctor has cleared you. I'm thinking mostly of blood pressure. When you're ready, find the heaviest weight you can use steadily and comfortably at target heart rate for five minutes, lop off a pound for safety, then use that weight for about 10 percent of your workout time!

The Joys of Being a Fit Grandfather

I can't rhapsodize enough over this. I believe I could gain a spot in Guinness's records as the best and most durable Wiffle Ball pitching and batting coach of 4-year-olds! Snicker all you want. Two of my grandsons, Jeremy and Ryan, demand high workloads for a couple of straight hours, and hot summer sun is fine by them. The other day while dutifully pitching strikes (every once in a while I got a liner right in the kisser), it occurred to me that were I a few METs less fit I'd be panting at high heart rate doing what for me is the purest pleasure. Retired and well-intentioned grandfathers have plenty of time; but if you're not fit, where do you get the flat-out energy it takes to be an active companion for a child who hasn't learned to comprehend the word "tired?" On baby-sitting days I'm a super batting instructor. When they scream and laugh hysterically with each contact between bat and ball, my heart skips a beat which isn't due to workload! At age 4, they're learning the joys and successes that come from practice, and I feel fulfilled. If the lists of reasons for exercise were suddenly truncated, my grandchildren's energy requirement from me would provide more than enough justification. And we've got cross-country skiing and body surfing and rowing to explore in the years ahead, so I've gotta stay in shape. Fathers and mothers are too busy and tired!

The Health-Fitness Enigma

As you doubtless know, there are those who believe that fitness and health are absolutely separate issues. It is a crucial question, because your answer will help determine how you live your life. The question is not simple. If, for instance, you have coronary artery disease, are you healthy or sick? Don't answer: The question is a trap. Healthy people may contain partly clogged coronaries, and I for one think some people lead unhealthy lives despite healthy coronaries!

One of my dearest friends, Fred Marks, a pediatrician nearing 60, has been an athlete and fitness freak for several decades. Despite his Greek physique and tremendous work capacity, Fred was diagnosed two years ago as having severe coronary artery disease. Cardiac catheterization revealed two vessels that were 95 percent obstructed, and a third on the decline. He underwent open heart surgery, during which his heart muscle (in exceptional shape) was "revascularized." Fred's family history is ridden with similar stories: His parents were and both brothers are also afflicted.

Today, Fred's workouts are performed at an average intensity that would place him in the 99th percentile for "healthy" men in his age group. Question: Is Fred Marks healthy or not? While there is little doubt that he retains the familial basis of vascular disease, I consider him one of the healthiest humans I've had the privilege to know. I tell the story to make the point. In settling "heavy" questions like the relationship between fitness and health, we have to carefully decide whether we're keying on the whole person or just a few admittedly crucial grams of his tissue. What excites me about my friend's life is that a devastating disease has scarcely affected the ferociously energized lifestyle he insists upon. Often the doctors can help rescue us from the ravages of clogged coronaries. But good equipment, whether inherited or surgically grafted, doesn't guarantee health as some choose to define it!

For some of us, health without fitness would leave something amiss. Health and fitness are different indeed; but that narrow perspective in modern humans becomes increasingly artificial and I believe it's downright dangerous. Anyone can effectively argue that health and fitness deserve separate space in the dictionary. The trick is to make them co-contributors to the good life.

Dutiful Aging

I am paranoid enough to believe that our society subtly encourages old timers to "act their age!" And we dutifully respond like puppets on a string. But what will happen when we defeat Alzheimer's and discover the physiologic bounty that lies dormant in our senior citizenry? I don't know, but I'd damn sure like to be around to see!

Both age and overweight make conventional types of high energy exercise improbable. Both tend to lead to deconditioning. Both are often associated with physical deteriorations of one sort or another. Lastly, obesity and aging, for quite different reasons, tend to affect the motor and mental functions. While the aging process and extra adipose tissue surely create separate problems, the similarities make the advantages of Heavyhands Walk apply to both: few injuries; more muscles and plenty of heart training; optimal calorie expenditure; convenience and small expense; good in groups or in majestic isolation; ease of beginning; a varied psychic stimulant.

While group exercise for the elderly makes all kinds of sense, the instructors need special kinds of knowledge and sensitivity. In a youthful aerobics class, instructor indiscretions are apt to be nicely absorbed by the physiologic resilience of young, fit bodies. In a class of seniors, however, the average participant may be on three or more potent medications, some of which make the response to unusual physical activity uncertain, to say the least. I've often thought that the new wave of one-on-one instruction should be concentrated on our senior citizens, who may not realize the risk involved in their sometimes bubbly enthusiasm over "getting in shape!"

A good exercise test in this age group is not suggested; it's a *must*. I would add that a day spent wearing one of the new variations of a Holter monitor is an excellent investment (see Chapter 3, page 23, for more information on this). Its computerized analyses—detecting any erratic heart behavior, printing out ECG samplings from certain moments during the day, tracking the heart rate over a 24-hour period, and most importantly, identifying when the heart muscle is not getting sufficient blood—are all invaluable. I suggest this procedure in this age group because the incidence of "silent" heart problems is, of course, more frequent.

Your doctor should be aware of the specifics of your exercise and know of all the prescription medications you take, as well as chemicals you consume on an irregular basis, like caffeine, aspirin, etc. If you have high blood pressure, get your doctor to help you learn the effect of your exercise upon your blood pressure. He can easily measure your response, say, to pump 'n' walk with tiny weights today (after four minutes or more), and again after some weeks or months of practice, to determine how well your body "likes" Heavyhands Walk.

Embark on your Heavyhands Walk program with enthusiasm tempered with common sense and caution. Warming up is more important for the elderly, because it takes a bit of care to stoke the metabolic fires properly in our later years. Start with very light weights, and progress to heavier ones as you feel comfortable. Don't challenge yourself with heavy weights. Outsized strength is not important for most of us; if anything, it's less necessary for older Heavyhanders.

Exercise caution when working out in any weather extremes. Slick sidewalks are even more hazardous when swinging handweights. They should simply be avoided. Hot, humid weather is more apt to cause sudden, untoward effects in older folks. Just to be on the safe side, try to work out where there are others present, even if you're working out solo. It just makes good sense.

Don't attempt to lose large amounts of body weight quickly through exercise. Likewise, abandon ambitious dieting strategies. There can't be any rational hurry! If you experience any sense of heart irregularity (sometimes it's readily sensed

Jogging: A Risky Proposition for the Over-50 Set

A high heart rate is sure to occur in those who jog for the first time at any age. It happens at the same instant the jogger feels breathless and abandons the effort momentarily. The problem in over-50 joggers is that unless they've been recently stress-tested, they may be incurring some risk. At a high heart rate, and given some degree of "silent" (meaning symptomless) heart disease, there's a greater chance that the 50-plus person's heart rhythm will be disturbed, sometimes dangerously. While such disturbances are possible in younger joggers as well, the statistical likelihood mounts rapidly in older folks who decide to jog. Incidentally, a well-trained Heavyhands Walker will be able to do harder workouts at relatively low heart rates. While that could be a safer way to go, it's not a good excuse to begin *any* vigorous exercise without an exercise ECG.

Why I'm an Exerciser
- Movement always improves my mood.
- I love to eat and refuse to starve, even marginally.
- It lets me grocery shop, clean my car, shovel snow, and carry out garbage without blinking.
- Friends say I look better, and I'm a sucker for flattery.
- I'm an energetic grandfather and a tireless baby-sitter.
- I think I've already lived longer than I otherwise would have.
- I can literally "dahnse all night!"
- I feel strong as a bull.
- I'd like to avoid the post-coronary lifestyle.
- I can control my blood pressure.
- My cholesterol levels are very healthy since I began exercising. I move "young."
- In my 62nd year, I can play softball or touch football with anyone.
- I'd like to become a role model for our young people.
- My fitness allows me to treasure hard rowing at sunrise.
- Something tells me that fitness has increased my mental capacity.
- People listen to me when I talk exercise: My body lends credence to my credentials.
- My wife tells me I'm sexier.
- I like being a visual contradiction: bald head; bold bod.
- I believe being fit is something I owe to the community.
- Being fit makes me energetic; being energetic allows me to give.
- My fitness eliminates dozens of worries that would waste my time.
- Fitness makes me a better worker—at any task.
- Fitness increases my tolerance for weather extremes.
- Fitness allows me to rest more effectively.
- I believe my interest in fitness makes me a better doctor.
- I love bargains: Fitness is the best wellness bargain around.

subjectively), chest discomfort, dizziness, or any kind of pain, halt your exercise proceedings. If the symptoms persist, see your doctor.

━━━━━━

I think our overall success in making our seniors fitter will reflect, more than anything else, the progress we make toward producing a fitter crop of children, who will in turn be fitter *adults* and fitter *seniors.* I don't think this is idle conjecture. The motor patterns that make for movement pleasure and facility are established early in life, as are many learning patterns. The blatant deficiencies in our physical education are transmitted along our developmental histories and come to rest resoundingly during aging. This is not to suggest that exercise isn't good enough and safe enough to begin at any time. But for a host of powerful reasons, the advantages of starting early can't be dismissed.

Predictions on the Future of the Fitness Movement

Canny readers will quickly diagnose the double intention of these remarks. They are predictions and wishes! Some of these predictions are obvious; others are pretty dicey.

- The exercise revolution will get serious. Despite numerous growing pains, its reasons for existing are multiplying rapidly.
- People will begin to understand that the higher risk for cardiovascular disease in our children is related in part to poor exercise habits.
- The effects of aging will be delayed by lifelong activity.
- Increasing medical costs will make all wellness strategies more attractive.
- We will learn safer and more convenient ways to exercise.
- There will be more exercise, more knowledge about exercise, better equipment, and better instruction to choose from.
- Muscle "loading," as I've come to call it, will become part of a general approach to exercise.
- Along with muscle loading, combined Panaerobics will become an accepted exercise formula.
- Exercisers will work harder. The continuous intensity of exercise will increase.
- Combined exercise will become a major preventive measure and treatment for certain forms of high blood pressure, and will be a major component of cardiac rehabilitation programs.
- Customized, computerized exercise prescriptions will become popular. In addition, four-limbed exercise testing will become standard practice.
- The diet industry will take a turn for the worse.
- Educators will take new interest in the teaching and development of exercise.
- Major research dollars will be devoted to the psychic effects of exercise. The numbers of both conventional walkers and runners will decrease.
- The practice of heavy weightlifting will diminish among all but those for whom it is specifically useful.
- Strength-endurance training will become a central part of every exercise program.
- Exercisers will spend less time doing static stretches.
- Heavyhands Walk, Walkdance, and other variations of Panaerobics will become the most popular forms of exercise.
- Exercise injuries will diminish in proportion to the increase in use of Panaerobics.
- Obesity will diminish, and with it the obsessive interest in technologies aimed at measurement of skinfold fat.
- The split between sport and fitness will gradually disappear.
- Medical research will provide better means of identifying those at risk of sudden death during exercise: Earlier diagnosis of coronary artery disease and more accurate means of assessing the immune system's response to various levels of activity will be two areas of improvement. Exercise will become safer.
- Multiple, 10-minute exercise sessions per day will be recognized as a preferable method of training the cardiovascular system, and controlling body weight.

Here's hoping your multiple successes with Heavyhands Walk will help make these guesses correct!

Epilogue: The Joy of Exercise

So there you have it. Plenty of movements to keep you busy for a lifetime. But people tell me that the psychic factors, things like enjoyment, will probably determine whether you live an active life or not. This "soft" area, far from the solid numbers generated in the laboratory, is what I find the most challenging.

The joy of exercise is for me far and away the most difficult area in the exercise domain to study with confidence. Exercisers are fickle, often ditching one loyalty after another while seeking the ideal. Even habitual exercisers find that the sense of joy they derive from exercise varies greatly from day to day. That makes sense to me, because we start each workout in a subtly different way.

It's been hard to understand what these ardently felt joys are all about. Language fails for most of us, and there are those standard clichés that hardly identify the subtle differences between us. I have tried dozens of times to document the pleasures associated with exercise, and have shredded each attempt!

It might be useful to differentiate passive from active joys. Passive joys might be thought of as the joys that accompany various sensations. These sense data are constantly "playing" upon our central nervous system. I think of active joys as ones associated with body movement, the utilization of relatively large amounts of energy.

Beginning exercisers are often amazed at how pleasant their initial experience is, and feel infatuated, even hooked, from the first bead of sweat. I've also learned to distinguish between the early joys of exercise and those hard-won kinds that come only after the habit has become established. The early pleasure is high on enthusiasm that often borders on the dramatic. The late joys are sedate, reflective, complicated, often wed to knowledge, and infinitely more stable.

Exercise is fun for many during the phase when improvement is obvious, if not striking. Teachers in the field might be well advised to watch closely the exerciser whose gains are leveling off. That's the time to offer encouragement along with advice as to where to look for improvement. Sooner or later, rapid, hard-edged gains come to an end. Weight loss, pulse rate, and blood pressure reductions plateau, feats of strength and flexibility top off. That's when humor and imagination should enter the exercise picture: a willingness to try novel things and think in novel ways.

Mood can make or break the joy of exercise. Upbeat people tend to like exercise (and other things); cynics may like it, too, but must keep it secret! Which is not to say whether happy folks or curmudgeons make the larger share of habitual exercisers. I have known many who never missed an opportunity to grouse over what seemed to me a pleasant workout, and I have wisely learned to keep my suspicions to myself! Evidently, there are those who derive pleasure from their steadfast willingness to continue despite the suffering they wear proudly on their sleeves.

I am convinced that true exercisers are the *least* likely to rhapsodize over it. The joy of exercise should, I believe, simply be reflected in your growing wisdom, determination, and, yes, willingness to groan occasionally over something you deem worthwhile. The key energies required to keep you at it are psychic: They consume almost no oxygen! They start with the premise, "Exercise is good stuff and I want to stick with it!" After that, it's a lifetime of shrewdly juggling propositions that keep the commitment alive and well.

Here's hoping your successes with Heavyhands Walk will help you to experience the subtle joys that come from working hard toward a lifetime of fitness.

Who's the Machine?

While you're shuffling around looking for an exercise program, you might be tempted to enlist the services of one of the more popular exercise machines. I was going to write a few paragraphs about them, but my efforts ended up looking like this:

Here it is for all to witness:
This wild and woolly surge toward fitness.
Only a few can resist its momentum,
Exploiting the gifts Mother Nature has lent 'em,
Seeking the blessings of leanness and tone,
Shaping what's sandwiched between skin and bone,
Muscling up to be handsome and strong,
Slim and flexible—what could be wrong
With this popular quest for ultra-improvement?
Nothing recent can rival the exercise movement.
And God knows I'd be the last to wax cynical;
On the subject of fitness I'm damn near rabbinical!
For mine is a system that poses as total,
Keeps you slender, healthy, and rhapsodically motile!
But I'm eager to learn how *you* think on this issue
That goes beyond enzymes and biopsy tissue.

I'm talking of gadgets that help us to work;
There are gadgets to clean and gadgets to jerk,
Machines for your hamstrings and obscure rotators,
Machines to train swimmers and skiers and skaters,
Machines you can row or cycle or both,
Machines for the eager and those who are loath!
Machines to climb stairs by and those for your belly:
All will convert you to sinew from jelly!
Some count your heartbeat and signal alarm;
Some gauge the fat at the back of your arm.
Every catalog brims with devices galore;
Choosing the right one's becoming a chore.
Workouts sans hardware appear to be "out,"
Pulleys and cams and gears must add clout.
But something inside me rebels at the scene,
And I hope you won't dub my analysis mean,
But the residual shrink that inhabits my soul
Thinks this tendency's getting quite out of control
And may symbolize something we need to discuss!
You ask, "Why the panic, why all the fuss?"
Someday the perfect machine will be born,

One that the stubbornest skeptic won't scorn.
It'll be solid as rock, without any rattle,
Make hardly a sound while you're doing battle.
It'll sop up your moisture if you dare to sweat,
Ply you with sugar, pay your oxygen debt,
Mollify muscles when your lactic is high,
Transfuse you with red cells in case they are shy.
In a manner of speaking the machine is quite human,
An object of envy that doesn't need groomin';
It's skin is pure silk and its weight doesn't alter,
And it doesn't lose patience when we tend to falter.
What I'm stewing about in case you still wonder,
Is not that machines will soon put us asunder.
It's more what a vulnerable prey we've become,
To depend on a gadget that's dumber than dumb,
Our body machinery is slicker than slick:
It can ape any movement, can do any trick.
Its price is just right and it travels with ease;
If you work it just right it'll aim just to please.
But the best part of all and the part you won't barter:
The body-machine will just keep getting smarter!

INDEX

Entries referring to entire chapters appear in **boldface** type;
entries referring to boxed text and illustrations appear in *italics.*